KEEPING
THE
CATCH

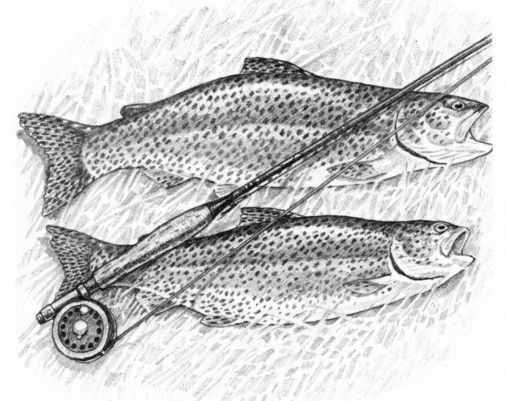

PATRICK SAWYER

KEEPING THE CATCH

Kenn and Pat Oberrecht

Winchester Press
Tulsa, Oklahoma

Library of Congress Cataloging in Publication Data

Oberrecht, Kenn.
  Keeping the catch.

  Bibliography: p. 218
  1. Cookery (Fish) 2. Fishes, Dressing of.
3. Fishery products—Preservation. I. Oberrecht,
Pat. II. Title.
TX747.023   641.6'92   81-4606
ISBN 0-87691-339-7   AACR2

Published by Winchester Press
1421 South Sheridan Road
P.O. Box 1260
Tulsa, Oklahoma 74101

Book design by Janice L. Merz

Printed in the United States of America

1 2 3 4 5 85 84 83 82 81

In fond memory of

F. W. Connaughton and Helen Oberrecht

CONTENTS

Chapter 1

THE PLEASURES AND PROBLEMS OF KEEPING THE CATCH

Home economists, nutritionists, and dietitians like to point out to consumers that fish and shellfish are among the most healthful of foods and best sources of protein and some of the most economical food buys today. Moreover, they are delicious and can be prepared in an infinite variety of ways.

Most nutritionists maintain that, for a balanced diet, one third of the daily amount of protein should come from animal sources. Pound for pound, fish is higher in protein and lower in calories than beef, pork, or lamb. In fact, a single four-ounce serving of fish contains from one third to half the daily adult requirement of protein—essential for growth, maintenance, and repair of body tissues. For that reason, some nutrition specialists now recommend that fish be a part of the diet at least three times a week.

Fish is low in saturated fats and cholesterol, which have been linked with heart disease and vascular disorders. Fish is also high in polyunsaturated fatty acids, which help break down cholesterol in the bloodstream.

Fish flesh contains calcium, iron, potassium, manganese, copper, cobalt, zinc, and other trace minerals, as well as thiamin, riboflavin, niacin, vitamin B_{12}, and pantothenic acid. Fatty fishes are also high in vitamins A and D.

Fish flesh is easily digested because its connective tissues are more readily assimilated than those of beef, pork, and lamb. Moreover, fish is naturally tender and requires only minimum cooking times.

All fish, even the saltwater species, are low in sodium, which make them ideal for low-sodium diets.

All this, of course, should make fish an attractive food and dietary mainstay of the American consumer, which goes double for the angler or the angling family.

1

Fish is considered a bargain these days, even when the different cuts of various species range anywhere from about two dollars to five dollars or more a pound. Smoked and pickled products, as well as most shellfish, can cost even more. But in comparison to the alternatives, they are cheap.

The angler is not only able to enjoy the many aesthetic values of his favorite sport, but he can put nutritious and delicious foods on his table at no additional cost. Furthermore, the angler can serve a much fresher product than the average consumer can buy. His canned fish can be far better than commercially canned products. His frozen fish can be of superior quality. He can smoke fish to suit his personal tastes, and he can pickle far more varieties than are commercially available.

The angler is not only able to catch and prepare fresher fish than he could ever buy, but he can also preserve seasonal surpluses for optimum storage life, maximum variety, and minimum waste. He also has access to numerous species that are never sold commercially and others that are sold fresh only in certain areas.

In most parts of the country, there are species that are underutilized. For example, catfish and bullhead populations in many states could easily stand much greater harvest. Elsewhere, bluegill, crappie, and yellow perch could be taken in far greater numbers. There are even areas in which bass and pike populations go nearly untouched. The angler can tap these resources and, in the process, significantly reduce his family food costs.

Despite all that fish and shellfish have going for them, according to Sam Gillespie, seafood marketing specialist at Texas A & M University, seafood accounts for only 6% of the total meat consumption in the U.S. Furthermore, most seafood—approximately 70%—is consumed in restaurants, which means that home consumption amounts to only 30% of all the seafood eaten in the U.S., or less than 2% of the total meat consumption. If fish and shellfish are such healthful and savory foods, why don't Americans eat more? "Consumer attitudes about seafood are formed by the experiences they have when buying and eating fish," Gillespie maintains. "Unfortunately, these experiences are not always happy ones." Gillespie also points out that "Many people hesitate to buy seafood, because they don't know how to prepare it and are afraid of the reaction they'll get at the dinner table." Although Gillespie was speaking mainly about the average consumer who would normally purchase seafoods rather than catch them, there are some noteworthy parallels regarding the angler who catches his own fish and shellfish.

First, many anglers do not know how to properly care for fish and shellfish from the time they are caught until the time they are eaten or preserved for later consumption. Few are truly adept at dressing the catch, and most have misconceptions about the methods of preservation. Too often, the angler returns from a trip to the mountains or his favorite lake with vivid memories of his streamside or lakeshore lunches of sizzling, pan-dressed trout or scrumptious fillets of walleye or smallmouth bass only to grossly disappoint himself and his family when he serves up the same fish and finds that it's not even fit to feed the cat. "There's nothing like fresh-caught fish, cooked over the coals, right on the bank," he'll apologize.

That's right. There is nothing like fish that's pulled from the water, killed, cleaned, and fried—as fresh as it could ever be. But there are many things that come mighty close. They include fish that have been properly cared for and kept as fresh as possible until they were cooked. They include fish that have been wrapped the right way for the freezer and then have been used within the recommended limits for freezer storage. They include fish that have been canned fresh, fish that have been smoked correctly, and fish that have been pickled the right way. They include fish that have been expertly dressed, and fish that have been cooked the way they should be.

And that's precisely what this book is all about. It is simply a book that will tell you how to care for your catch, how to preserve it, and how to prepare it to ensure that it will be as tasty and healthful as it can possibly be. As an angler, you are able to prepare a far better product than you could ever buy, providing you pay attention to the essential requirements for proper handling, storage, and cooking of the catch.

In our formative years, we made all the usual mistakes with the fish we caught. We failed to recognize how fast fish deteriorate after they die. We didn't take all the care we should have in dressing the catch. Worse, we paid little attention to the limits for keeping fish frozen. And we made the most common mistake of all—we overcooked just about every fish we prepared. But gradually we learned—the hard way—and what we've learned we want to pass on to others.

Fish are a precious commodity, and far too many go to waste because they are carelessly handled and prepared. And there's no reason for any fish to go to waste. We admit that we have prepared fish that truly weren't fit to eat, but that was before we had learned all we needed to know. We can honestly say that during recent years we have not prepared any fish or shellfish that we caught ourselves that haven't met our hearty approval, and we eat fish at least once a week and sometimes three or more times a week during periods of seasonal abundance. During the past five years, the only fish we have been dissatisfied with have been some we've purchased when our own stocks ran short and some we've had in restaurants.

Deterioration and Spoilage

Fish is among the most perishable of foods, and shellfish—particularly clams and mussels—are the most perishable of seafoods. Fish deteriorate rapidly after death and continue to deteriorate until they are consumed. Proper handling and preparation methods retard the process, but do not stop it.

Fresh fish have firm flesh, and the saltwater species are usually firmer than freshwater species. Mushy flesh is an indication that the fish has deteriorated too far for human consumption.

Fresh fish also have a clean, pleasing, often tangy aroma. The so-called "fishy" smell—a strong, unpleasant odor—often indicates that the fish is beginning to spoil.

Deterioration and spoilage of fresh fish is caused by bacteria and enzymes. If the fish is not properly cleaned and dressed, the bacteria and enzymes will continue to act on the flesh until it spoils. Frozen fish is also prone to oxidation and dehydration and if not correctly packaged will spoil rapidly. Improperly canned fish and some smoked fish not stored correctly can harbor deadly toxin-producing bacteria.

Although fish flesh is normally free of bacteria, the gills, entrails, skin, and slime do harbor bacteria. Bacterial growth is kept in check as long as the fish is alive but rapidly increases when the fish dies. For that reason, fish should be gutted, gilled, and washed immediately after they're killed.

Spoilage occurs most rapidly in temperatures from 70° F. upward, coupled with high humidity or moisture. Fish keep best at temperatures below 40° F. Consequently, icing the fish thoroughly—immediately after they're gutted, gilled, and washed—will help keep them fresh until they are consumed or preserved in some way.

Enzymes found in the digestive tract are kept in check as long as the fish remains alive. After the fish dies, though, enzymes in the digestive juices begin attacking the stomach wall and will eventually eat through to the stomach cavity and body of the fish. If the fish was feeding when caught, as with most school fish and troll-caught species, enzymes can eat into the flesh of the dead fish within an hour, producing a brownish discoloration and mushy texture commonly called "belly burn." Stop the enzyme action by immediately gutting, gilling, and removing the kidneys from the fish as soon as you kill it. Then wash the fish thoroughly to remove most bacteria and residual enzymes.

Rough handling of fish can also lead to spoilage. Careless gaffing (into any fleshy part of the fish) and bruising of fish allow bacteria to enter the flesh through breaks in the skin, and bacterial growth can then lead to spoilage. So avoid using a gaff if possible, but if you must gaff your catch, do so carefully, and try to gaff it in the head or jaw area.

Since bacteria and enzymes exist in high concentrations in the wastes left after dressing fish, it is important that you keep your cleaning and handling area free of blood, slime, and all visceral residues. Wash cutting boards and utinsels frequently and keep tables and counter tops free of blood and slime.

Contaminants in Fish

Although the subject of contamination of fish is the source of some controversy, the presence of pesticides, chemicals, and other contaminants in fish flesh is serious enough to be of concern to the angler who keeps his catch.

PCBs

Among of the most serious threats to some species of fish in certain waters are the chemical compounds known as polychlorinated biphenyls (PCBs). These are industrial chemicals that have been in commercial production since 1929 and are used in plastics, paints, sealants, carbonless copy papers, and other types of coatings. They are also used as coolants in electrical transformers and capacitors. They contain varying amounts of chlorine and are toxic.

Although PCBs are no longer manufactured and marketed in the U.S., some foreign manufacturers who had large stockpiles of products containing PCBs on hand when the importation of such products was banned have been allowed exemptions and continue to ship these products to the U.S. While there are strict laws in the U.S. and other countries that closely regulate the use of PCBs, these toxic compounds were widely used for many years, and many products containing PCBs have since been discarded at dump sites and junkyards where they continue to contaminate the environment.

Our polluted waterways carry PCBs, but the compounds also leak into soils at dump sites and are eventually washed into watersheds by rain and melting snow. They are also among the airborne particulates that contaminate the air and in this form have been carried to all parts of the globe and into wilderness areas far beyond industrialized civilization. PCBs are found "in Arctic polar bears, New York chickens, England's rainfall, human blood plasma, the world's oceans and mother's milk."[1]

_____

1. *ABCs of PCBs*, University of Wisconsin Sea Grant College Program, WIS-SG-76-125 (Madison, 1976), p. 2.

PCBs enter the aquatic food chain by adhering to small particles in the water that are consumed by the lower life forms. These plankton are then eaten by small fish that, in turn, are eaten by larger fish that man catches and consumes. Since PCBs are so widespread and are present in so many life forms, our concern is with excessive levels that are potentially dangerous.

Although all our large river systems carry PCBs and the compounds can be found in most of our lakes, reservoirs, impoundments, and coastal bays and estuaries, the highest concentrations are found in the St. Lawrence-North Atlantic drainage basin and the waters of the southeastern coastal states.[2] The Hudson River, the Mississippi River, and the Great Lakes are the major problem areas in the U.S. Large carp, salmon, and lake trout from some parts of these areas contain potentially dangerous levels of PCBs, and some state fish and game agencies have posted and published warnings to that effect.

The threat to humans is the build-up of high levels of PCBs. Consequently, health authorities are now advising against the consumption of possibly contaminated fish more than once a week. If you fish in any area where there are high levels of PCBs, you should check with your local fish and game agency and your state health department to determine if it is safe to consume fish from these waters and which fish in which areas have been most affected.

Studies have shown that the fatty species of fish are more prone to PCB contamination than the lean species. Moreover, larger fish are more likely to be affected than smaller ones. In the midwest and Great Lakes region, for example, large carp, salmon, and lake trout have been most affected, and these are the only fish believed to be any real threat at the moment.

Mercury

Mercury occurs naturally in the environment and is found in minute quantities in all life forms—plants and animals alike. It is assumed that these normal levels of mercury have always been present and have had no recognizable effect on man or his food supply. It is the misuse of mercury and its improper disposal that have caused serious contamination of fish populations in some parts of the world. Because of an epidemic of mercury poisoning in the villages on Minamata Bay, Japan in 1953, we were made aware of the potential hazards involved in the industrial pollution of our waterways with mercury.

The U.S. Food and Drug Administration has conducted studies and set levels for allowable mercury content in fish. Industrial and agricultural uses of mercury are also strictly controlled, so that mer-

---

2. *Ibid.*, p. 4.

cury appears to be posing no great threat to our supply of food fishes.

Although the potential for mercury poisoning has received much publicity in the U.S., no cases have been reported that were caused by the consumption of fish.

Cleaning and Cooking to Reduce Contaminants

Even if you keep fish that possibly contain high levels of PCBs, DDT, Mirex, or other contaminants, you can greatly reduce contaminant levels in the way you dress and prepare the catch. Since the fatty tissue will contain about ten times more contaminants than lean tissue, you should trim away all visible fat when you dress the fish. This means removing all belly meat (where fats are highly concentrated) and all dark meat along the lateral line and along the dorsal side or back of the fish.

Avoid preparing the fish in any way that prevents the fats and juices from draining. The dry cooking methods—range broiling and charcoal broiling—will allow the fats to drain away while cooking. You can also steam the fish, but discard the water after cooking. If you bake the fish, place it on a rack inside the roasting pan to allow for sufficient drainage. You can also deep fry fish to remove much of the fat, but you should discard the cooking oil afterward.

Red Tides and Paralytic Shellfish Poisoning

Another type of contamination you should know about that occurs naturally and results from so-called "red tides" is paralytic shellfish poisoning. Although red tides occur with some frequency in American coastal waters during the warmer months of the year, most are harmless. Red tides are actually blooms of microscopic organisms known as dinoflagellates. Although these organisms (as small as 25,000 to the inch) are normally transparent or only slightly tinted in normal concentrations, during population explosions they can color the coastal waters in small patches and streamers for great expanses of the ocean and bays. The term "red tide" is something of a misnomer, since the blooms might be red, rust, blue, green, yellow, black, brown, pink, or any of a number of hues, depending on the species of organism and the stage of the bloom.

Of the hundreds of species of dinoflagellates, many cause red tides, but only a few are harmful to aquatic life. Fish kills and other problems result from many factors arising from red tides, including the release of neurotoxins by the organisms and the reduction of oxygen content in the water where the bloom occurs. At least one species of dinoflagellates is known to cause paralytic shellfish poisoning. The shellfish themselves are not normally harmed by the organism, but

7

other animals feeding on the toxic shellfish can be poisoned. In these animals, including man, the toxin can cause temporary paralysis, or even death, when a sufficient quantity has been consumed.

A visible red tide is only a warning that shellfish *might* be poisonous. The red tide could be a bloom of harmless organisms. Worse, the shellfish could be poisonous when too few organisms are present in the water to produce a visible red tide. Since it is impossible for the public to determine whether or not shellfish are safe to eat, health departments and fish-and-game agencies in coastal states monitor coastal waters and frequently test shellfish for toxicity. In some states, warnings are posted, published, and broadcast when shellfish have been found to be affected. In other states, quarantines on the taking of certain shellfish are enforced during the months when the potential for red tides exists.

Mussels are the shellfish with which you must be most concerned and careful. Most dangerous red tides occur on the open ocean where mussel colonies are plentiful rather than in the bays where other species of clams are normally dug. Moreover, the toxin accumulates in the dark digestive glands of shellfish. Since mussels are normally consumed whole, the poison is consumed with the mussel.

The first safeguard against possible poisoning is to check with the local health department or state fish and game agency to learn if there are any current quarantines on shellfish. Find out what areas are affected and what species. Often, only open ocean beaches and coastline areas are off limits, while bays remain open to the taking of shellfish. Also, mussels are often the only shellfish to have been declared unsafe.

It's a good idea, though, to take some extra measures with all clams during any quarantine period. If only certain areas or only mussels have been declared unsafe, we prefer not to take chances on others. So we don't prepare any clams for steaming then. Rather, we completely clean all clams, removing all dark parts where any poison would be concentrated, and keep only the white meat.

Some people go a step further by testing all mussels they gather, regardless of whether or not they are under quarantine. If you gather mussels during the warmer months, you might want to make the same test, even if the shellfish are supposedly safe to eat. Since the severity of poisoning is proportionate to the amount of shellfish consumed, you can check your catch by steaming only one mussel and refrigerating the rest of your catch until the next day. If, after eating one mussel, you experience a tingling in your lips and slight numbness in your tongue, discard the rest of the mussels.

Chapter 2

CUTLERY AND ACCESSORIES FOR DRESSING THE CATCH

The secret to dressing fish quickly, efficiently, and safely is top-quality cutlery that is kept sharp and in good working order. In addition to one or more good knives, you'll also need sharpening implements and the ability to use them skillfully.

Fillet Knives

The most important kind of knife for anyone who keeps the catch is a fillet knife. You'll need at least one good fillet knife, but if you bring home fish in quantity, you'll find it saves time to have several sharp knives ready for dressing the catch. If you take a variety of species and fish of different sizes, you might need knives with blades of different lengths and designs.

Although all major cutlery manufacturers and a number of custom knifemakers now offer fillet knives, this style of knife is a relatively recent development. According to *The Gun Digest Book Of Knives*, by B. R. Hughes and Jack Lewis, the first fillet knife was probably made in the late 1950s for Abercrombie and Fitch. But it took several years for what is now considered the classic fillet knife to become widely available to sportsmen everywhere. Prior to that time, serious anglers and commercial fish processors used professional boning knives for fish-filleting tasks. While it seems that the ubiquitous and very popular Rapala Fish 'n Fillet knife has been around forever, it made its debut in 1965.

Today, there is a staggering array of fillet knives on the market. What might come as a surprise to those who have become accustomed to this era of planned obsolescence and the lack of quality in many of our manufactured products is that most or all of these knives are good ones that will serve and last for years. In fact, of the many fillet knives

9

we have owned or tried over the years, we haven't found one that couldn't accomplish the job for which it was designed. Of course, some were better than others for a number of reasons, and some were better suited to our personal requirements. But all were good or at least adequate.

Selecting Fillet Knives

Since the fillet knives from all the reputable manufacturers are well made, selection is, to a great extent, a personal matter. You'll have to pick knives that suit your purposes. A few guidelines should help you make your choice.

Type of blade steel is not as important a consideration with fillet knives as it is with other kinds of cutlery because most fillet knives have stainless-steel blades. There are a few fillet knives made of high-carbon tool steel, and some anglers prefer these for one reason or another. Most of the fillet knives we own are made of stainless steel, but a couple of old favorites have softer, nonstainless blades. These are knives, however, that we selected for a specific task, not for the type of steel. If given the choice between two nearly identical fillet knives, but one with a nonstainless and the other with a stainless-steel blade, we would pick the latter for two reasons. First, the edge-holding ability of modern stainless steel has been greatly improved over earlier stainless steels. Second, stainless steel is simply easier to maintain.

Blade flexibility is one of the most important considerations and is a source of some confusion. Just about every piece of writing about filleting fish stresses the importance of using a fillet knife with a very flexible blade. Blades of fillet knives, as compared with other types of cutlery, should be relatively narrow, thin, and somewhat flexible. But a fillet knife can be too flexible for general purpose filleting. Some fillet knife blades are so thin and flexible that they can be easily bent into a semicircle, but these should be considered special-purpose knives. Such a knife is not a good choice for the person who will own only one fillet knife. A flexible blade is important for trimming the rib sections on most fish, but a certain amount of rigidity is required for the initial filleting of most species and is essential for skinning the fillets.

Blade length is another important criterion in the selection of a fillet knife. If you'll only be dressing small trout and panfish, a blade of four inches is sufficient. For the average bass, pike, walleye, and many in-shore marine species, a six-inch blade will do. But for large trout, salmon, striped bass, lingcod, and others, you'll want a knife that is up to the task—a nine-inch blade or larger. For general purposes, you won't go wrong with a Case Model 607-5½ F SSP, a G96 Mariner Cuda Fillet Model 2078, a Rapala Fish 'n Fillet Model FNF6, or similar knife.

These knives are in the six-inch range and have enough flexibility to take care of rib trimming while still maintaining the rigidity necessary for the average filleting job.

You might prefer one of the knives with an extremely thin and flexible blade for trimming ribs, and if you fish the salt chuck for the flatfishes—sole, flounder, halibut, and the like—such a knife is essential for filleting these species. A good choice here is the Olsen Model 213F6 or any similar knife.

For filleting big fish with heavy ribs and for steaking large fish, we prefer a blade with a bit more heft and rigidity. Our favorite for these tasks is the John Zakovich fillet knife with a nine-inch blade.
safe filleting of large fish.

For filleting big fish with heavy ribs and for steaking large fish, we prefer a blade with a bit more heft and rigidity. Our favorite for these tasks is the John Zakovitch fillet knife with a nine-inch blade.

Handle design and size are two more noteworthy considerations but are largely personal matters. Of course, you should pick a handle that is comfortable, but you should also consider that during fish-dressing operations your hands will usually be wet and might be slimy as well, so the knife should have a good grip that isn't likely to slip. If you pick the largest handle that you can comfortably hold, you'll find the greater size gives you added leverage and better control. We personally prefer large-handled knives that are contoured to fit the grip.

Other Useful Knives

Several major cutlery manufacturers (Camillus, Case, and Western, to name three) offer versions of the classic fisherman's or angler's knife—a two-bladed folding knife. One blade is a clip blade suitable for cutting bait, gutting and gilling any fish, and filleting small fish. The other blade is a scaler with a hook disgorger and cap lifter. It's a handy knife to keep in a tackle box, but we recommend only those models made of stainless steel because they are the easiest to care for.

For cleaning clams, you need a good knife that will get inside the shell quickly to sever the adductor muscles and trim meat away from the shell. Although there are so-called "clam-and-oyster knives" on the market, these are designed more for prying than cutting. Our personal choice is a small fillet knife with a four-inch blade, such as the Rapala Fish 'n Fillet Model FNF4.

One specialty knife that certainly deserves mention is the "Zak" Fish & Deer Knife. This unique tool is especially suitable for effortlessly opening any fish for gutting and gilling without damaging any entrails. For that reason, it is ideal for any angler who keeps fish roe for food or bait. In fact, inventor and manufacturer, Felix Zak, told us that

11

several fish-and-game agencies throughout the U.S. and Canada are using this knife for opening ripe fish to remove the roe needed in hatchery operations.

Honing Stones

You'll need one or two oilstones for sharpening your knives, and here again, you will have to make some personal choices, the first being whether to select natural or synthetic stones. Some people prefer the Washita or Arkansas natural stones that are quarried from deposits of novaculite. The soft Arkansas stone is recommended for general purpose honing and producing a keen edge quickly. A hard Arkansas stone is then used to polish the sharp blade to a razor edge. If you prefer a manmade whetstone, you'll find carborundum stones in various sizes and grits or combination stones that are one grit on one side and another grit on the other side. A good choice for sharpening fillet knives is either a combination stone with medium and fine grits or two different stones of these grits. For final polishing to razor sharpness, a ceramic stone, such as the Case Moon Stone, is a good choice.

Keep a good-quality honing oil on hand and always use oil on your stones when sharpening any knife, unless the stone manufacturer advises otherwise. The oil helps to get a good edge on your knife quickly by keeping the fine dust and particles of stone that are loosened from becoming imbedded in the pores of the stone. After sharpening, wipe the excess oil away from the surface of the stone.

Incidentally, never use any kind of powered grinding stones for sharpening your knives because they can ruin the temper of the blade if you don't know how to use them properly.

Steels and Strops

You have probably heard or read that steels don't actually sharpen a blade, but rather, realign the edge. While this is true of the traditional butcher's steel, it is not the case with the various makes of hone steels available from several manufacturers.

A hone steel is made of very hard steel to which some kind of abrasive has been bonded during the manufacturing process. Most are flat bars of steel with two different sharpening edges: the narrow edges are for removing material and putting an edge on a knife quickly, while the broad surfaces are for fine finishing. We have found hone steels the best choice for quickly renewing the edge on a fillet knife, and for this reason we keep a hone steel handy during any fish-dressing operation. We prefer oilstones, though, for major resharpening, which is periodically necessary.

A butcher's steel is another handy item to have on hand whenever you're using knives. With use, the edge of a blade will begin to turn or curl. Several strokes over a butcher's steel will reset the edge to its original alignment.

If you want the finest edge on a knife, use a strop for final polishing. Razor strops are available through barber supply dealers and are excellent for stropping all sorts of blades. You can make a simple strop by gluing a piece of leather to a block of wood, or you can even use a leather knife sheath for stropping.

Honing with Stones

Honing a blade with an oilstone is a fairly simple task that becomes even easier with practice. It is essential, though, that you address the stone with the right blade angle and that you draw the blade across the stone in the right direction.

Most cutlery manufacturers recommend that the blade be held at a 10- to 15-degree angle to the stone. To get the proper angle, lay the blade across the stone and lift the back of the blade while the cutting edge remains on the stone. In the beginning you will have to carefully watch to make sure you are maintaining the correct angle, but with practice it will come naturally to you.

To sharpen the blade, start by laying it across one end of the stone. The heel of the blade (the part nearest the handle) should be on the stone with the point of the blade extended beyond. Tip the back of the blade to achieve the 10- to 15-degree angle; then draw the blade across the stone, cutting edge first, as if you are taking a slice out of the stone. You should draw the blade diagonally across the stone—from heel to point—so that in one stroke the length of the stone the entire cutting edge will be stroked against the stone. When you reach the other end of the stone, turn the blade over and draw it over the stone back to your starting point, thus honing the other side of the blade.

Continue sharpening in this fashion until you have put a good cutting edge on the blade. Always count the strokes and make sure each side of the blade gets an equal number of strokes. Use more pressure during the first few strokes and gradually reduce pressure until you are only lightly running the blade across the stone, removing less and less material as you progress. After you have put an edge on the blade with a soft Arkansas or medium-grit synthetic stone, polish the edge with a hard Arkansas or fine-grit synthetic stone, using the same technique and maintaining the same blade-to-stone angle.

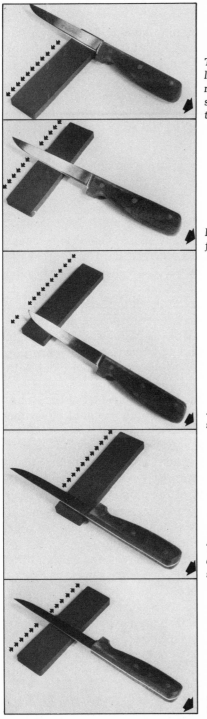

To sharpen a knife with an oilstone, begin by laying the blade across the face of the stone near one end, with the heel of the blade on the stone and the blade at a 10- to 15-degree angle to the stone.

Draw the blade across the stone diagonally, from heel . . .

. . . to point, so entire edge is honed in one stroke.

Turn the knife over, lay the blade across the end of the stone opposite of where you started . . .

. . . and sharpen the other side the same way—heel to point.

Using a Hone Steel

In some ways, using a hone steel is much the same as honing with an oilstone. You should maintain the same 10- to 15-degree angle and you should draw the blade across the steel in the same slicing motion, from the heel to the point. But instead of turning the blade over after the first stroke and drawing the blade back in the opposite direction, simply return the blade to its starting position, but on the opposite side of the steel, which will then be in contact with the other side of the blade. Then make another stroke. Continue sharpening by alternating strokes of the blade, first on one side of the steel, then on the other, and count your strokes.

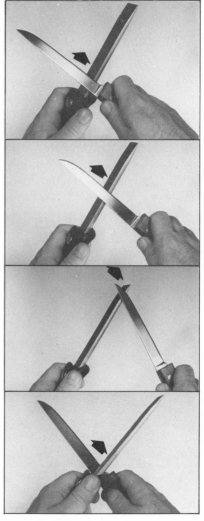

When using a hone steel, begin sharpening by laying the blade across the coarse edge of the steel, with the blade heel near the steel handle.

Draw the blade diagonally across the steel, from heel . . .

. . . to point.

Shift the blade to the opposite side of the steel and hone the other edge the same way.

As with using an oilstone, keeping track of your strokes will enable you to determine how many strokes it takes to put an edge on any given knife. For example, when our favorite fillet knives just begin to lose their keen edges, we know that eight to ten strokes on a hone steel, depending on the knife being used, will return that edge to its original sharpness. Then another half dozen strokes on the fine surface of the steel will polish the edge sufficiently for resuming fish-dressing tasks.

The manufacturers' directions that accompany some hone steels are distressing to us, because they recommend a potentially dangerous way to use the steel. They picture or suggest drawing the blade across the steel toward the hand holding the implement, the same way a butcher's steel is used. While this is fine for the long butcher's steels and might be all right for sharpening small pen knives on a hone steel, it is an unsafe method for sharpening the long blades of fillet knives. Always draw the blade away from the hand holding the hone steel.

Using the Case Safety-Sharp

If you have any worry about being able to maintain the proper blade angle during the sharpening process, you might prefer to invest in a more foolproof sharpener, such as the Case Safety-Sharp. This sharpener consists of a wooden base with predrilled holes into which two ceramic sharpening rods are inserted. The angle of the holes assures that the rods will be positioned at the proper angle to the knife blade.

To use the Safety-Sharp, extend the wood base to its open position

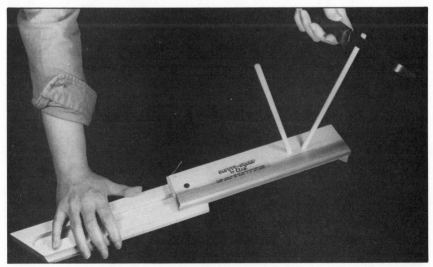

To sharpen a knife with the Case Safety-Sharp, extend the base to the open position and hold it secure with one hand well away from the sharpening rods. Hold your knife blade with the heel against the top of one rod, keeping the blade perpendicular to the base.

and grasp the end opposite the rods with one hand. In your other hand hold the knife with the heel of the blade against the top of one rod, making sure the blade is perpendicular to the base of the sharpener. Then draw the blade straight down, keeping it perpendicular to the base, and bringing the knife toward you to sharpen the entire edge, from heel to point. Then move the blade to the opposite rod and repeat the process. Continue sharpening, alternating from one rod to the other, until a fine cutting edge has been achieved. These hard, extremely fine-grit rods will put a keen edge on a blade. They require no oil, but they should be cleaned after each use with a household cleanser, such as Comet or Ajax.

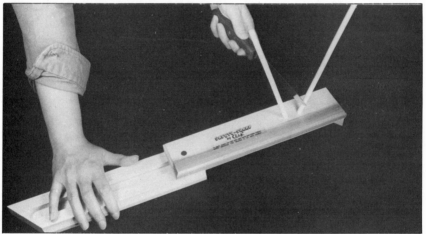

Draw the blade downward, along the rod, from heel to point. Move the blade to the top of the opposite rod and sharpen the other side of the blade the same way.

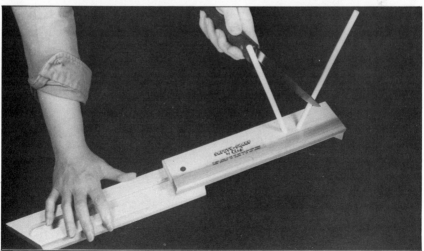

Stropping the Blade

Finely polishing the edge of the blade with a strop requires a different technique from those recommended for stones and steels. Instead of drawing the cutting edge of the blade across the strop first, start at the top of the strop and pull the blade across it with the back of the blade first, tilted upward at about a 10-degree angle to the strop. When the blade reaches the other end of the strop, pivot it on the back until the opposite edge touches the strop at a 10-degree angle. Then run the blade back up the strop. Do this several dozen times along the entire cutting edge of the knife, from heel to point.

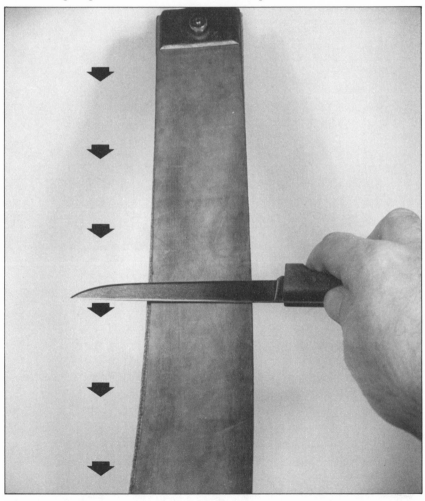

When stropping a blade, draw it across the strop with the back of the blade leading and the cutting edge trailing.

18

Turn the blade over and run it up the strop in the opposite direction, blade back first.

Using a Butcher's Steel

When you use a butcher's steel to realign the edge on a blade, you should maintain the same 10- to 15-degree angle recommended for oilstones and hone steels and you should draw the blade into the steel as if cutting off a thin slice. Since the butcher's steel is rather long, you can safely stroke it in the traditional manner. That is, you can hold the steel in one hand, pointing upward, while using the other hand to draw the knife down the steel toward the handle of the steel.

As with the hone steel, start at the heel of the blade and draw the blade down the length of the steel in a diagonal motion to steel the blade from heel to point. Do likewise on the other side of the steel to steel the other side of the blade. A half dozen or so strokes on each side of the blade are usually sufficient to reset the edge.

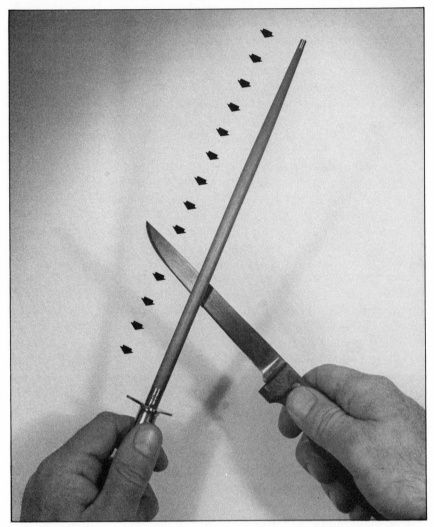

When using a butcher's steel, draw the blade from the tip of the steel toward the hilt.

Care of Your Cutlery

Fillet knives should be washed in hot, soapy water after each use and dried immediately. We recommend washing them by hand. Although many fillet knives are "dishwasher safe," the jostling they get from the high pressure of the water spray in a dishwasher could cause the blades to be dulled or nicked when they bang against other blades or utensils. Dishwashers are also hard on wooden knife handles.

Although stainless-steel blades are relatively corrosion resistant, they will stain and corrode if mistreated, especially if they're used around salt water. Generally, if you keep them clean stainless steel blades won't corrode.

Blades of high-carbon tool steel, on the other hand, are very susceptible to tarnishing and rusting and should be given a thin coat of vegetable oil after they are cleaned in hot, soapy water.

You should periodically clean and oil your folding knives, too, even if they are made of stainless steel. If you use a folding knife to cut bait or clean fish, clean it immediately afterward. Wash the knife in hot, soapy water, using a brush to clean all crevices. Dry the knife thoroughly and use the corner of a folded paper towel to reach difficult spots. Then let the knife air dry for an hour or more with the blades open.

After each cleaning, and from time to time between uses, put a drop or two of oil or a squirt of WD-40 into the joints of your folding knives. This will help remove dirt particles that act as abrasives and will retard corrosion. Moisture-displacing lubricants, such as WD-40, will also drive out residual moisture that causes rust.

If the blades of your folding knives are not stainless steel, you should keep them lightly coated with oil to prevent corrosion.

Use a Cleaning Board

Whenever you dress fish you should use a cleaning/cutting board of some kind to protect your knife blades and to make the fish easier to handle. Although any board of sufficient size will do, one of the fish-cleaning boards equipped with a steel holding jaw is the best choice, because it will hold the fish securely while freeing your hands for cleaning operations.

Plastic cleaning boards should be scrubbed in hot, soapy water after each use, then rinsed in hot water and dried. Wooden boards should be cleaned the same way, but other measures might be required to eliminate fishy odors in the board. An excellent way to remove slime and that fishy smell from a board is to make a paste of equal parts salt and baking soda moistened with fresh lemon juice. Then use the squeezed lemon half to scrub the board with the paste. Rinse the board with hot water and towel dry it. It also helps to put a cleaning board out in the open air and sunshine for an hour or two after you clean it.

Catalog of Cutlery and Accessories

In the following section, you will find a wide assortment of cutlery specifically designed for the angler, as well as various sharpening implements and other accessories you should find useful. Although we have included prices on all items, they appear only for comparison purposes. Prices change so rapidly these days that it is impossible to produce a book in which prices will be current. Furthermore, we have listed the suggested retail prices, and you might be able to find some of these products at reduced prices in mail-order catalogs and discount department stores. If you are unable to find any product of interest at a local outlet or in a mail-order catalog, write to the manufacturer for information. We have included addresses for your convenience.

Barbee Knives
Box 1702
Ft. Stockton, TX 79735

Brochure—$1.

Louisiana Special Fillet Knife, Model 900-B. Available with a choice of Micarta handles and features a seven-inch blade of 440-C stainless steel. Delivery time is from five to six months. Price with sheath: $75.

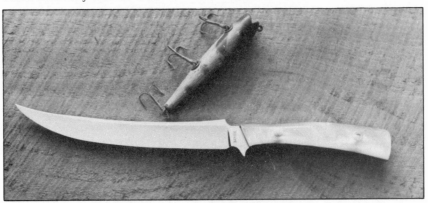

Barbee Louisiana Special Fillet Knife, Model 900-B.

Buck Knives, Inc.
P.O. Box 1267
El Cajon, CA 92022

Free brochure

Fisherman, Model 121 Knife. Features a gently curving 5½-inch blade. Contoured handle is molded of ebony-colored phenolic, which is impervious to heat, cold, and shock. A dural butt is used for lightness and balance. Price with sheath: $21.

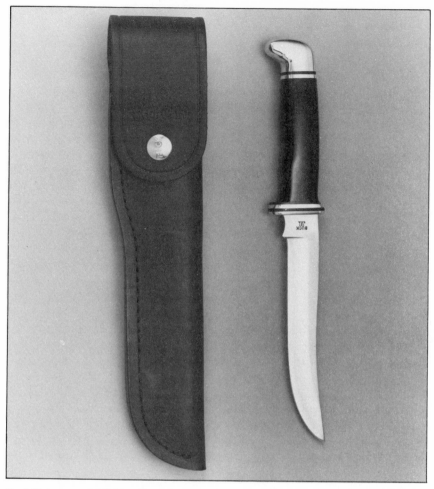

Buck Fisherman, Model 121.

Buck Honing Oil, Model 132. For use with all honing stones and available in three-ounce bottles. Price: $1.

Mounted Washita Honing Stone, Model 134. A 2-inch by 5-inch stone, mounted on a wooden base. Price: $9.

Mounted Hard Arkansas Stone, Model 135. A 2-inch by 5-inch stone, mounted on a wooden base. Price: $12.

Buck Honing Oil Kit, Model 133. Combines a Washita stone, hard Arkansas stone, and Buck honing oil in a plastic case. Price: $9.

Buck honing tools and materials.

Honemaster, Model 136. Attaches to any blade over ⅝-inch wide to maintain the proper angle while honing. Price: $7.

Washita Stone, Model 131. Stone measures 1⅝ inches by 4⅜ inches and comes in a plastic case. Price: $4.

Steelmaster, Model 137. A five-inch flat steel with metal handle and cam lever to secure steel. Price with sheath: $15.

Camillus Cutlery Co.
Camillus, NY 13031

Catalog—$1.

American Wildlife Angler's Folder, No. 32. Is five inches long closed and features ivory Delrin stag handle with inset Sid Bell pewter bass under acrylic. Has a clip blade with serrated tip and a flexible fillet blade, both stainless steel. Knife has a brass lock and nickel silver bolsters. Price: $18.

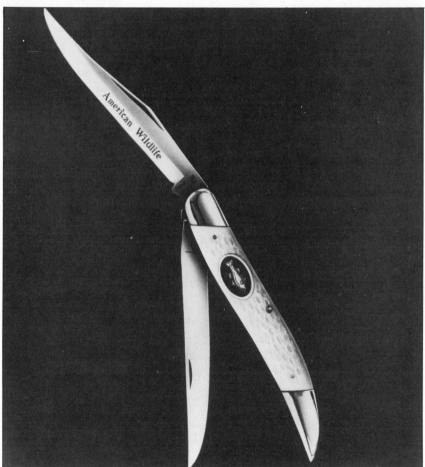

Camillus American Wildlife Angler's Folder, No. 32.

American Wildlife Fish Fillet, No. 1006. Overall length is 11 inches. Knife features a 440-A stainless-steel blade and ivory Delrin stag handle with inset Sid Bell pewter bass under acrylic. Price with sheath: $19.

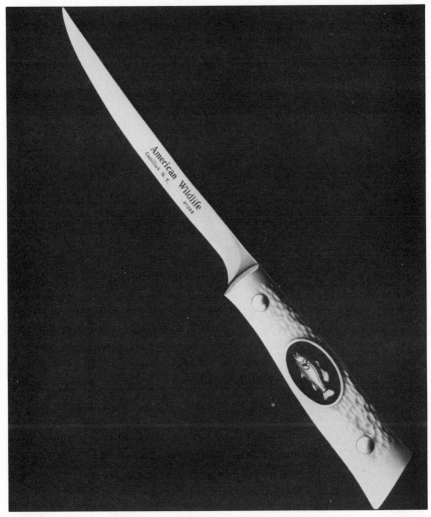

Camillus American Wildlife Fish Fillet, No. 1006.

Fisherman's Folder, No. 5. Features a 440-A stainless-steel sabre clip blade and smooth maize Delrin handle with hook-sharpening stone. Bolsters are nickel silver. Price: $10.75.

Angler's Folder, No. 31. Is five inches long closed and features a Delrin Indian stag handle, stainless-steel sabre clip blade with serrated tip, and scaler with hook disgorger and cap lifter. Bolsters are nickel silver. Price: $15.

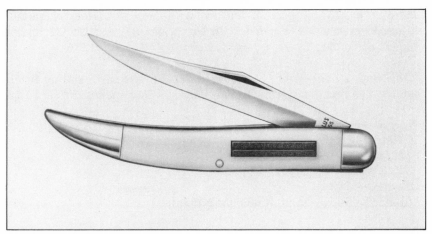

Camillus Fisherman's Folder, No. 5.

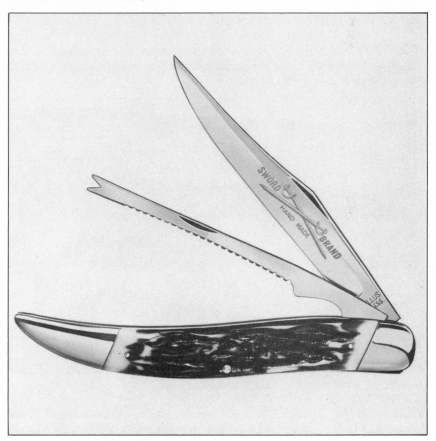

Camillus Angler's Folder, No. 31.

Sheath, No. 131. Top-grain leather with belt slot. Heavily saddle-stitched and riveted. For use with No. 5, No. 31, and No. 32 folding knives. Price: $4.

"Cam-Stone" Sharpening Steel, No. 9380. An abrasive coating firmly bonded to a steel mandrel. Overall length is four inches. Price: $4.50.

W. R. Case & Sons Cutlery Co.
20 Russell Blvd.
Bradford, PA 16701

Brochure—25¢
Full-line catalog—$5.50 (Collector's item)

Fillet Knife, No. 607-5½ FSSP. Features a 5½-inch, flexible, surgical-steel blade and shaped, natural walnut handle. Price with sheath: $18.50. Price without sheath: $10.50.

Fillet Knife, No. 607-9 SSP. Features a nine-inch, flexible, surgical-steel blade and shaped, natural-walnut handle. Price with sheath: $21.25. Price without sheath: $13.50.

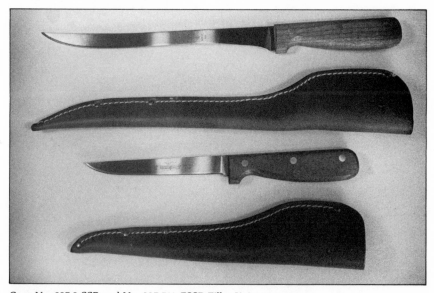

Case No. 607-9 SSP and No. 607-5½ FSSP Fillet Knives.

Fillet Knife, No. 124-6 SS. Has a six-inch, glazed stainless-steel blade, spoon end for cleaning fish, and hardwood handle. Price with sheath: $21.50.

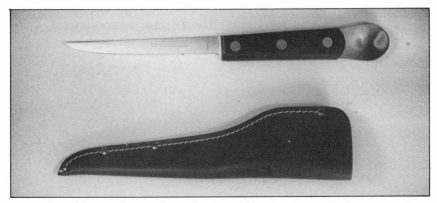

Case Fillet Knife, No. 124-6 SS.

Fillet Knife, No. P 204-6. Has a flexible, six-inch, mirror-finished blade and Pakkawood handle. Price with sheath: $19.35.

Folding Fisherman's Knife, No. 32095 F SS. Is five inches long closed and features cream-colored composition handle with hook hone. Stainless-steel blade and springs and stainless-steel scaler with disgorger and cap lifter. Price: $22.75.

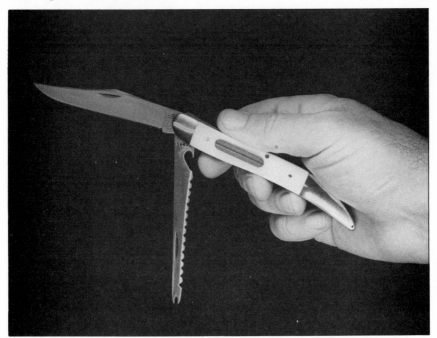

Case Folding Fisherman's Knife, No. 32095 F SS.

Sportsman Shear, No. 47. Measures 8½ inches overall and comes apart for easy cleaning. Chrome over nikel-plated forged steel. One blade serrated. Price with sheath: $23.25.

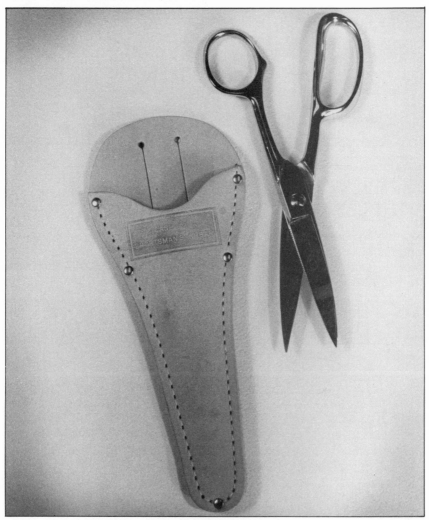

Case Sportsman Shear, No. 47.

Honing Oil. Is formulated to Case specifications for use with all stones. Comes in four-ounce cans. Price: $1.80.

Manufactured Oilstone. Measures 6 inches by 11½ inches by ½ inch and is used for sharpening all types of knives. Price: $7.75.

Washita Stone. Is a natural, soft Arkansas (novaculite) oilstone, measuring 5⅜ inches by ⁷⁄₁₆ inch by 1⅝ inches. Comes with plastic case. Price: $9.25.

Moon Stone. Measures 3⅞ inches by 1⅞ inches by ½ inch. Is a man-made stone that is harder than natural novaculite and has a more uniform "bite," with fewer surface imperfections. Produces a superfine edge. Price: $10.50.

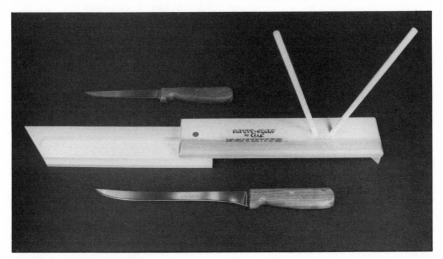

Case Safety-Sharp Sharpener.

Safety-Sharp Knife Sharpener. Features two nine-inch sharpening rods in a hardwood block that swivels open to keep hands safely away from knife blades when in use. Sharpening rods fit into predrilled holes to give proper angle for quick and easy sharpening. Compartment in base provides storage and protection for rods. Price: $16.50.

Gerber Legendary Blades
14200 SW 72nd Ave.
P.O. Box 23088
Portland, OR 97223

Free brochure

Tb/Trout & Bird Knife. Features exclusive Gerber nonslip Armorhide handle with stripping spoon and 3¼-inch, surgical stainless-steel blade. Overall length is eight inches. Price with scabbard: $16.50.

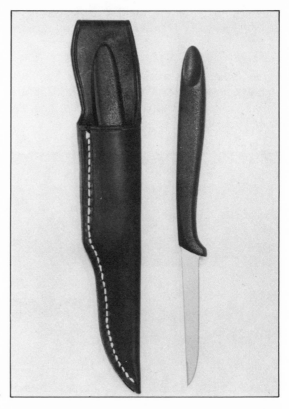

Gerber Tb/Trout & Bird Knife.

Mu/Muskie Knife. General purpose fillet knife, features nonslip Armorhide handle and six-inch, surgical stainless-steel blade. Overall length is 11¼ inches. Price with scabbard: $26.50.

Co/Coho Knife. Designed for cleaning and filleting large fish like salmon, features nonslip Armorhide handle with stripping spoon and six-inch, surgical stainless-steel blade. Overall length is 11¾ inches. Price with scabbard: $26.50.

F-5/Fisher 5. For filleting and steaking smaller fish, features a five-inch, drop-point blade. International orange, unbreakable handle with stripping spoon is molded onto notched blade tang. Overall length is 11 inches. Price without scabbard: $12.50. Scabbard price: $6.

F-8/Fisher 8. For filleting and steaking larger fish. Features are same as F-5, but blade is eight inches long. Overall length is 14 inches. Price without scabbard: $14.50. Scabbard price: $6.50.

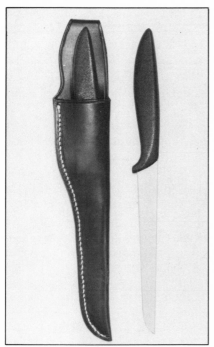

Gerber Mu/Muskie Knife.

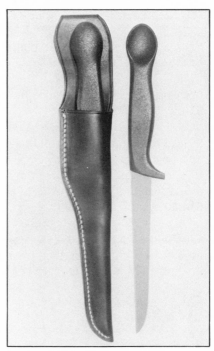

Gerber Co/Coho Knife.

Gerber F-5/Fisher 5 and F-8/Fisher 8 Knives.

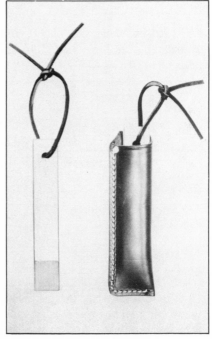

Gerber 5 St Sportsman's Steel.

8 Sth Sportsman's Steel. An eight-inch folding steel with leather handle and tie thong. Price: $18.50.

8 St Sportsman's Steel. An eight-inch steel in a leather scabbard. Price: $18.

5 Sth Sportsman's Steel. A five-inch folding steel with leather handle and tie thong. Price: $15.

5 St Sportsman's Steel. A five-inch steel in a leather scabbard. Price: $14.50.

Fsk Field Sharpening Kit. A complete sharpening kit, including a five-inch steel with leather thong, a double-edged (coarse grit and medium grit) whetstone, and leather scabbard. Price: $27.50.

J. A. Henkels/Zwillingswerk, Inc.
1 Westchester Plaza, Box 127
Elmsford, NY 10523

Free brochure

Fillet Knife, Model 32432-180. Features a seven-inch, high-carbon, no-stain steel, ice-hardened, hand-honed blade; and black wood handle. Price: $17.50.

Henkels Fillet Knife, Model 32432-180.

IPCO, Inc.
331 Lake Hazeltine Dr.
Chaska, MN 55318

Catalog—25¢

IPCO Clean-A-Fish Boards. Nine different models of cleaning boards, from Scalin' Boards for panfish to yard-long Lunker Boards, in hardwood and molded wood-grain models. Equipped with heavy steel power jaw for holding fish firmly, leaving both hands free to work. Also available are Clean-A-Fish combos that come with fillet knives. Price: $5.95 up.

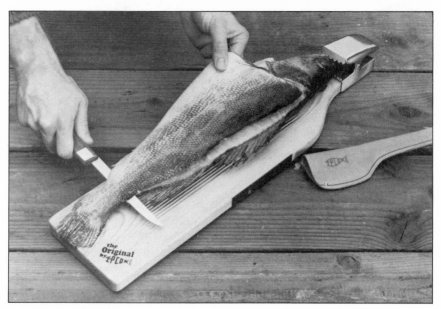

IPCO Clean-A-Fish Combo.

Jet-Aer Corp.
100 Sixth Ave.
Paterson, NJ 07524

Free brochure

Mariner Fillet Knife, Model No. 2083. Features full-tang construction and 6¼-inch, stainless-steel blade. Nonslip, high-impact plastic handle has brass rivets. Price without sheath: $3.75.

Mariner Cuda Fillet, Model No. 2078. Features classic style, 6¼-inch, high-carbon, rustproof blade and finger-grip handle. Price with sheath: $8.95.

Mariner Cuda Magnum, Model No. 2079. Heavy-duty fillet knife features a 7½-inch, flexible, high-carbon, rustproof blade and finger-grip handle. Price with sheath: $9.95.

Mariner Cuda Flex Fillet, Model No. 2099. Combines flexible blade action with broad blade shape and features a 6¼-inch, 440-C stainless-steel blade and finger-grip handle. Price with sheath: $9.49.

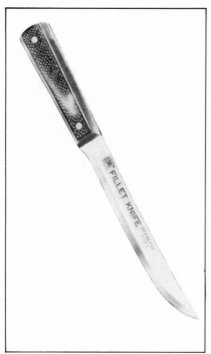

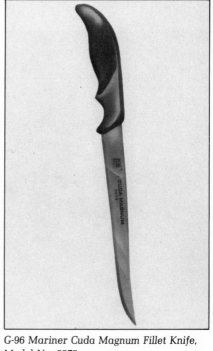

G-96 Mariner Fillet Knife, Model No. 2083.

G-96 Mariner Cuda Magnum Fillet Knife, Model No. 2079.

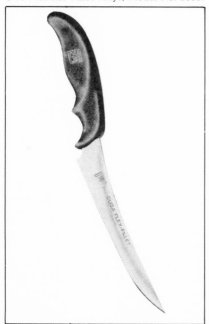

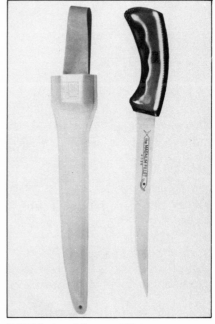

G-96 Mariner Cuda Flex Fillet Knife, Model No. 2099.

G-96 Mariner Magnum Fillet, Model No. 2025.

Mariner Magnum Fillet, Model No. 2025. A larger version of the classic style fillet knife, with a nine-inch blade. Price with sheath: $12.95.

Mariner Floater, Model No. 2075. Classic style fillet knife features a 6¼-inch, rustproof blade and nonslip, finger-grip, floating handle with high-visibility yellow butt plate. Price with sheath: $11.95.

Mariner Regal Fillet, Model No. 2011. Constructed entirely of 420 stainless steel to clean quickly without absorbing odors. Classic style blade is 6½ inches long. Price with sheath: $17.95.

Mariner Sure-Grip Fish Skinner, Model No. 2098. Features extra-heavy-duty tempered spring and wide-spread, reverse-curve handle for added leverage and comfort. Jaws have interlocking teeth. Made of heavy chrome-plated steel. Price: $3.98.

G-96 Mariner Sure-Grip Fish Skinner, Model No. 2098.

G-96 Mariner Floater, Model No. 2075.

KA-BAR Khyber Fish Fillet Knives, #0860 and #0862.

Ka-Bar Cutlery, Inc.
5777 Grant Ave.
Cleveland, OH 44105

Free brochure

Khyber Fish Fillet Knife #0860. Features a six-inch, flat-ground, stainless-steel blade with a molded, nonslip handle permanently bonded to the blade. Price with sheath: $8.95.

Khyber Fish Fillet Knife #0862. Same as the Model 0860, but with an eight-inch blade. Price with sheath: $9.95.

KA-BAR Fish Fillet Knife #1383. Features a six-inch, flexible, stainless-steel blade with contoured Honduras rosewood handle. Price: $11.

Al Mar Knives
5861 SW Benfield Ct.
Lake Oswego, OR 97034

Free brochure

Fisher Knife. Features full tapered-tang construction with a 4¼-inch, high-carbon, stain-resistant blade and ivory-colored Micarta handle. Made in Japan in the time-proven tradition of the Japanese Samurai sword makers. Price with sheath: $70.

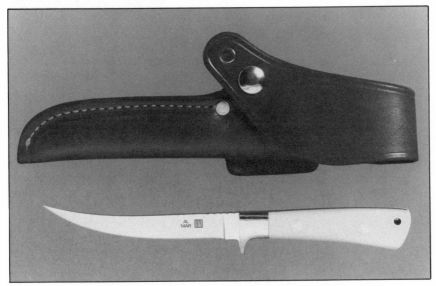

Al Mar Fisher Knife.

Normark Corp.
1710 East 78th St.
Minneapolis, MN 55423

Free brochure

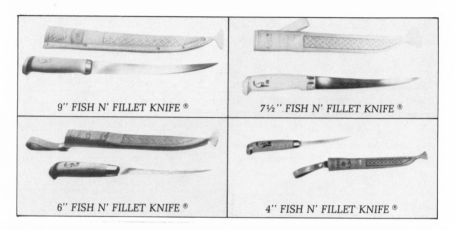

9" FISH N' FILLET KNIFE ®	7½" FISH N' FILLET KNIFE ®
6" FISH N' FILLET KNIFE ®	4" FISH N' FILLET KNIFE ®

Fish 'n Fillet Knife, FNF4. Trout and panfish knife features a four-inch, hand-ground blade of Swedish stainless steel. Handle is varnished, reinforced birch. Comes with tooled-leather Laplander sheath. Overall length is 9½ inches. Price with sheath: $8.95.

Fish 'n Fillet Knife, FNF6. Same as model FNF4, but with six-inch blade. Overall length is 12½ inches. Price with sheath: $10.95.

Husky Fish 'n Fillet, FNF7. Same as above models, but with 7½-inch blade. Overall length is 13½ inches. Price with sheath: $13.95.

Big Fish Fillet Knife, FNF9. Same as above models, but with nine-inch blade. Overall length is 15½ inches. Price with sheath: $17.95.

Fish 'n Fillet Board, B-24. Hardwood fish-cleaning board with deep-ribbed grooves to keep fish from sliding. Rust-resistant, deep-jaw, steel clamp holds fish firmly in place. Board is 24 inches long and 6 inches wide. Price: $13.95.

Fish 'n Fillet Board, B-24/6. Same as model B-24, but comes with FNF6 knife that fits into slot in side of board. Price: $19.95.

Fish 'n Fillet Board, B-36. Same as model B-24, but measures 36 inches long and 7 inches wide. Price: $14.95.

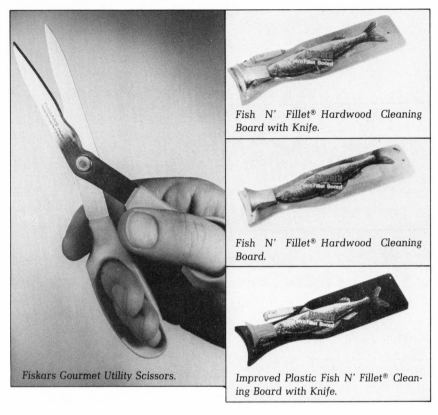

Fish N' Fillet® Hardwood Cleaning Board with Knife.

Fish N' Fillet® Hardwood Cleaning Board.

Fiskars Gourmet Utility Scissors.

Improved Plastic Fish N' Fillet® Cleaning Board with Knife.

Fish 'n Fillet Board, PB-24. Same as model B-24, but made of poly-molded plastic. Price: $8.95.

Fiskars Gourmet Utility Scissors. Lightweight, super-sharp shears with comfortable, contoured grips. Stainless-steel blades are precision ground. Exclusive ball-bearing pivot assures long life and easy, comfortable operation. Price: $10.95.

Olsen Knife Co., Inc.
Howard City, MI 49329

Free brochure

Fillet Knife, No. 213F6. Features six-inch, high-carbon, Swedish tool-steel blade with riveted wood handle. Price with sheath: $10.95.

Fillet Knife, No. 213F9. Same as Model 213F6, but with nine-inch blade. Price with sheath: $12.95.

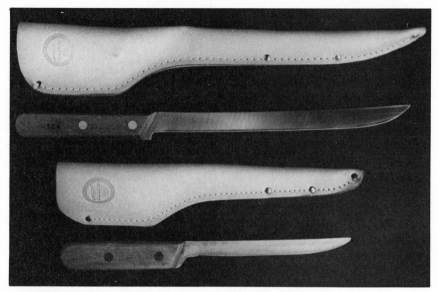

Olsen Fillet Knives, No. 213F6 and 213F9.

Randall Made Knives
P.O. Box 1988
Orlando, FL 32802

Free catalog

Salt Fisherman, Model 10. Available with either five-inch or seven-inch blade of ⅛-inch stock. Blades are fully handcrafted from high-carbon stainless steel. Duralumin handle has comfortable, slip-proof grip. Available with Micarta or rosewood handle at no extra cost. Delivery time is five to six weeks. Price with sheath: $40.

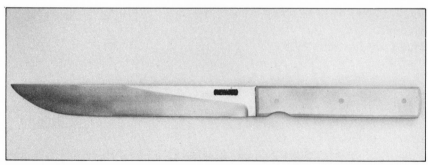

Randall Salt Fisherman, Model 10.

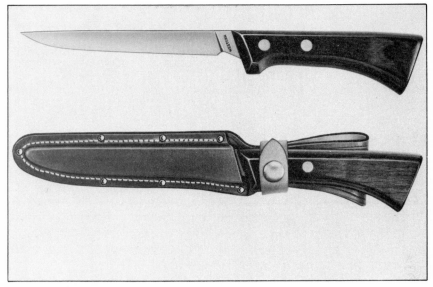

Western Fish Fillet Knife, No. SW766.

Western Cutlery Co.
1800 Pike Rd.
P.O. Box 1539
Longmont, CO 80501

Free catalog

Fish Fillet Knife, No. SW766. Features a six-inch, flat-ground, satin-finished stainlesss-steel blade that is thin and flexible. Large handle is resin-impregnated hardwood. Overall length is 11 inches. Price with sheath: $12.95.

Super Fillet Knife, No. SW769. Same as model SW766, but with nine-inch blade. Overall length is 14 inches. Price with sheath: $14.50.

Fishing Knife, No. S-751. Features stainless-steel blades and springs, yellow Delrin handle with hook hone, master clip blade, and scaler blade with hook disgorger and cap lifter. Closed length is 4⅜ inches. Price without sheath: $15.95. Price with leather belt sheath: $18.95.

Ceramic Hone, No. 992. Sapphire-hard, fine-grained ceramic with three different surfaces: flat top and bottom, rounded sides, and V-groove. The hone is 6½ inches by 1 inch by ⅜ inch and comes with leather thong. Price: $6.95.

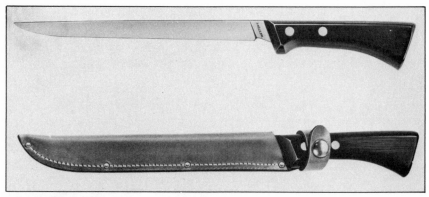

Western Super Fillet Knife, No. SW769.

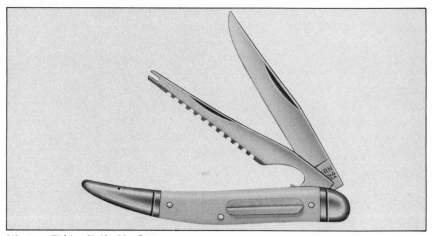

Western Fishing Knife, No. S-751.

Handi-Hone, No. 991. Combination stone measures 3 inches by 1½ inches by ½ inch and has leather grips attached for holding stone while sharpening. Grips can also be used for stropping. Price with sheath: $12.25.

Zak Tackle Mfg. Co.
235 So. 59th St.
Tacoma, WA 98408

Free brochure

"Zak" Fish & Deer Knife. Extremely efficient and guaranteed for easy, fast, clean, and safe opening or cleaning and skinning of fish. Ideal for drawing and dressing fish of any size. A must for the angler who keeps

the roe for food or bait. Used and recommended by many fisheries biologists. Long-lasting blade is reversible for extra-long life. Price with plastic sheath: $2.50.

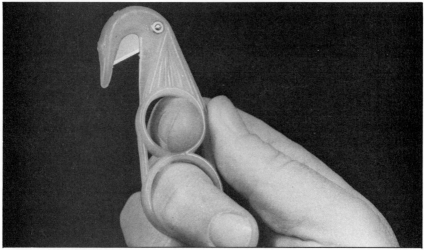

"Zak" Fish & Deer Knife.

John Zakovich
Box 353
Biwabik, MN 55708

Fish Fillet Knife. Available in models with 7½-inch or 9-inch blades, handcrafted of high-carbon tool steel. Full-tang construction with riveted hardwood handle. Ideal for those who prefer a stiffer blade for cutting through heavy ribs on bass and all large fish. Prices: $7.75 for 7½-inch blade, $8.75 for 9-inch blade (hardwood scabbard extra).

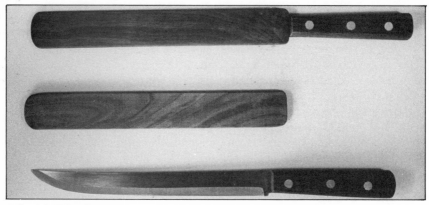

Zakovich Fish Fillet Knife.

45

Chapter 3

KEEPING THE CATCH FRESH

After watching how people keep fish from the time they're caught until they're eaten, we've come to the conclusion that more fish are probably ruined because of poor handling in the field than for any other reason. Since fish flesh deteriorates so rapidly after the fish is killed, it is imperative that the angler take every possible measure to keep the catch fresh from the time it's taken from the water until it is cooked or preserved for later consumption. Otherwise, the quality will decrease, or worse yet, the fish will spoil.

Keeping or Releasing the Catch

It should be apparent to any right-thinking angler that most fish should be released unharmed and that we should keep only as much fish as we can consume in a reasonable period. Lugging home limits of fish that will be foisted on friends and neighbors or shoved into a freezer to sit for a year is hardly in the best interest of maintaining the resource. In fact, wasting fish is not only pointless, but criminal.

On the other hand, you should have no qualms about keeping enough fish for a meal or two and a few more to freeze for later use. You should have no pangs of conscience about taking advantage of seasonal surpluses, as long as you properly care for your catch and preserve it for maximum quality. And, by all means, you should take as many of the underutilized species as you can put to good use, particularly where these fish tend to overpopulate. In short, there's nothing wrong with keeping the catch, as long as you do so wisely and within reason, and as long as you use what you keep.

Landing or Boating the Catch

Whether you plan to keep or release a fish, you should bring it in quickly without unnecessarily horsing it and handle it as little as possible. If you plan to release the fish, try to do so without removing the fish from the water. Use an efficient hook remover—such as a pair of forceps, longnose pliers, or the Zak's Flipgun—to get the hook out while the fish remains in the water. If you must handle the fish, do so carefully. Avoid using a landing net, if possible, and never gaff a fish that will be turned loose unless it is an extremely large fish that can only be held with a gaff for hook removal. Be sure to gaff the fish cautiously by running the point of the gaff into the thin mandibular membrane on the lower jaw.

Even if you plan to keep the fish, use nets and gaffs with discretion, only when they are the best means of safely and efficiently landing or boating a fish. Fish that will be kept alive on a stringer or in a livewell should be treated just as carefully as fish that are released.

Don't let fish flop around on the bank or the deck of a boat where they can become bruised. Keep a tight line on fish that are netted to prevent their entanglement in the net mesh.

Wet your hands before handling small fish because dry hands can remove protective slime from the fish's body or even knock scales loose. Such spots are then often attacked by fungi that can ultimately kill the fish. If you handle a large fish with wet hands, though, you might do even worse damage when you squeeze the fish to get a good grip on it. Try not to handle large fish at all, unless you plan on keeping them.

Fish that are too large for a stringer or livewell should be killed at once with a sharp rap to the head with a "priest" or fish billy. Then they should be gutted, gilled, and iced at once or iced and dressed as soon as possible.

Keeping the Catch Alive

Fish can be kept alive on stringers if they are properly strung and kept in water that is deep enough for their survival. Fish that die on stringers deteriorate rapidly, so you should be careful in how you string them and should use an adequate stringer.

The angler has a choice of two types of commercially available stringers: the bayonet type, which is a length of rope with a large metal ring at one end and a pointed shaft or bayonet at the other, or the safety-pin type, which is six or more snap clips that close like safety pins and are attached to a length of rope or chain. Except for a few specific purposes, the latter is by far the better choice.

The problem with many stringers is that they are too short and, if used unaltered, will keep fish in water that is too shallow, too warm, and too low in oxygen. It just doesn't make sense to bring a fish up from

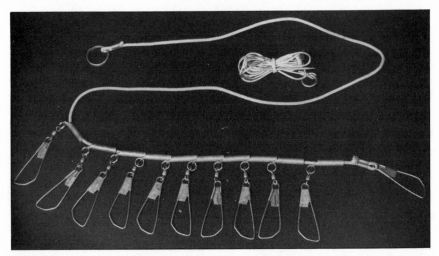

The best stringer for most purposes is a top-quality safety pin-type at least six feet long and equipped with swivels. A long (six to nine feet) bayonet stringer gives added length for keeping fish alive in deeper water.

depths of 10, 15, 20 or more feet and expect it to remain in good shape in two feet of water, often in the blazing sun. Most cheap safety-pin stringers are nothing more than a four-foot length of light chain to which a half dozen or so snap clips are directly attached. Such stringers not only keep fish in water that is too shallow, but they allow fish to twist and snarl the chain, which impedes movement and usually results in death.

We recommend that you invest in the best safety-pin stringer you can find. It should be no less than six feet long, and all snap clips should be equipped with swivels that prevent the fish from becoming entangled. We prefer the kind that has the snap clips attached to rings or tubes that slide up and down the length of the stringer. With such a stringer, it is possible to keep vacant clips in the boat and add fish to the stringer without bringing up the entire catch every time. If you fish from a boat, you can add a length of rope to a stringer to allow fish to seek the cooler depths and lie in the shade of the boat. Of course, you must be careful to place the stringer amidships or far enough forward to keep it out of the way of an electric motor or outboard.

String your fish by running the snap clip through the mandibular membrane in the lower jaw only. This allows the fish freedom of movement and maximum oxygen intake. No matter what kind of stringer you use, never run it through the gills of a fish because the stringer will damage the gills and cause the fish to hemorrhage and die.

Fish kept on a stringer need not be brought aboard when the boat is moved at slow speeds, such as when you're trolling or slowly maneuvering a boat along a shoreline. Before getting underway at any but idle or trolling speed, however, hoist your stringer aboard. We have found that a large piece of wet burlap does wonders in keeping strung fish alive when we're moving from one spot to another. We use a large enough piece to cover the deck where the fish will be placed, with plenty left over to cover the catch. This not only cushions the fish, but it prevents them from flopping about while keeping them wet and cool.

String a fish by running the snap clip through the mandibular membrane of the lower jaw.

We put the bayonet type stringers to two uses. When we're fishing from shore we like to attach a nine-foot bayonet stringer to the upper end of a safety-pin stringer to greatly increase stringer length and allow fish to seek out deeper waters. We also use heavy-duty, nine-foot bayonet stringers for stringing large fish, one fish per stringer. Big, powerful fish should never be stacked on a stringer of any type, and they shouldn't be trusted to safety-pin stringers that can snap open under heavy pressure.

If you enjoy wading streams or the shallow backwaters of lakes and bays, attach one end of a length of rope to a belt and the other to a stringer and let your catch trail behind you in the water. If you stop to fish any particular spot, find a deep, sheltered pool and tie the rope and stringer to a nearby tree root or log.

Stringers are impractical for most panfish. Since these fish are often taken in large numbers, stringing each one would be a time-consuming nuisance. Moreover, these small fish don't keep well on stringers. A far better choice is a wire-mesh fish basket. We use one that has a spring-loaded lid that opens easily for dropping in the catch and snaps closed to keep fish from escaping.

On extended fishing trips we also use live boxes to keep the catch alive and well until we can clean them. A live box is easy to make from a framework of 2 × 2 lumber to which galvanized wire screen is attached with heavy-duty staples. The box should have a hinged lid that locks shut. It should be kept in water that is deep enough for the fish to remain comfortable, such as a shaded area near a dock or boathouse. The live box not only keeps fish healthy and allows them freedom of movement, but it keeps them out of the reach of predators. More than one angler has learned the hard way that fish kept on stringers for too long near docks and boathouses are likely to end up as meals for hungry turtles, mink, otter, and other opportunists.

Creeling the Catch

Some stream fishermen, particularly trout anglers, like to keep their catch in a creel. A creel is a handy item, indeed, and will keep fish relatively fresh—within limits. Use only the wicker-type creel for holding fish. The canvas pouches lined with plastic or rubber that are called creels are not at all good for holding fish because they do not permit sufficient air circulation and cooling.

Creels work best when the weather is cool. Use plenty of damp moss or small pieces of damp burlap to separate the fish and promote cooling by evaporation. Despite recommendations for lining the creel with damp grass, leaves, and other foliage, this is a poor practice. Dead grass does not hold moisture well and will do little to cool your catch; dead leaves are just as inefficient. Green foliage will start to rot immediately, thus increasing the temperature in the creel and the possibility of spoiling your catch.

All creeled fish should be gutted and gilled as soon as possible. Leave the heads on for easier handling. On a warm day, when temperatures are 70° F. or above, kill your fish as soon as they're caught, gut and gill them at once, and get them out of the creel and into a frying pan within an hour or two. If you'll be keeping them for later consumption, put them on ice.

Killing and Cooling the Catch

The best way to retard deterioration and prevent spoilage of fish is to kill the catch as soon as possible and ice it down. If you don't have access to ice, fish should be killed, gutted, gilled, and hung in a cool place and kept dry.

If you will be traveling to a remote area to fish where no ice is available, you should take along plenty of salt, paper towels, fine-mesh cheesecloth or deer bags, and a roll of masking tape. If temperatures are below 70° F., you should be able to keep fish fresh for 24 hours or more by first eviscerating them and wiping the stomach cavity clean with paper towels. Then rub an ample amount of salt into the stomach cavity and on the outside of the fish. Find a cool, shaded area where you can hang the fish from a pole made of a trimmed sapling and lashed horizontally between two trees or other uprights. Prop the stomach cavities open with small twigs to facilitate air circulation and make sure none of the fish are touching each other. Then cover the fish with cheesecloth or a deer bag and seal any openings in the cloth by tying or taping it with masking tape.

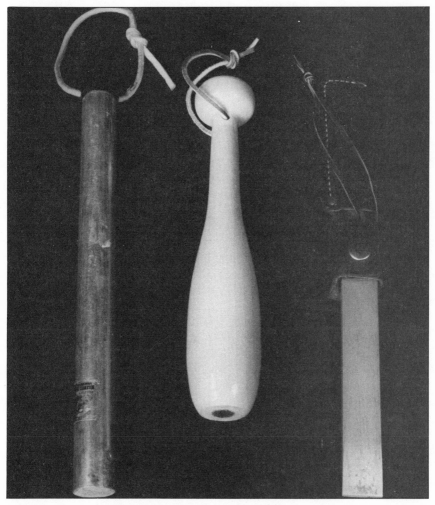

Three handy items for quickly dispatching a fish. The two on the left are "priests" specifically designed for killing fish. One is a length of aluminum tubing filled with lead. The other is a lead-weighted billy. The hone steel on the right is also useful as a fish billy.

On trips of one day or less, if you don't have room in your boat for an ice chest or don't want to lug one along if you fish from the bank, wet burlap will help immensely in keeping the catch cool and fresh. Fish kept under wet burlap will be as much as 10° F. cooler than the air temperature.

Although it's best to gut and gill fish immediately after they're killed, most whole fish will keep well for several hours on ice and can be cleaned during lulls in the angling action. Fish that have been actively feeding, however, should be gutted and gilled promptly to prevent enzymes in the fish's digestive fluids from acting on the fish's flesh.

Nothing beats clean ice for cooling fish quickly and efficiently, and you should try to ice your catch whenever possible. Studies have shown that properly iced fish keep better than fish refrigerated at 32° F. You will need about one pound of crushed or shaved ice for every two pounds of fish, and you'll need to add more every few hours as the ice melts.

When you pack fish in ice, line the bottom of your cooler with about four inches of ice. Follow that with a layer of gutted and gilled fish, making sure each fish is separated from the others by at least an inch. All but the smallest panfish should have their stomach cavities packed with ice. Continue packing the cooler in alternating layers of ice and fish and top it off with a final layer of four or more inches of ice.

Generally, the quicker you cool your catch and the colder you keep it, the better. Even seemingly minor temperature rises will dramatically increase the rate of deterioration and spoilage. For example, commercial fishermen have found that fish that keep well on ice at 32° F. for as long as 10 days will last only about half that time at 37° F., a difference of a mere five degrees. At 45° F. the same fish will keep only about two days.

Saltwater fishermen who have access to ice have an added advantage when it comes to cooling the catch. They can use ice and salt water to create a slush brine that will quickly chill the catch. To make a slush brine, fill an ice chest or washtub with crushed or shaved ice and pour sea water over it to the level of the ice. Stir the ice and sea water, creating a slush. Then immerse the gutted and gilled fish in the slush and keep them there for about 30 minutes. Remove the quick-chilled fish from the slush and pack them in clean ice in an ice chest.

Freshwater and saltwater fishermen alike can use salt and ice to help keep the catch fresh. For this process, the folks at the University of North Carolina Sea Grant College Program recommend lining the bottom of an ice chest with about four inches of crushed ice, leaving the drain cock open. Use a washtub or another cooler to make a mixture of salted ice, consisting of one pound of coarse dairy salt for every

20 pounds of crushed or shaved ice. Then lay fish on the bottom layer of ice in the ice chest, making sure that the fish are separated from one another by at least a couple of inches. Cover with a layer of about four inches of salted ice and follow that with another layer of fish. Continue packing in alternating layers of fish and salted ice until the chest is full. Top it off with a layer of salted ice. Keep the chest in a cool, shaded area where salt water draining from the open drain cock as the ice melts will pose no problems. Check the fish at least twice daily and repack with salted ice as required.

Gutted and gilled fish can be kept fresh in this way for up to one week. Fish packed in ice only, however, will keep only for about 48 to 72 hours before they begin to spoil. You can also use the salted ice method for keeping fillets and steaks fresh, but these should be sealed in plastic bags first and then layered the same way as whole fish.

Transporting the Catch

For one-day trips to nearby fishing spots, you should have no problem keeping your catch fresh and cool. If you have kept your fish alive, you can leave them whole and ice them down in a cooler if you have to transport them only a short distance. You can safely transport most fish this way if your travel time is no more than an hour or two.

For shorter distances, you can keep your fish wrapped in wet burlap. In fact, we use wet burlap during all but the hottest weather for transporting fish from nearby lakes to our home and have had no problems. In fact, when we're fishing at spots no more than a half-hour drive from home, our fish are usually still alive when we get them home.

For long distance trips, you will have to ice your catch or freeze it. If you prefer to dress your catch at home, it will keep well for even the longest of trips if you ice it thoroughly and check it frequently, adding more ice as required.

Whether you use the salted ice method or ice only, if you do a lot of fishing and frequently transport large quantities of iced fish, you would do well to make a drainage rack or false bottom for your ice chest. Use galvanized wood screws or nails to attach wooden slats the length of the cooler to 2 × 2 cross members cut to the width of the cooler. Cut V-notches in the bottoms of the 2 × 2s to facilitate drainage.

To use the drainage rack, put a layer of crushed ice in the bottom of the ice chest; then push the rack down into the ice—slats up—and pour another two or three inches of ice over the rack. Put a layer of fish on the ice and a layer of ice over the fish and continue packing in this manner. Or you can pack with salt and ice, as described earlier. Then, every two to four hours, open the drain cock on the cooler and let all water run out. Add more ice as necessary. In this way, fish will be kept packed solidly in ice and the bottom layer of fish will not be able to sink into the ice water where they could become waterlogged.

If you prefer to dress and freeze your catch before heading home, package and label it according to the directions in Chapter 6. Then freeze it quickly and let it stand in the freezer for 24 hours or until frozen solid.

If you're no more than a day's drive from home, wrap your packaged frozen fish in several layers of newspaper and pack in an ice chest. If you don't have a full cooler of fish, fill the cooler to the top with wadded newspapers, which will eliminate dead-air space and will help to insulate the fish. Fish packed this way should remain frozen solid for at least 12 to 14 hours, with no need for using dry ice. If the weather is warm, wrap your ice chest in a sleeping bag or a couple of heavy blankets to further insulate it and prevent the fish from thawing.

If you'll be traveling for two or more days, you should make prior arrangements to put your fish in a freezer when you make overnight stops, or you will have to use dry ice. The Chamber of Commerce in any city where you plan to stay overnight should be able to provide you with information about short-term freezer storage. Phone them prior to your trip to make necessary arrangements. Dry ice is solid carbon dioxide and is used as a refrigerant. It is available at ice companies in most cities but is sometimes hard to find in small towns or in remote areas, so any angler planning to transport his frozen catch packed in dry ice should make prior inquiries as to availability. Sometimes marinas and charter services sell dry ice. Also, be sure to check with commercial cold-storage facilities.

Since dry ice will burn your skin, never handle it directly. It will also burn fish and can burn through the plastic walls of an ice chest if not wrapped adequately in several layers of newspaper. A cooler full of frozen fish can be kept at below-freezing temperatures with one five-pound chunk of dry ice for 24 to 30 hours. If you'll be traveling longer than that, make prior arrangements to add more dry ice along the way.

Chapter 4

KEEPING THE ROE

While many anglers discard the roe with the entrails when cleaning the catch, others keep the roe for food or bait. Indeed, some fishermen hold the roe of certain species in higher regard than the fish's flesh. In some parts of the country, fish eggs are among the most popular of baits to use.

Fish Roe as Food

Personally, we are not big fish roe fans. But individual tastes and food preferences and prejudices notwithstanding, we have occasionally enjoyed caviar and other fish-egg dishes in moderation and have handled and prepared more roe than the average angler will in a lifetime. When we worked as commercial fish buyers we bought hundreds of pounds of salmon eggs that were exported to Japan, where they were sold at premium prices and were usually served cured but uncooked. If you haven't tried fish roe, we suggest you experiment with the roe of several species and judge for yourself. You might soon join the ranks of anglers who relish this bonus food.

Popular American Roe Fish

In the U.S., the roe most often consumed are the eggs of sturgeon, shad, and salmon, but others are popular in various parts of the country. The roe of panfish—bluegill, crappie, rock bass, and the like—is prized by some anglers. You might also try the roe of trout (particularly steelhead), black bass, striped bass, white bass, whitefish, walleye, sauger, alewife, and sucker.

You should exercise caution with the eggs of saltwater species, because not only are some inedible, but the eggs of certain otherwise popular food and sport species—the cabezon, to name but one—are toxic. Check with the local fish and game agency or county extension agent in any coastal area before you keep the roe of saltwater fishes for food.

Making Caviar

Strictly speaking, only the roe of sturgeon is true caviar. In fact, in the U.S., the roe of other fishes cannot be labeled as caviar. But for our purposes, we'll loosely use the term to describe the roe of any fish that is brine-cured and consumed uncooked.

Certainly, if you are fortunate enough to land a gravid sturgeon, you'll want to save the roe and prepare this connoisseur's delight. But you might also wish to make "caviar" from the roe of other species. Salmon, trout, shad, and whitefish eggs are among the most popular for this method of preparation.

No matter what species of fish, if you plan to keep the eggs for human consumption, you should dress the fish as soon as it's caught. Carefully remove the egg skeins, being cautious not to crush or puncture any of the eggs. Seal the eggs in clean plastic bags and store them on ice until you get them home. Don't wash them.

To prepare your caviar, follow these steps:

1. Carefully remove individual eggs from the skeins and put them into a nonmetallic bowl. Although this can be done by hand, some people prefer to split the skein with a knife point, then carefully rub the skein over a fine-mesh screen (¼- to ½-inch mesh will do for most species). This allows the eggs to break away from the membrane and fall through the screen, leaving the inedible portions of the skein behind. No matter how you do it, be sure to remove all pieces of membrane, bits of intestine, skin, and blood from the eggs.
2. For each cup of eggs, make a brine by dissolving one cup of curing salt in one quart of cold (about 40° F.) water.
3. Pour the brine over the eggs and let stand for about 30 minutes or until the eggs become firm. Stir occasionally and check the eggs for firmness about every five minutes after the first 15 minutes. If the eggs are runny when pinched, they are not firm enough; they should be gelled.
4. Pour the eggs into a strainer and rinse very lightly in cold water, carefully removing any bits of membrane or other material.
5. Let excess water drain off the eggs for several minutes. Then pack your caviar in tightly covered jars or freezer containers and store in the refrigerator. Thus preserved, the cavier should keep well for several weeks in the refrigerator.

Fried Egg Skeins

The small skeins of immature eggs and skeins from small fishes are quite tasty when lightly breaded and pan fried or deep fried. As usual, you should remove the skeins immediately after catching the fish and store them in plastic bags on ice. At home, remove any bits of intestine from the skeins and soak the skeins in a brine made from one cup of curing or dairy salt dissolved in each quart of cold water. Refrigerate the brined skeins and let them soak for about one hour; then rinse them under cold, running water and lay them on paper towels to drain for several minutes. After the skeins have drained, they can be placed in air-tight containers and refrigerated for use within two days, or they can be wrapped and frozen for later use within 90 days.

To prepare the skeins, beat an egg (chicken type) with a half cup of light cream or buttermilk, which you can season with garlic salt, onion salt, fines herbes, and freshly ground black pepper. Dip the skeins in this mixture and roll them in your favorite breading (see Chapter 12—Frying the Catch). Then fry quickly in oil at 350° F. until golden brown on all sides. This is a favorite fish camp dish, served with scrambled eggs and buttermilk biscuits for breakfast.

Sautéed Fish Eggs

We learned this method from a salty old commercial fisherman some years ago. Although he used fresh salmon eggs, you might want to experiment with the eggs of any species available locally.

As with the above methods, make sure the egg skeins are removed from the fish as soon as the fish is caught. Keep skeins iced and when you get home, brine, rinse, and drain them as you would for fried skeins (above).

To prepare this simple dish, first chop a medium onion and sauté it in a skillet with one quarter pound of butter for each pound of eggs. Add a finely chopped clove of garlic, if you like. Then add the egg skeins and sauté them, turning frequently, until they "set up." Salt and pepper to taste and serve with wedges of lemon or lime.

Fish Roe as Bait

Although the eggs of salmon and trout are the ones most frequently used as bait, other roe is also productive and is a staple in the diets of many species of game fish and panfish. Sturgeon, for example, seasonally consume large quantities of herring and shad eggs, and during the spawning runs of the smaller fishes, their eggs make excellent sturgeon bait. Many panfish, particularly bluegill, are notorious nest raiders that gorge themselves on the eggs of other species. They, too, can be taken on fish-egg baits. In the cold waters of our northern states, whitefish are caught on salmon eggs. In Montana and Alaska, grayling relish single salmon eggs impaled on tiny hooks and drifted through likely pools. The eggs of bluegills, suckers, and other freshwater fish make excellent bait for several species of catfish and bullhead.

Freezing Bait Roe

If you're pressed for time, you can freeze roe and thaw it later to make your baits according to any of the following methods. You can increase the storage life of already cured baits by freezing them. You can also make spawn sacks with fresh roe and freeze them for later use.

As with the freezing of fish, you should carefully wrap bait roe to maintain quality and you should freeze your baits quickly. If you're freezing whole skeins, wrap them in plastic cling wrap and spread the packages in a single layer on a cookie sheet or shelf in your freezer and leave them overnight. The next day, overwrap them in freezer paper, date and label the packages, and return them to the freezer immediately.

To freeze fresh cluster baits, first pat the whole skeins dry with paper towels. Then use a pair of sharp scissors to cut the skeins into bait-size clusters, making sure you leave a bit of the membrane attached to each cluster. Spread the clusters on a cookie sheet and allow to air dry until a glaze appears. Turn the clusters so that all sides become glazed. Total drying time should be about one hour, but the drying process can be speeded up by blowing air over the clusters with a small electric fan.

Once the clusters have dried, place the cookie sheet in the freezer and quick-freeze the clusters for about four hours. Frozen clusters can then be packaged in "trip-size" portions. You can wrap them in plastic cling wrap and overwrap with freezer paper, but you might find it more convenient to pack them in plastic margarine tubs that will later fit in a tackle box or pocket of your fishing jacket. Fill any air space in the top of the margarine tubs with crumbled cling wrap to displace as much air as possible.

You can also tie spawn sacks and freeze them for later use. This saves you the time, trouble, and mess associated with tying them while fishing and losing precious fishing time. Make the spawn sacks according to the directions provided later in this chapter; then quick-freeze them on a cookie sheet as described above. When they're frozen solid (about four hours), pack them in plastic bags or margarine tubs for later use.

If you're freezing the eggs of bluegills and other small fishes, leave the skeins intact and treat them as clusters. You'll find that they will stay on the hook much better if tied into spawn sacks, so you might want to do this before freezing them.

If you properly wrap your bait roe, it should keep well in a freezer for up to one year.

Preserving Eggs With Borax

Borax is widely used by salmon and steelhead anglers to preserve the eggs of those species for bait. If you plan to cure eggs in this way, be sure to use only pure borax, which is available at most grocery and drug stores, not Boraxo or any other similar laundry product. Although you can use borax as it comes, you'll get even better results if you first whir it in an electric blender, a cup at a time, rendering it into a talcum-fine powder.

Borax toughens eggs and retards the growth of spoilage bacteria while helping them retain their natural appearance, odor, and "milking" qualities. Soft-cured and medium-cured eggs are the best milkers because they crush easily and allow their scent trails to drift in the currents. But these baits are not as durable as hard-cured eggs.

To soft-cure eggs with borax, spread a layer of the powder on a cookie sheet or large sheet of waxed paper. With one hand, hold a skein of eggs above the powdered cookie sheet and use the other hand to snip off bait-size clusters with a pair of scissors. Sprinkle a layer of borax over the clusters. Or, you can put a cupful of borax in a plastic bag, drop the clusters into the bag, and shake the bag to completely coat the clusters. If using the latter method, return the clusters to the cookie sheet and place them in a cool room to stand and dry overnight. A pestproof garage or basement is ideal. If you want a hard-cured bait, allow the clusters to dry for 24 to 36 hours, until the desired firmness is achieved.

Once your baits have properly cured, they can be packed for freezing. Lift a few at a time from the cookie sheet, shake them gently in your hands to remove excess borax, and spread them on another cookie sheet or large piece of waxed paper. Sprinkle them with fresh borax and then pack them in plastic margarine tubs or similar containers to within about a half inch of the rim. Sprinkle more fresh borax on the clusters, put the lid on the container, and store bait in the freezer until needed.

Hard-cured eggs will stay on a hook reasonably well, but you might find the soft clusters easier to use if you tie them into spawn sacks. You might prefer to do this prior to freezing rather than while fishing.

Preserving Single Salmon Eggs

Single salmon eggs are often used as bait for trout, salmon, and other species in many parts of the country. For this bait, use loose eggs found in the stomach cavity when you dress your fish or the largest mature

Spread a layer of borax on a cookie sheet and use a fork to break up any chunks of borax. Hold a skein by one end above the cookie sheet and use scissors to snip off bait-size pieces from the other end of the skein.

Sprinkle a layer of borax over the egg clusters and let stand in a cool place overnight or until cured to desired hardness.

eggs that you remove from the skein by hand. Remove the eggs from the skeins by immersing them in water at about 120° F. for several minutes, which causes the membrane to coagulate and lets you remove the eggs by hand without damaging them.

To cure the eggs for refrigerator or freezer storage, make a brine of one cup of sugar and four cups of salt for each gallon of cold (40° F.) water. Put the eggs in a bowl, pour the brine over them, and let them stand for one to two hours, stirring occasionally, until they are firm enough to stay on a hook. Pour them into a strainer and rinse them lightly under cold water. Then spread them on paper towels and let them drain for several minutes. Pack them in jars or other suitable containers and store them in a refrigerator for several weeks or in a freezer for up to one year.

If you want eggs that keep without refrigeration, the following ingredients and method are recommended by Robert J. Price at the University of California Cooperative Extension:

A. A preservative bath, consisting of one part commercial (40%) formalin (available at most drug stores) to 20 parts water at about 90° F.

B. Dye (if red eggs are desired), consisting of ¼ teaspoon of powdered Safranin—O (available at many drug stores) dissolved in two quarts of water.

C. A neutralizing-fixing bath, comprised of eight tablespoons of sodium bisulfate (found at photo supply stores and some drug stores) dissolved in one gallon of water at 60° F.

D. A glycerine-formalin bath, consisting of six drops of commercial (40%) formalin mixed with one ounce of glycerine.

E. Optional fish-attracting scents and flavors, such as anise oil, which may be added to the glycerine-formalin bath.

Process as follows:

1. After separating the eggs from the membranes in the skeins, immerse them in the preservative bath for 30 to 45 minutes. Processing time will vary, so process eggs in small batches and begin checking them after 30 minutes. Properly preserved eggs should be soft but with no trace of a liquid center when sliced in half.

2. Eggs can be dyed now by dipping them in the dye solution for several minutes, until they reach the desired hue. Rinse excess dye from eggs with cold water.

3. Immerse eggs in the neutralizing-fixing bath for 20 to 30 minutes to halt the action of the formalin and prevent excessive hardening during storage.

4. Drain the eggs and pack loosely in screw cap jars (many anglers use baby food jars). Do not rinse the eggs or allow surface eggs to dry before sealing.

5. Pour a small amount of the glycerine-formalin mixture into each jar, only enough to moisten the eggs, but not enough to cause a noticeable accumulation at the bottom of the jar.

6. Cap the jars and store at room temperature or in a refrigerator.

Single salmon eggs prepared in this fashion will keep well for several weeks at room temperature. In a refrigerator they will keep for more than a year.[1]

How to Tie Spawn Sacks

Some anglers prefer fresh egg baits to cured eggs for salmon and steelhead fishing. We're among their ranks, but we're also well aware of the attendant problems with such delicate baits and admit that cured eggs generally make a much more durable bait.

Laboratory experiments have shown that trout prefer fresh eggs to cured eggs, but whether salmon and steelhead in the wild exhibit such preferences is up for debate. So you'll just have to decide for yourself and prepare your egg baits accordingly.

If you make fresh-egg clusters or spawn sacks, you'll need salmon or trout eggs cut into bait-size clusters, fine nylon netting or other suitable material, nail clippers or angler's clippers, light monofilament line, scissors, and storage containers. Maline cloth is a red nylon mesh material sold specifically for tying spawn sacks. You can also use fine-mesh nylon netting (veil material) available in suitable shades of red or orange at most fabric shops, which is cheaper than Maline cloth. About the cheapest and most readily available material is sheer nylon stockings. Keep discarded hosiery for such purposes, or buy the cheapest you can find. Patches of cloth that are four inches square or larger are the easiest to use. If you're using nylon stockings or veil material, though, you need not cut them into patches. Simply leave the material intact during the tying process and cut the completed sack away from the material.

Here's how to tie a spawn sack:

1. Cut fresh egg skeins into bait-size clusters: dime-size pieces for small trout, quarter-size pieces for steelhead, and half-dollar–size pieces for large salmon.
2. Place a cluster into a piece of cloth and gather the cloth up around the cluster. Twist the top of the cloth until the eggs have been molded into a tight sphere, but not so tight as to squash the eggs.
3. Wrap the top of the sack several times with thread or light monofilament line and tie off the line with several tight overhand knots or a square knot.
4. Use scissors to trim the cloth away from the top of the sack just above the thread or monofilament wrap.

---

1. Fish Eggs For Caviar And Bait, Leaflet 21114, Division of Agricultural Sciences, University of California (Davis, 1979), pp. 2-3.

Pack the finished spawn sacks in margarine tubs and keep them in a freezer until needed. If you wish, you can separate layers with small pieces of cling wrap or waxed paper. Large, one-pound margarine tubs

Place a cluster of eggs in a swatch of netting and gather the material up around the cluster. Carefully and gently twist the top of the cloth to mold the eggs into a snug sphere.

Wrap the top of the sack several times with light monofilament line and tie off the line with several overhand knots.

will hold as many as three dozen spawn sacks. The smaller tubs hold about 1½ dozen.

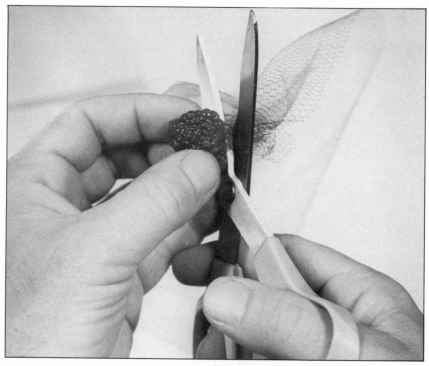

Snip off the ends of the monofilament line with clippers or scissors. Trim the spawn sack away from the netting with scissors.

Chapter 5
DRESSING THE CATCH

Among the various factors affecting the quality of fish flesh is the dressing of the catch. The angler who knows how to properly care for the catch and who takes the time to learn the various techniques for pan dressing, steaking, filleting, and the like will be rewarded with a product that is not only pleasing to the palate, but one that is nutritious and attractive as well—all of which combine to make any dish appetizing.

Planning to Keep the Catch

On any fishing trip you should go just as prepared to care for your fish as you are to catch them. So, in addition to carrying your usual tackle and baits, you should take along certain cleaning tools and materials to assure that you'll return home with a catch that is as fresh and wholesome as possible. If you're embarking on an extended fishing trip, of course, you should have all the usual paraphernalia required for dressing and packaging your catch—fillet knives, wrapping materials, freezer containers, and the like. For the usual day trip you won't need quite as much gear, but what is required is every bit as important.

Many public fishing areas now have fish-cleaning stations where there are cleaning benches or sinks, running water, and trash cans for waste. You can use these facilities to do the bulk of your fish-cleaning chores or simply to field dress your catch and do the rest at home. Either way, you should plan ahead.

If you'll only be gutting and gilling your fish, all you'll need is a sharp knife and possibly a teaspoon for removing the kidneys from large fish. If you plan to scale your catch, you'll need a scaling tool. Most important, you'll need a cooler and ice. In cool weather you can get by without the ice chest by using wet burlap to keep your catch cool.

Some folks like to do all the work away from home so that all they bring back is a mess of fillets, ready for the freezer. If that's your preference, you should plan to take a fillet knife along and some sort of sharpening tool, such as a hone steel. You will also need plastic food storage bags for the fillets, which should be packed in ice for the trip home.

If you will be fishing where there are no cleaning facilities, take along several plastic trash bags in which to put the waste. You would do well to have a fillet board to make the dressing job easier and quicker.

Although we live only 15 minutes from seasonally good saltwater fishing, 20 minutes from our favorite lake, and within a half hour's drive of four coastal rivers, and consequently do most of our fish-cleaning chores at home, during the fishing season we are always prepared for taking care of the catch. We keep a fillet board and an old ice chest in the back of the pickup truck just for hauling fish. We carry several large pieces of burlap, two fillet knives, a scaler, a hone steel, plastic food storage bags, plastic trash bags, twist ties, and several cleaning rags—all of which fits neatly into a large plastic bucket with a lid. It really doesn't take much effort or planning to go prepared, and it certainly pays handsome dividends in top-quality fish.

Organizing Your Fish-Dressing Area

It's just as important to be prepared and organized at home for the fish-cleaning operations because by being systematic you will be able to dress your fish quickly and get them preserved while they are still fresh. You'll also find it much easier to keep your cleaning area tidy, which is also important for assuring fish of peak quality.

Before we get down to fish-cleaning tasks we get all our needed tools and materials ready, while the fish are kept cool on ice or in wet burlap. If we have a lot of fish to dress, we get out all the fillet knives so that when one dulls we just put it aside and use another. We keep a steel handy for resetting the knife edges as we go.

We set up a fillet board at the sink, and on a nearby counter we have a cleaning brine in a large bowl for soaking fillets and steaks. Next to that is a plastic bucket, lined with a small plastic trash bag, into which all the waste goes.

As dressed fish, fillets, steaks, or roasts are accumulated, they are soaked in the brine as required, rinsed, and immediately refrigerated. After all fish are dressed, we clean all our tools, wipe down the counter tops, and discard the scraps. Then we set up for wrapping and freezing, canning, smoking, pickling, or whatever method of preservation and preparation we plan to use.

During periods of seasonal abundance, when our catches are large, or when we have other anglers visiting us, we often set up simultaneous wrapping operations, so that as soon as the fish are dressed, they're wrapped, labeled, and frozen as fresh as they can possibly be. At all times, we keep the fish-dressing area clean and sanitary and we work quickly.

Fighting Fish Slime

If fish had handles they would be a lot easier to grip. Not only are fish handle-free, but they're sleek—tapered at both ends—and covered with slime. In addition to making fish difficult to handle, slime houses bacteria. Although this bacteria is not harmful to live fish, once the fish have been killed, the bacteria in the slime can be transferred to the exposed flesh, where it causes spoilage. So it's important to keep fish slime cleaned up. Wash your hands frequently to remove slime and rinse the slime from fillets, steaks, and roasts.

Some fish are more slimy than others. Consequently, they are more difficult to handle and more susceptible to invasion by spoilage bacteria. Halibut and other flatfishes, for example, are covered with a relatively heavy coating of slime, comprising as much as 6% of the body weight in large specimens. You can remove much of the slime from such fish by scraping it away with the back edge of a knife blade. Slime is not as great a problem with fish such as bass, trout, and most panfish, but these fish will be much easier to handle if you wipe them down with a cloth dampened in a desliming solution made of one part vinegar to three parts water.

There are several other tricks that make handling slimy fish easier. One is to keep a plate of salt nearby when you're dressing fish. As your hands get slimy, dip them into the salt, which will cling to your hands, providing an abrasive coating that keeps fish from slipping out of your grip. Most commercial fishermen and fish processors wear ordinary cotton work gloves when handling fish. The cloth clings to slippery fish much better than bare flesh does, and as the gloves get too slimy they can be quickly rinsed out under running water. If you prefer to work barehanded, make a slime-cutting solution by mixing one cup of vinegar in three cups of water, into which is dissolved two tablespoons of alum. Dampen a towel in this mixture and use the towel to wipe the slime from your hands as required.

Drawing or Field Dressing the Catch

The simplest and most essential fish-cleaning process is drawing or field dressing. A drawn fish is merely one that has had its entrails and gills removed. Normally, the head is left on to facilitate handling.

All fish, large and small, are drawn the same way. Kill the fish with a sharp rap on the head with a "priest" or similar blunt instrument. If the fish is large, lay it on its back or side. A small fish can be held in one hand.

Use only the point of a sharp knife or "Zak's" Fish & Deer Knife to make an incision the length of the fish's belly. Start at the anus and slit forward, all the way to the gills, making sure the knife penetrates only deep enough to cut through the belly meat, but not so deep that it punctures entrails or egg skeins.

Cut the gills free near the chin and at the base of the skull. Then grip the gills firmly and pull them back toward the anterior end of the fish, and in so doing extracting all attached entrails. Then remove all remaining viscera by hand.

The kidneys—the dark, bloody material along the backbone in the stomach cavity—are easily stripped out of small fish with a thumbnail. Start at the rear of the kidney and press a thumbnail into the backbone. Push your thumb forward for the length of the backbone, puncturing the thin membrane and forcing out the kidneys as you do so. On larger fish, use a teaspoon or a knife with a stripping spoon in the handle to scrape out the kidneys. On the largest of fish, you will need to slit the membrane open for the entire length of the kidneys before stripping them. Rinse the stomach cavity out with cold water and your drawn fish is now ready to be iced down.

To draw or field dress a fish, begin by inserting the point of a knife in the vent or anus.

Slit the belly open from the vent forward to the gills, being careful not to cut into the viscera and ovaries or egg skeins.

Cut the gills free near the chin and at the base of the skull.

After entrails are removed, use a stripping spoon, teaspoon, or tablespoon to scrape the kidneys away from the backbone. On small fish, use your thumbnail to strip the kidneys. If further cleaning is necessary along the backbone, use an old toothbrush.

Pan Dressing the Catch

Pan dressing is among the easiest of preparations. In fact, for some fish it requires no more than drawing. Small trout, for example, are pan dressed simply by gutting and gilling them. You can remove the heads from slightly larger trout if you have trouble fitting them into the frying pan. Most other pan-size fish—bass, bluegill, perch, and various saltwater species—should have their heads removed as part of the pan-dressing process. After removing the head, simply cut away the pelvic and pectoral fins from the flesh. To remove the dorsal and anal fins, make incisions along each side of the fins and a half inch or so into the flesh, keeping the knife blade as close as possible to the fin base for each cut. Then use a pair of pliers to make a quick pull toward the head, removing the fins and bones to which they are attached. Pan-dressed fish should also be scaled.

Dressing Whole Fish for Baking

Larger fish that will be baked whole are prepared the same way as pan-dressed fish. Whether to leave the heads on or remove them is the chef's choice; normally it depends on the type of fish and the chef's artistic bent. Lingcod and similarly homely creatures normally look more appetizing without their heads. Such handsome fish as salmon, trout, and striped bass, however, are often baked with the heads on and are creatively garnished prior to serving. Fish dressed for baking should be scaled.

Scaling the Catch

Fish that are to be filleted and skinned need not be scaled. All others should be scaled. Before scaling a fish, soak it in cool water for several minutes because wet scales are more easily removed than dry ones.

Use a scaling tool, the scaling blade of an angler's knife, or a teaspoon to scale fish. Scrape from the tail toward the head, being careful to remove scales along the belly, at the base of each fin, and near the head. If you're scaling indoors, you can keep scales from flying about by scaling fish under water. Use a suitable washtub, large dishpan, or a sink filled with cold water. If you have trouble scaling large, heavily scaled fish, try immersing them in boiling water for a few seconds before scaling. This will soften and loosen the scales.

Salmon that are caught offshore in salt water or in the open waters of the Great Lakes before their spawning migrations have immature scales that are easily removed by spraying the fish with a garden hose. Direct the stream of water from the tail toward the head and the scales will simply wash away. Stream-caught salmon, however, have mature scales that must be removed in the traditional fashion.

Cutting Steaks and Roasts

Most large fish of five pounds or more can be cut into steaks and roasts with little effort. To prepare any fish for such use, you need only draw and scale it.

To cut steaks, simply lay the fish on its side and make a straight cut across and all the way through the fish, just behind the head. (Meat left behind the head can be boiled or steamed and flaked for chowder or other flaked-fish dishes.) Move the knife toward the tail, about one inch from your first cut, and slice through the fish again, rendering an inch-thick fish steak. Continue making cuts in this fashion to steak the entire fish.

Any large chunk of fish is suitable as a roast. Roasts are cut the same way steaks are, but in larger sections, the size of which depends on your personal needs and how many people you plan to serve.

Since we like steaks to be of uniform size, we prefer to cut both steaks and roasts from the same fish. On a 10-pound fish, for example, we make the initial cut two or three inches behind the head. We then cut the head away from this section, leaving a small roast, perfect in size for two persons. Next, we cut steaks from the central portion of the fish, all the way to where the stomach cavity ends and the anal fin begins. This yields steaks that are all nearly identical in size. The remaining tail section makes a good roast that will serve four persons, or the same section can be quickly turned into two, large, boneless fillets.

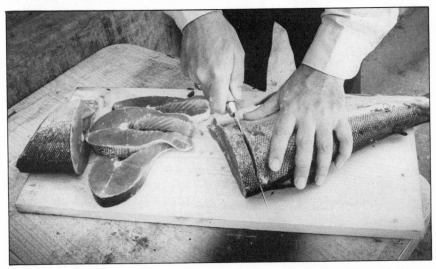

To cut steaks and roasts from a large fish, begin by laying the fish on its side and making a straight cut across and all the way through the fish, behind the head. Cut inch-thick cross sections from the fish. To keep all steaks uniform in size, stop cutting when you reach the anal fin or the end of the stomach cavity.

Here, one 12-pound salmon has yielded eight large steaks, a "shoulder" roast large enough to feed two persons, and a tail roast that can be rendered into two large fillets.

Filleting the Catch

Since we don't like picking the bones out of fish, the boneless fillet is our favorite cut. Although filleting appears to many to be a baffling art, mastered only by Indian guides of the north country and deck hands on charter boats, it's quite a simple process that is easily learned. Moreover, with a little practice, any angler can become quick and efficient at it.

Over the years, we've seen at least a half dozen ways to fillet fish and have tried them all. While all methods did indeed work, the one described here is certainly the fastest, and it works for most species. With a little practice, you should be able to render any fish of one to five pounds into two boneless, skinless fillets and a pile of scraps in about one minute. Smaller fish often go faster, and larger fish take only a little more time. Just follow these easy steps:

1. If the fish is alive, hold it firmly and kill it with a sharp blow to the top of the head with a "priest" or fish billy.
2. Lay the fish on its side on a cutting board. (A fillet board equipped with a fish-holding clamp is ideal.) Use a sharp fillet knife with a fairly rigid blade to make a cut just behind the head, down to the backbone. Continue the cut down behind the gill cover to the belly.
3. Turn the blade with a cutting edge toward the tail and angled slightly into the backbone and cut in a sawing fashion through the rib bones, being careful to keep the blade working along the backbone to leave as little meat as possible on the skeleton.

72

Filleting, Step 1.

Filleting, Step 2.

Filleting, Step 3.

Filleting, Step 4.

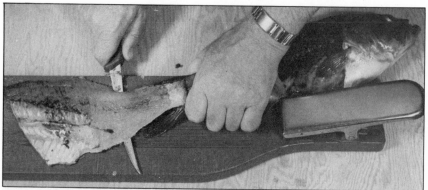

Filleting, Step 5.

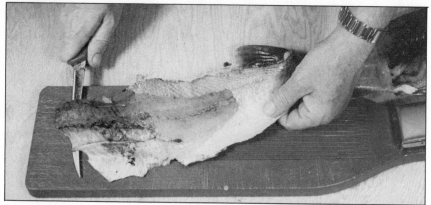

Filleting, Step 6.

4. Once you have cut through the rib section, a sharp blade will move quickly along the backbone to the tail. Stop cutting just before you reach the caudal or tail fin.

5. With the fillet still attached by a small bit of skin at the tail, flip the whole fillet beyond the tail so that it now rests skin side down, flesh side up. Now carefully cut into the flesh at the tail end of the fillet, down to the skin but not through it. Then, holding the blade at a very slight angle to the skin—in fact, almost flat against the skin—begin pushing the blade forward while lightly sawing back and forth. With your other hand, grasp the skin of the fillet firmly and pull it back toward the carcass of the fish.

6. Continue pushing the knife in one direction and pulling the skin in the opposite direction, separating the flesh from the skin until the skin pulls free. Turn the fish over and repeat the process on the opposite side.

7. In most species, the only bones in the fillets at this point are the ribs. The simplest way to remove them is to just cut them away. Make a cut along the natural lateral division of the fillet for the length of the rib cage. Then turn the knife and make a right-angle cut to remove the ribs.

You now have two boneless, skinless fillets. Such fillets from small fish of a pound or less, particularly bluegills and other panfish, are ready for the freezer or frying pan. Fillets from larger fish should be cut into serving size pieces for best results.

Some people simply freeze the fillets at this point and cut them into smaller pieces just before cooking them. We like to keep our fillets fairly uniform in size and thickness to make cooking them as foolproof as possible. So when we have a good batch of fillets, we cut the thinner tail sections away and package them together, labeled "tail fillets." We do the same with the thick back sections and label them "back fillets."

We discard the rib sections of small fish, simply because there isn't enough meat there to bother with. But with fish from one to about four pounds, we shave the meat off the ribs and package them as "rib tidbits," which when breaded and fried make dandy snacks or appetizers. The ribs from fish of five or more pounds have quite a bit of meat on them. We bone these pieces and package them as "rib fillets."

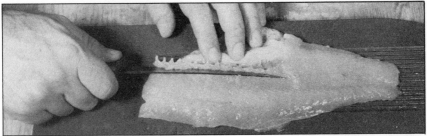

To cut large fillets into serving-size pieces, start by cutting through the forward end of the fillet, as near the ribs as possible.

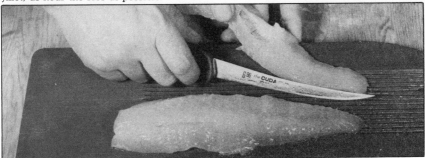

Continue the cut, lengthwise through the fillet, along the natural lateral division.

Cut one fillet half in two just behind the rib cage. Then cut the other half in two to yield two tail fillets of equal size, one back fillet, and the rib section.

To remove the meat from rib sections, you'll need a fork and a sharp fillet knife, preferably one with a flexible blade. You'll be cutting from the top of the ribs to the bottom, or from the thick end to the thin end, so position the ribs with the thick end along the edge of your cutting board and hold them in place with the tines of the fork. Now, make a cut along the top edge of the rib cage, as near the protruding bone ends as possible, and perpendicular to the rib bones. Turn the knife blade and push the cutting edge toward the end of the rib section, shaving the meat away from the bones as you do so. Simple, eh?

To remove the meat from the rib section, start by positioning the ribs along the edge of the cutting board and making a cut along the edge of the rib cage, near the protruding ends of the ribs.

Holding the ribs with the tines of a fork, turn the knife blade and shave the meat away from the bones.

Filleting Drawn Fish

The above method is for fish that have been kept alive until filleted. If you have field dressed and iced your fish, you'll fillet them in a similar fashion with one slight alteration. Make your initial cut as described in Step #2, above, but when you start Step #3, use the thumb of your free hand to hold the side of the fish up and out of the way of your knife. By looking into the cleaned stomach cavity, you'll be able to make sure your blade is closely following the backbone. All other filleting steps are the same as described above.

Filleting Flatfishes

The flatfishes—halibut, flounder, sole, and the like—pose a problem, albeit minor, to the unsuspecting angler. If you try to fillet one of these fish in the conventional way, you're going to waste a lot of meat. Furthermore, these fish are so broad that one of any size would require a blade far longer than those on most fillet knives to reach from one side to the other.

When we were buying fish commercially, we learned this method from one of our fishermen. It's simple, fast, and leaves little meat on the bones. You'll need two fillet knives—a conventional fillet knife with a fairly stiff blade and another with a thin, flexible blade. You'll also need a cutting board and a fork or ice pick.

Follow these steps to yield four boneless and skinless fillets from each flatfish:

1. With the stiff-bladed knife, make an incision along the backbone, from the gill cover to the tail.

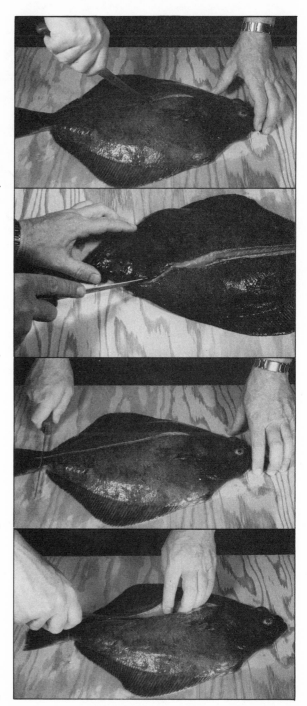

Filleting Flatfishes, Step 1.

Filleting Flatfishes, Step 2.

Filleting Flatfishes, Step 3.

Filleting Flatfishes, Step 4.

Filleting Flatfishes, Step 5.

Filleting Flatfishes, Step 6.

Now you have four boneless fillets ready for skinning.

2. Then cut at an angle through the fleshy section behind the head.
3. With the same knife, make a cut across the caudal peduncle, down to, but not through, the backbone, just forward of the tail.
4. Now, with the flexible-bladed knife, begin at the head and gently ease the blade between the flesh and the skeleton, allowing the blade to bend along the bones. Then, gently move the knife toward the tail, letting the knife slice the meat away from the skeleton.
5. All that holds the fillet to the carcass now is the skin. Lift the fillet and cut it free.
6. Now remove the opposite fillet on the same side the same way.
7. Turn the fish over and repeat Steps #1 through #6.

And that's all there is to filleting a flatfish, leaving four boneless fillets ready for skinning and a pile of scraps.

Skinning Fillets

Regardless of the size of the fish or species, any fillet that has been removed from the fish can be quickly and easily skinned. Use a fork or ice pick to hold the tail end of the fillet in place on a cutting board. Now use a stiff-bladed knife to cut into the flesh, down to the skin but not through it. Turn the blade so that it is only at a slight angle to the cutting board, and push it forward and through the fillet, separating the flesh from the skin.

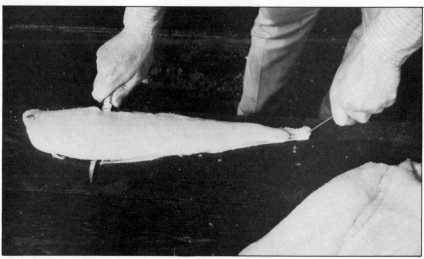

To skin any fillet that has been removed from the carcass, lay it out on a cutting board, skin side down. Use an ice pick or fork to hold the tail end of the fillet and cut down to the skin but not through it. Turn the blade so that it is only at a slight angle to the skin and push it through the fillet, separating flesh from skin.

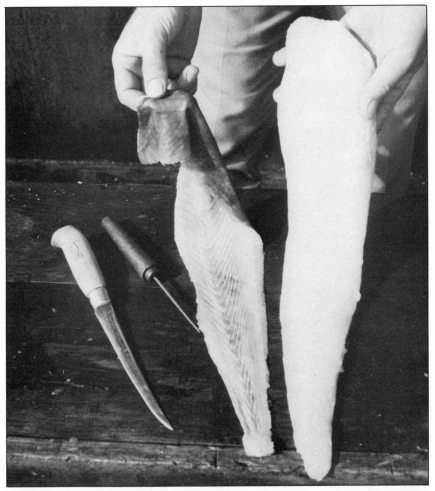

Done properly, this method of skinning leaves no skin on the flesh and no flesh on the skin.

Try an Electric Knife

Some anglers have found that an electric knife makes short work of a long catch. Although we normally prefer to use traditional cutlery for filleting fish, there have been instances when the electric knife proved to be quite a time and labor saver. We find it particularly useful for quickly filleting large catches of panfish.

It takes a little practice to get used to the unwieldy apparatus, but once you get used to it, you'll be able to zip the fillets off small fish in practically no time at all. Use the same filleting method described in this chapter and you'll be able to accomplish everything but rib removal; use a standard fillet knife for that.

The electric knife is also a dandy tool for cutting steaks and roasts. It saws through the backbone with a minimum of effort and produces beautifully uniform steaks.

Chapter 6

FREEZING THE CATCH

Freezing is the most popular method of preserving fish and shellfish at home and with good reason. It is the easiest and least time-consuming technique as well as the safest. And the result of proper freezing is a product that comes as close as possible to tasting freshly caught. But, as with other methods, freezing requires meticulous care of the catch if the highest quality is to be maintained. Freezing in no way improves poor-quality fish and shellfish. It effectively retards deterioration, but only within recommended limits.

Before freezing, bacteria and enzymes are the primary causes of spoilage. Many bacteria are not killed by freezing, but are rendered inactive until the fish is thawed. Freezing also retards enzyme action. After freezing, however, oxidation and dehydration can adversely affect the quality of the frozen product. And the longer the product is held in the freezer, the greater the effects of oxidation and dehydration.

Oxidation and Dehydration

Other high-protein foods, such as beef and pork, that are higher in saturated fats than fish and shellfish are not as susceptible to rancidity caused by oxidation. The same polyunsaturated oils that make fish and shellfish such healthful foods are also subject to oxidation when these foods are frozen. When these oils oxidize, they become rancid, giving the product an offensive taste.

Air is the chief cause of oxidation. So to alleviate the problem you must eliminate all air, or as much as possible, from the product before freezing. This means that great care must be taken during packaging, and the proper packaging materials must be used.

Frost found in packaged frozen foods is an indication that dehydration is taking place; moisture has been drawn from the product and has

d to frost. In its advanced stages, dehydration is known as
zer burn." In fish, freezer burn is characterized as a brownish
u.. loration of the flesh. The result is a tough, dry product.

Improper packaging materials and techniques are the main causes
of dehydration. Since inefficient packaging allows air to reach the fish
and moisture to escape, oxidation and dehydration occur simultaneously, combining the tough, dry texture with an unpleasant taste.

Packaging Materials

The best packaging materials are those that allow a minimum of
moisture to escape and a minimum of air to invade the product. Consequently, materials that are lowest in permeability to air and water are
those that usually are best suited to packaging fish and shellfish for
freezer storage.

Materials should also be durable and strong, as punctures in the packaging will only hasten oxidation and dehydration. They should be able to
withstand the low temperatures inside the freezer without becoming too
brittle and should be able to hold up under moderate handling.

Some inefficient packaging materials are in wide use, primarily
because of popular misconceptions, and are the chief sources of com-
plaints about fish and shellfish having a "fishy taste." Waxed paper
and cartons are highly permeable to water and moderately permeable
to air and are not good packaging materials, although they are used by
many people and recommended in far too many books and articles.
Common polyethylene bags, such as those used for bread wrappers or
those found in supermarket produce departments, are widely used in
home freezing, but are not recommended. While they provide a cheap
(free) wrap, they are relatively permeable to water and air and do not
adequately protect fish and shellfish in the freezer. Aluminum foil,
another popular wrap commonly used in home freezing is a bad choice
on several counts. Although it is impermeable to air and water, it is not
a strong wrap. It is easily punctured by bones, fins, other packages,
and even by freezer shelves. It will break where it is creased or seam-
ed. Additionally, it is about the most expensive wrapping material on
the market.

Among the best packaging materials are the polyvinylidene chloride
(Saran) wraps and polyester bags, commonly called plastic wraps and
bags. The ordinary plastic food wraps, such as Saran and Glad, are ac-
ceptable for primary (inner) wrapping, but we recommend the heavier-
duty clear freezer wraps because they are thicker, stronger, and
easier to use. Common food wraps are usually about 0.5 mil in thickness, whereas the clear freezer wraps are 0.9 mil or thicker. Look for
plastic bags of one mil or more in thickness.

To assure a proper seal and durable wrap, all fish and shellfish should be double-wrapped. Although the same material used for the primary or inner wrap can be used for the outer wrap, we recommend freezer paper for the second wrapping. This paper, which is coated with wax or plastic on one side, provides a strong outer wrapper that is easy to date and label.

Plastic pint and quart freezer containers with tight-fitting lids are also useful for freezing fillets, flaked fish, and shellfish. Larger freezer containers can be used to package soups and chowders. These containers are relatively inexpensive, easy to use, and reusable and will last for many years. We keep a good supply on hand at all times.

Wrapping the Catch for Freezing

Plastic wrap is also commonly called cling wrap, because it clings to the product, conforming to its shape, and when wrapped, the plastic then clings to itself. This characteristic is just one more good reason for using plastic wrap as a primary packaging material, especially when you're wrapping drawn fish, pan-dressed fish, and odd-shaped roasts.

Drawn and pan-dressed fish, as well as roasts cut from any section of the fish forward of the anal fin, are more susceptible to oxidation than are fillets and steaks because the stomach cavity creates a troublesome air pocket. To wrap fish dressed this way, you must press the plastic wrap into the stomach cavity, eliminating all air space between the wrap and the fish. Continue wrapping around the fish or roast until the wrap overlaps by about four inches. Allow at least four inches of wrapping material at each end and fold the ends over, being careful to force out all visible air pockets. Use transparent tape (Scotch Magic Tape is best) to seal the ends if necessary.

Steaks can cause similar air-pocket problems because of the stomach cavity, but they are a bit easier to wrap. By tucking one flap of the belly strip into the stomach cavity on each steak and bringing up the other flap against the tucked one, you can form a compact piece that is relatively free of air pockets. Large steaks can then be packaged individually, and small ones can be wrapped several to a package.

Fillets are the easiest of all forms to wrap because they can be easily arranged to eliminate all air pockets. Large fillets can be wrapped individually, and small ones can be wrapped several to a package.

To facilitate quick thawing and easy handling, we recommend that small steaks and fillets be separated from one another in the primary wrap. You can use small pieces of waxed paper between the steaks and fillets that are being stacked in one package. Or you can use the continuous-wrap method, in which you start with one steak or fillet and roll the piece in the wrapping material until it is covered; then place another piece atop the wrapped one and roll the package again until the second piece is covered. Continue wrapping in this way until all pieces are wrapped. Then tuck and fold the ends of the wrap and seal them with transparent tape if necessary.

You'll find it much easier to make neat and tightly sealed packages if you keep the packages small. A pound of steaks or fillets is much easier to wrap than three or four pounds. And the smaller packages will thaw much faster when you need them.

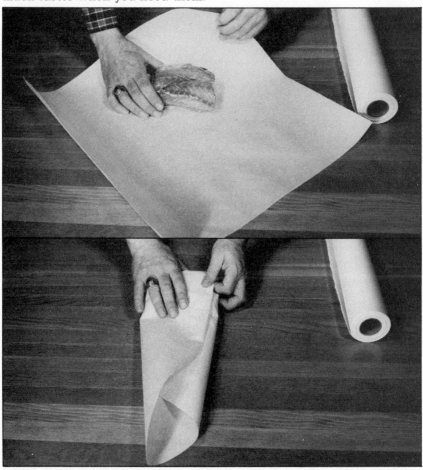

When using freezer paper for the outer wrap, tear off a piece of sufficient size, lay it on a table or counter top, shiny side up, and place the plastic-wrapped package of fish on the freezer paper, slightly rear of center. Bring the rear corner of the freezer paper up and over the fish. Fold both side corners over the fish and tuck under any excess paper. Roll the package forward, tightly wrapping the remaining paper around the package. Tape the flap to the package with freezer tape.

When using freezer paper for the outer wrap, tear off a piece of sufficient size, lay it on a table or counter top, shiny side up, and place the plastic-wrapped package of fish on the freezer paper, slightly rear of center. Bring the rear corner of the freezer paper up and over the fish. Fold both side corners over the fish and tuck under any excess paper. Roll the package forward, tightly wrapping the remaining paper around the package. Tape the flap to the package with freezer tape. Although the outer wrap is primarily for protection of the more delicate and vulnerable inner wrap, try to eliminate all air pockets when making this final wrap.

Ice Glazing

One of the most effective and inexpensive ways commercial fish processors and cold-storage operators have found to prepare fish for the freezer is to glaze them in ice. Although you will find ice glazing highly touted for the home freezer in some articles, pamphlets, and books, we do not recommend it as a viable method for several reasons.

First, commercial processors have the facilities and equipment to make glazing highly cost-effective. They have huge vats to hold the glazing solution, into which whole, drawn fish are dipped. Sometimes the fish aren't even drawn before glazing, but are left "in the round." Then the fish are flash frozen at -40° F. They are dipped again and put back into the freezer. Subsequent dipping and freezing produces a substantial coating of ice that effectively seals the fish and protects it from oxidation and dehydration. The fish are then stacked like cordwood in giant, walk-in freezers and are held at temperatures of -20° F. to -40° F., where they will remain in top quality for as long as a year or more if necessary.

While we concede that this is certainly about the best method there is for sealing large fish, it is not practical for the home freezer. To begin with, you would have to find a container large enough for dipping big fish. Secondly, since your home freezer is incapable of flash freezing, you will have to add thickening agents to the glazing compound to promote the glazing process. Moreover, it's a messy project when done at home, and there's a good chance you just don't have sufficient space in your freezer for ice glazing. And since it might take 12 or more hours to freeze a large fish solid with the first coating of ice, and it might take several coatings to build up a sufficient glaze, it is certainly a time-consuming process. But most important, the ice glaze is relatively fragile. If you have to move the fish about when rearranging items in your freezer, chances are the glaze will get chipped or cracked, rendering it worthless in the protection of the fish.

Freezing Fish in Water

One method that is similar to ice glazing, but far more practical for the home freezer, is freezing fish in water. Since freezer containers are reusable, this is one of the least expensive packaging methods. Additionally, freezing in water is easy, perhaps the least time-consuming of all freezing methods, and, if done right, the most efficient.

We couldn't begin to count the number of times we have seen recommendations for using milk cartons for freezing fish in water, but we are not going to follow the crowd on that suggestion. Quite the contrary, we recommend against using milk cartons. One reason is that milk cartons are bulky and awkward to store. They are also difficult to adequately clean and sanitize. But most important, they are poor barriers against dehydration and oxidation. No matter what sort of container you use, some fish in the package will touch the bottom and sides. Since milk cartons do not adequately impede the transfer of gases, the fish touching the sides will dehydrate and begin to oxidize.

Use plastic freezer containers. They're easy to sanitize. They're easy to store. And they can be used over and over again. They will also provide maximum protection for your frozen fish and shellfish. We use this method for freezing virtually all fillets of lean fish. You can also freeze small, pan-dressed fish in water. We find the pint and quart containers the best suited to our purposes.

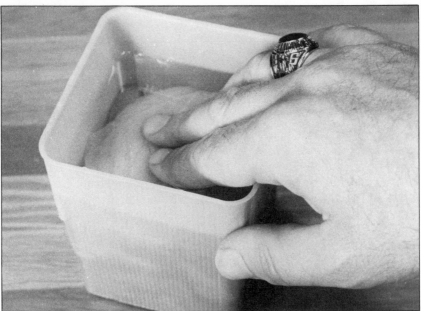

To freeze fish in water, arrange fillets in a plastic freezer container and cover with water to a point ½ inch below the fill line. Then press the fish to remove air pockets.

For best results, pack fish or fillets solidly in the containers and use as little water as possible because water tends to draw nutrients from the fish. For the same reason, freeze the fish quickly and thaw them properly.

Most freezer containers have "fill lines" ½-inch from the top of the container. Since freezing causes expansion, containers should not be filled byond this point. But it is best to pack the fillets or fish to a point ½ inch below the fill line or an inch below the rim of the container. Then add enough cold water to cover the fish. Gently press the fish into the containers with your fingertips to eliminate air pockets. Continue pressing and prodding until no more bubbles float to the top. Put the lids on the containers, label and date them, and carefully carry them to the freezer, trying not to jostle them.

After the containers have stood in the freezer overnight, remove the lids. Inside most you will find that one or two fillets have emerged slightly from the surface as the water froze and expanded. If left this way, the exposed fish would soon begin to dehydrate and oxidize. To remedy the situation, add water to the fill line, put the lids back on the containers, and return them to the freezer until you need them.

If you use fish preserved in this way within the prescribed limits for frozen storage, you'll find them comparable or nearly equal to fish that are fresh out of the lake or stream.

We recommend this method for any lean fish. The fatty varieties are better frozen in a double wrap after an ascorbic acid treatment, (see later in this chapter).

Freezing Clams and Mussels

Shucked clams and mussels are relatively easy to freeze. If you plan to fry them later, you can freeze them whole. If you'll be using them in chowders or for fritters, you can grind them before or after freezing.

Preclean the clams in clean sea water or brine as you normally would (see Chapter 11). Then shuck them over a pan to catch the juices. Clean them as required and wash in cold, running water. Strain the clam nectar through linen or several layers of cheesecloth to remove grit. Save the nectar.

Pack whole frying clams in pint or quart plastic freezer containers as described above, but do not cover with water. Instead, cover with the clam nectar, using only enough to adequately cover the clams. Label and date the containers and freeze overnight. Check the following day and add nectar to the fill line. The necks of gaper clams can be frozen whole in nectar, or they can be minced for use in chowder and fritters. Minced clams and mussels should be packed in plastic freezer containers with an ample amount of nectar added, since the nectar is used in chowders and other dishes.

If you're rushed and have a lot of clams on hand or if you want to lay up a batch of steamers for later use, you can freeze them in the shell. Since freezing will kill them, make sure the clams you're freezing are alive and healthy. Let the clams self-clean in sea water or brine and cornmeal for 12 to 24 hours. Then check to make sure that all clams close when you touch them. Discard any that don't.

Use a stiff brush to scrub the clam shells under cold, running water. Fill a bucket or kettle with cold water. Then put the clams inside a plastic food storage bag. Slowly ease the bag of clams down into the bucket of water until the clams are beneath the surface and the top of the bag extends above the surface. The pressure of the water will collapse the bag around the clams, forcing out most of the air. With the clams still beneath the water, twist the top of the bag to seal it; then tie it off with a twist tie. Place the bag inside another plastic bag and submerge this one the same as the first. Seal and tie it, and it's ready for the freezer.

Freezing Crabs

Crabs are best when eaten the day they're caught. They can be cooked soon after they're caught and kept in the refrigerator for a couple of days and still be quite tasty. Our third choice—which becomes our first choice when we have an abundance—is to can them. If we're rushed we will freeze them, but frozen crab meat is not of the highest quality and will not keep well beyond a month or two. Frozen crab meat rapidly changes in texture and flavor. Extended frozen storage often renders the meat inedible.

If you plan to freeze crab meat, cook, clean, and pick the crabs as you normally would (see Chapter 10). If you plan to use the crab within a couple of weeks, you can freeze the meat in plastic bags or in plastic wrap with an overwrap of freezer paper. If you will keep the meat frozen up to two months, use plastic freezer containers and cover the meat with a brine made of $2/3$ cup of salt to each quart of water.

Recent studies at Texas A & M University have shown that crab cores can be rapidly frozen and stored with no significant loss of quality. The core is the body meat left intact after the crab's legs, claws, and back have been removed and the body has been cleaned. The recommended method calls for debacking, cleaning, and washing the crabs, then boiling them in brine ($2/3$ cup of salt to each quart of water) for about 10 minutes. Allow the cores to cool; then wrap and freeze them and consume them within two months. Meat from the legs and claws can then be consumed fresh or canned for later use.

Although you will find frozen or previously frozen whole crab, crab legs, and crab claws in supermarkets and fish markets, we do not recommend freezing any part of the crab with the shell still on mainly because the abundant air spaces in the shells lead to rapid oxidation. Moreover, the sharp points and edges on crab shells will puncture just about any kind of wrapping material you use. If you're ever tempted to freeze crab in the shell, don't take our word for it. Go buy a crab that has been frozen this way. Your first bite will make a believer of you.

Freezing Smoked Fish

Smoked fish doesn't last long around our house, so unless we have a lot of fish to smoke, we don't normally freeze it. Smoked fish will keep well in a refrigerator for several weeks, wrapped in a common brown paper bag.

If you have more smoked fish on hand than you can use in a few weeks, freeze the excess. But be sure to use it within three months because it does not keep well beyond that point. To keep it longer, we recommend canning it. To freeze smoked fish, cool it to room temperature as soon as it comes out of the smoker. Then brush a thin coat of vegetable oil on each piece and wrap portions as you would fillets or steaks in clear plastic wrap and overwrap with freezer paper.

After thawing smoked fish, remove it from its air-tight packaging and store unused portions in the refrigerator in a more permeable material, such as brown paper bags, or in a jar with a ventilated lid. Since some smoked methods do not completely destroy *Clostridium botulinum* spores that thrive in an air-tight environment, refrigeration for several weeks in the freezer packaging could lead to the production of harmful botulism toxin. We find that smoked fish in brown paper bags keeps well in the meat drawer of our refrigerator, and the light oil coating keeps it from drying out too much.

Treating Fish with Ascorbic Acid

Ascorbic acid is the chemical equivalent of vitamin C and is used in the freezing of fruits to aid their preservation. It is also an effective antioxidant for fish that will be frozen. You can find ascorbic acid at any drug store or at some supermarkets under the trade name, Fruit Fresh.

If you don't eat fish often and tend to store it in the freezer for its maximum recommended time, you would do well to dip your fillets, steaks, and pan-dressed fish in a .5% ascorbic acid solution prior to freezing. To make the .5% solution, dissolve four teaspoons of ascorbic acid in a gallon of ice water. It is important to work quickly and keep the solution and fish cold and wrap and freeze the fish as soon as possible. The ascorbic acid can become inactive if the treated fish are left at room temperature, and the solution will no longer protect the fish against rancidity.

In a large, shallow container made of plastic, glass, stainless steel, or aluminum, spread out a single layer of fillets, steaks, or pan-dressed fish, and cover with the ascorbic acid solution. Let the fish stand for about two minutes. Then remove, drain, wrap, and freeze the fish at once.

For large quantities of fish, do not reuse the solution because the fish will absorb the acid from the solution, causing it to become weaker. Discard used solution and use a fresh solution for subsequent batches.

For treating fatty fish, such as tuna and salmon, make a stronger solution of two tablespoons of ascorbic acid to each quart of water. Immerse the fish for 20 seconds prior to wrapping and freezing.

What Kind of Freezer?

Everything in this chapter pertains to storage of fish in a freezer, not a frozen-foods compartment in a refrigerator. The small, frozen-foods compartments in most refrigerators are inadequate for anything but brief storage of foods. Most maintain a higher temperature than freezers do, and since these compartments are usually opened more often than freezers, temperatures tend to fluctuate greatly. Fish and shellfish should be kept no longer than 30 days in any frozen-foods compartment.

If you already own a freezer, that's the best freezer for your purposes, but you can make it even better by keeping it organized. If you are shopping for a freezer, carefully consider your personal needs and weigh all advice in terms of those needs.

Chest-type freezers are considered to be more efficient than upright models, but their inherent efficiency dwindles when they're kept in disarray. Moreover, if your family is small and you have no need for daily access to your freezer, the upright can be just as efficient. Furthermore, the upright is easier to keep organized, and if you know where an item is and can get to it instantly, you won't have to keep the freezer open as long as you might if everything is just dumped in.

Whatever kind of freezer you own or buy, keep it neat and keep it closed. Plan the use of it so that you can put items in and take them out in a minimum of time. And, by all means, put a thermometer inside so you can keep track of how your freezer is operating.

Labeling and Inventorying Your Catch

If you have to guess at what various packages contain and how long they've been in the freezer, you're either going to end up wasting a lot of fish and shellfish, or you'll eventually eat some pretty awful stuff that's been stored too long. So you should label every package that will be put in the freezer with its contents, amount, and the date it was packaged and frozen.

Packages overwrapped with freezer paper are quite easy to mark with a soft pencil, crayon, grease pencil, or indelible felt-tipped marker. Don't use a ballpoint pen that can puncture the wrap or markers with water-soluble ink that will run and smear.

The lids of plastic freezer containers can be marked with crayon or grease pencil, and those markings can be scrubbed off later with hot, soapy water. We prefer to put a couple pieces of Scotch Magic tape on each lid, which we then mark with an indelible felt-tipped marker. The tape peels off easily when the lid is washed.

Just as important as proper labeling of all packages is a running inventory of the freezer's contents. For this we use a legal pad, snapped into the jaws of a clipboard. On it, we list all contents of the freezer, just as they are marked on the packages. As we use a package, we mark it off the list. This lets us know exactly what we have on hand. And it enables us to plan to use any item that is reaching its expiration date. Proper labeling and inventorying also makes it easy to locate desired items in a hurry so we don't have to have the freezer open for unnecessarily long times.

Storing the Catch in a Freezer

The general rule for storing and using any frozen food is "first in, first out." But this rule requires a bit of qualifying as regards fish and shellfish.

Although there are some exceptions, the higher in oil content a fish is, the more susceptible it is to oxidation and the resultant rancidity. For that reason, fatty fish have a shorter storage life than lean fish. Normally, any fish containing fat in excess of 5% is considered fat.

Since percentages of fat will vary among lean and fat species alike and since some fish and shellfish are susceptible to texture and other changes when kept frozen, we can only make general recommendations that you should consider guidelines. You might find that some fatty fish available in your area will keep longer than the general recommendation or that some lean fish will begin to deteriorate sooner. And, too, the temperature at which you are able to keep your freezer might be higher or lower than recommended. So keep track and set up your own guidelines.

Generally, though, you should keep fatty fish frozen for a maximum of three months and lean fish for a maximum of six months. All smoked fish should be used within three months, and shellfish should be kept frozen only from one to three months.

The length of time fish is held on ice before freezing also affects the storage life after freezing. For example, some lean species iced down for two days and properly packaged might keep frozen for as long as a year, whereas the same fish iced down for a week might only keep frozen for two months before deteriorating.

It is also important that you keep your freezer as cold as possible and that you not allow temperatures to fluctuate widely. Fish kept in commercial cold storage are usually held at temperatures from -10° F. to -20° F. and sometimes as low as -40° F. Most home freezers are designed to maintain a holding temperature range from 4° F. to -4° F., and some will hold at temperatures as low as -10° F., which is where we keep our freezer set.

Although fish begin to freeze at 28° F. and will be completely frozen at about 18° F., consensus is that the lower the storage temperature the better they will keep. Some fish, properly prepared and wrapped, that will keep for four months at 0° F., will keep up to six months at -10° F. or colder before they begin to deteriorate.

It is important that fish and shellfish be frozen quickly. Slow freezing can actually cause tissue cell walls to puncture. When the fish is thawed, the moisture within the punctured cells is lost and the fish or shellfish can lose much of its flavor and become tough. Rapid freezing prevents cell-wall destruction.

Don't overload your freezer with large quantities of unfrozen fish because this can cause the temperature to rise dramatically, thus preventing the fish from freezing quickly. Place unfrozen fish on shelves or against the back or walls of the freezer, not on top of already frozen foods. When putting a substantial quantity of fish or other foods into the freezer, set the unit for its lowest temperature. Then you can readjust the setting to normal the next day, if you wish.

If you have a large quantity of fish to freeze and your freezer is already relatively full, check with a friend or neighbor to "borrow" freezer space. Then transfer the frozen product to your own freezer after 24 hours. Your friend will probably appreciate it when you leave a couple packages of fish in his freezer as a way of saying thanks.

Thawing Frozen Fish and Shellfish

Fish and shellfish should be thawed as rapidly as possible, and the best method seems to be running cold water over the frozen package. If you are thawing fillets or steaks that have been separated with pieces of waxed paper or by the continuous wrapping method, you can thaw them under cold, running water until the pieces can be separated. Then place them in the refrigerator until you are ready for them.

The next best choice is to thaw the frozen product in a refrigerator, which can take as long as 12 to 18 hours for two to four pounds of fish.

Never thaw fish at room temperature because this can cause spoilage. And don't thaw fish in hot water, which can cause loss of moisture, flavor, and nutrients.

Fish that will be baked, steamed, or poached can be cooked frozen, but additional cooking time is required, usually double the normal time prescribed for thawed fish. Flaked fish and minced clams that are to be used in chowders and soups can also be used frozen. Any fish or shellfish that is to be breaded must be completely thawed first.

Refreezing Fish and Shellfish

Contrary to popular belief, refreezing of previously frozen foods does not necessarily render them unsafe for human consumption. As long as the food was not allowed to spoil, it can be refrozen and will still be safe to eat. For many foods, refreezing will destroy some of the nutrients and might cause the quality to diminish. Sometimes the flavor will also deteriorate, and fish and shellfish will often undergo changes in texture. So it is best to avoid refreezing if possible.

The general rule for refreezing fish and shellfish is that the product should not have been kept in the refrigerator for more than two days and ice crystals should still be present on the product. Fish and shellfish that have only partially thawed, for one reason or another, can be refrozen with little loss of quality and nutrients, but should be used sooner than products that have been kept completely frozen. After thawing and cooking, frozen fish and shellfish leftovers can be safely frozen but should be used within a month or two.

If you thaw more fish than you can use, instead of refreezing it, bake, steam, or poach it. Let it cool and flake it. Then pack it tightly in plastic bags or wrap it securely in plastic cling wrap. Overwrap with freezer paper and freeze it for later use in soups, chowders, and salads.

This is also an excellent way to get extended storage life with fish that is reaching its storage limits. When we have more packages of fish nearing the "pull date" than we can consume in a week or two, we thaw the fish and steam or poach it, then return it to the freezer and use it in a variety of dishes.

Sometimes we also extend the storage life of frozen fish by thawing it and smoking it. In fact, this moment, as we're preparing the final manuscript for this book, we have the smoker fired up with salmon and lingcod that was approaching the maximum recommended storage time.

Popular Freshwater Fishes

Species	Forms	Fat/Lean	Freezer Life
Bass, Largemouth	Filleted	Lean	6 months

Bass, Smallmouth	Filleted	Lean	6 months
Bass, Rock	Pan-dressed Filleted	Lean	6 months
Bluegill	Pan-dressed Filleted	Lean	6 months
Bullhead	Pan-dressed Filleted	Lean	6 months
Carp	Drawn Filleted	Lean	6 months
Catfish	Filleted Smoked	Lean	6 months 3 months
Crappie	Filleted	Lean	6 months
Eel	Pan-dressed Smoked	Fat	3 months
Muskie	Filleted	Lean	6 months
Northern Pike	Filleted	Lean	6 months
Perch, White	Pan-dressed Filleted	Lean	6 months
Perch, Yellow	Pan-dressed Filleted	Lean	6 months
Pickerel	Filleted	Lean	6 months
Salmon	Drawn Filleted Steaked Smoked	Fat	3 months
Shad	Drawn Filleted Smoked	Fat	3 months
Smelt	Pan-dressed Smoked	Fat	3 months
Sturgeon	Filleted Steaked Smoked	Fat	3 months
Sucker	Pan-dressed Filleted Smoked	Lean	6 months 3 months
Trout	Pan-dressed Filleted Steaked Smoked	Fat	3 months

| Whitefish | Pan-dressed
Filleted
Smoked | Fat | 3 months |

Popular Saltwater Fishes

Species	Forms	Fat/Lean	Freezer Life
Bluefish	Drawn Filleted Steaked	Lean	6 months
Cod	Filleted	Lean	6 months
Croaker	Pan-dressed Filleted	Lean	6 months
Flounder	Filleted Steaked Smoked	Lean	6 months 3 months
Grouper	Filleted Steaked	Lean	6 months
Haddock	Filleted Smoked	Lean	6 months 3 months
Halibut	Filleted Steaked	Lean	6 months
Lingcod	Filleted Smoked	Lean	6 months 3 months
Mackerel, King	Filleted Steaked	Fat	3 months
Mackerel, Spanish	Drawn Filleted	Fat	3 months
Mullet	Drawn Filleted Smoked	Fat	3 months
Perch, Ocean	Filleted	Lean	6 months
Perch, Surf	Filleted	Lean	6 months
Pollock	Filleted Steaked Smoked	Lean	6 months 3 months
Pompano	Drawn Filleted	Fat	3 months
Porgy	Pan-dressed Filleted	Lean	6 months

Rockfish	Filleted	Lean	6 months
Sablefish	Filleted	Fat	3 months
Sea Bass	Drawn Filleted Steaked	Lean	6 months
Sea Trout	Drawn Filleted	Lean	6 months
Shark	Filleted Steaked	Lean	6 months
Sheepshead	Filleted	Lean	6 months
Snapper	Filleted	Lean	6 months
Sole	Filleted	Lean	6 months
Spot	Pan-dressed Filleted	Lean	6 months
Striped Bass	Drawn Filleted Steaked Smoked	Lean	6 months 3 months
Swordfish	Steaked	Lean	6 months
Tuna	Drawn & Bled	Fat	3 months

Popular Shellfishes

Species	Forms	Fat/Lean	Freezer Life
Clams	Shucked Minced In Shell	Lean	3-4 months
Clam Necks	Skinned Minced	Lean	4 months
Crab	Picked	Lean	1-2 months
Crayfish	Peeled & Veined	Lean	6 months
Mussels	Shucked Minced	Lean	3 months
Shrimp	Peeled & Veined	Lean	6 months

Chapter 7

CANNING THE CATCH

While many kinds of canned fish and shellfish are available at the supermarket, home canning is not as popular a method of preserving the catch as it might be. Perhaps one reason for this is that canning is a bit more tedious and time-consuming than other preservation methods. It requires more equipment than freezing does. And there is the very real threat of botulism that the careless canner would do well to heed.

On the positive side, there are some distinct advantages to canning your catch. Canning, properly done, is one of the most efficient means of preserving fish and shellfish. Canned fish can be easily stored and will retain its quality much longer than frozen fish will. Some species lend themselves to the canning process and in some dishes are better than fresh or frozen fish. Indeed, we consider certain species to be far tastier after canning than they are when prepared fresh or after freezing.

If your only experience with canned fish is what you've bought at the supermarket, we think you'll be pleasantly surprised when you taste your own product. Just as your own fresh and frozen fish, properly cared for, will be far superior to anything you buy at the grocery store or fish market, so will your home-canned fish and shellfish be much better than the commercial products.

The time lapse between the catching and the canning is almost always briefer for the sport-caught fish than for the commercial catch. That means your fish will be fresher. Moreover, fish caught on a rod and reel are generally in much better shape than those taken in giant nets. As the commercial trawler or dragnetter hauls his catch aboard, fish in the periphery of the school are subject to net burn. Those at the bottom of the net are often squashed by the weight of the fish above them. As the net is hauled aboard, some fish are bruised as they flop and thrash on the deck. And, as in any other occupation, there are commercial fishermen who are absolutely meticulous in the care of the catch and those who are less than careful.

Fishing is largely a seasonal sport. Even in areas where anglers are fortunate to have some kind of fishing available the year round, some species will be most numerous only during certain times and often for relatively brief periods. Canning enables you to take advantage of these seasonal fluctuations and enjoy your catch for the whole year. By canning, you can preserve your surpluses and use them during the leaner months.

Canning also prevents waste. If you live in an area where fishing opportunities are plentiful and catches are reasonably large during any given season or during runs of particular species, you might end up with more fish than you might consume fresh or within the prescribed limits for frozen fish. Once you have frozen as much as you can use during the next three to six months, can the rest instead of freezing it and chancing later deterioration of fish that has been kept frozen too long. Also, as your frozen fish begins to approach its recommended storage time, you can thaw it and can it if you are unable to use it otherwise, thereby stretching its storage life. It should be noted here, however, that canning previously frozen fish is recommended only as a way of preventing waste. It's always better to can fish while they're fresh. So try to plan and coordinate your canning and freezing operations with this in mind.

Botulism is certainly something you must be concerned with, but it need not frighten you away from canning. If you are tidy and careful during your canning operations, if you use a modern pressure-canner that is checked at least once a year for its pressure-holding abilities, and if you use only those jars and lids recommended for modern home canning, you will eliminate the threat of potential poisoning from *Clostridium botulinum* bacteria.

Canning in Cans

Although we have put up fish in cans with excellent results, we're not going to recommend canning in cans for several reasons. First, the equipment used for closing and seaming cans is an added expense and it's not readily available everywhere. Canning with cans also requires a bit more skill than does canning with jars. And cans aren't as widely available as jars. Of course, if you have the equipment, the expertise, and the cans, certainly use cans if you prefer. But if you're that experienced and well-equipped, you probably won't need to read this chapter.

Canning in Jars

Use only standard jars manufactured specifically for home canning. Such jars are made of tempered glass that will withstand the high temperatures required for home canning. Avoid using ancient jars that might have tiny, invisible cracks in them, and never use jars that supermarket products come in.

Generally, we recommend using only Mason jars that are widely available in such brands as Kerr and Ball. You will only need half-pint and pint jars for canning fish and shellfish. Larger jars require longer processing times, and the large quantities they hold lead to waste. A pint of canned fish is a lot of food; it compares in volume to the large, one-pound cans of commercially processed salmon and mackerel. A half-pint jar holds a bit more than the standard 6½-ounce tuna can. So plan according to your family size and individual needs. You have a choice between standard and wide-mouth jars, and while either type is suitable for most canning operations, you'll find the wide-mouth type handier when canning large chunks of fish.

New jars come with lids and rings, but these can be purchased separately, as well. Rings should be replaced whenever they become bent or in any other way damaged so that they do not properly and effortlessly screw onto the jar top. Lids should be discarded after one use because the sealing compound will not effectively seal the jar after its first use.

Even new jars can be damaged by shippers, warehouse workers, or stock clerks, so it's a good idea to carefully inspect all new jars for cracks or chips. You should also inspect your jars before reusing them. Be especially watchful for any nicks or rough areas around the rims because such damage will prevent proper sealing of the lids.

The Canner

Canning fish and shellfish, whether in cans or jars, requires a pressure cooker/canner. Never use the simpler boiling-water method or oven methods of canning that are suitable for the canning of high-acid fruits and vegetables. Bacteria that cannot thrive in acids do, indeed, thrive in low-acid foods, including fish and shellfish. Consequently, they must be destroyed in the canning process.

While boiling will generally kill molds and yeasts, bacteria are harder to kill and require higher temperatures. Water boils at 212° F. at sea level and at lower temperatures at higher elevations. To attain sufficiently high temperatures while canning fish you must use pressure.

The *Clostridium botulinum* bacteria are able to grow in improperly canned foods, and the toxin they produce is one of the deadliest known.

It produces botulism, which is a severe and often fatal illness. A temperature of 240° F. kills this dangerous bacteria.

A pressure of 10 pounds at sea level corresponds to a temperature of 240° F., and that is the minimum pressure recommended for canning fish and shellfish. At higher elevations, though, higher pressures are required; 11 pounds at 2000 feet, 12 pounds at 4000 feet, and one more pound of pressure for every 2000 feet of elevation. If you live well above sea level and are unsure of what pressure to use, contact your county Extension Service or the Cooperative Extension Service at a nearby university. Extension agents are usually able to provide a wealth of information in such areas.

Remember, these are minimum recommendations. Some canner manufacturers recommend higher pressures and correspondingly shorter processing times. The manufacturer of our canner, for example, recommends 15 pounds pressure (250° F.) for all fish and shellfish. Always follow the manufacturer's directions. But if you have no owner's manual for your canner, you can use the recommended pressures and times in this chapter, provided that you have had your canner checked and that it is holding pressures properly.

Our recommendation is that you buy a new pressure cooker/canner rather than relying on a hand-me-down unit or something you might find at a garage sale or flea market. Old pressure cookers might not be suitable for pressure canning, and any you might buy as used equipment might have been damaged or not properly cared for. And an old or used canner seldom comes with the all-important owner's manual.

It is important that you carefully read the owner's manual before using any canner. And it's a good idea to test the canner to make sure it is functioning properly before actually canning anything. Run through all the recommended steps, only without processing any foods. Be sure the gauge is functioning properly and note the burner setting on your range required to maintain a constant pressure. For safety's sake, make such a test at least once a year or at any time you suspect that your canner might have been damaged in any way.

You should have your pressure-canner gauge checked once a year to be sure that it is correctly calibrated and to make sure your canner is holding the right pressure. Check with local hardware, appliance, or department stores to find out when manufacturers' representatives will be in your vicinity to perform such tests. They usually make their rounds in the spring, prior to the traditional summer canning season. Some canners come equipped with dial-type pressure gauges, and some don't. Although those with this type of gauge are a bit more expensive, they are easier to use and are more foolproof. We recommend a canner equipped with a dial gauge if you're just getting into canning.

Species Suitable for Canning

Numerous species of fish and shellfish are suitable for canning. Some are quite popular with sportsmen and canners alike and are widely available. Others are more restricted in their availability and are only locally popular. To learn what species are generally canned with good results in your part of the country, talk to other anglers who can their catches and, by all means, phone your county Extension Service or the Cooperative Extension Service at a local university.

Some of the most universally popular fishes for canning include the various species of tuna, salmon, the large trouts and chars, whitefish, striped bass, sturgeon, mackerel, shad, sucker, halibut, cod, rockfish, and large flounder and sole. Crabs, clams, and other shellfish can be canned with quite good results. You can even can soups and chowders if you wish, although you might prefer to freeze these products, especially if you will be using them within the limitations prescribed for frozen foods. You can also can smoked or pickled products, but you will want to alter your usual smoking and pickling processes if you plan to can these products.

Preparing Your Catch for Canning

As with any other method of preserving the catch, you should take care to keep your catch fresh, clean, and cold—from the time it's caught until it's packed in jars ready for the canner. Fish should be eviscerated and iced as soon as they're killed. Shellfish should be shucked, washed, and refrigerated as soon as possible.

Beyond the general recommendations for keeping the catch in the best possible condition, preparation for canning is guided both by proven and tested processes as well as by personal taste and preference. Here, and in the directions that follow, we'll try to tell you how fish are normally canned, what various sources recommend, and what we prefer to do. Then, you decide for yourself and perhaps do a bit of experimenting with different prescribed methods and recipes.

Since canning softens bones and renders them edible, many people prefer to simply cut fish into jar-size chunks, leaving the bones in. This certainly saves time, and if you don't mind the bones, leave them in. Personally, we don't care for the texture of bones, so we generally fillet our fish before canning. If we have a large amount of fish, we sometimes leave the bones in to save time. But we remove them later, before using the canned fish. The bones can be picked out with a fork.

Fish should be scaled before canning, or you can skin the fish, as we normally do. We sometimes leave the skin on smaller fish that we can and plan to use in chowders and soups, but skin-free fish looks much more appetizing in salads and other cold dishes. The decision to leave or remove the skin is up to you, but we do recommend that you *skin all large fish*, because you must remove the skin to find the fatty, darkened meat just beneath the skin on the large members of most species. This oily flesh is usually very strong in flavor and will affect the rest of the fish if left on. We trim it away with a fillet knife.

Preparing Your Work Area

It's important to clean your work area before beginning the canning operation, and you should make as much useful room available as possible. You'll need table space and counter surface, and with some precanning preparation, the job will run smoothly and efficiently. We have a roomy kitchen with plenty of counter space, but before getting to work, we clear away small appliances, cannisters, and other items that are normally kept on the counters. Then we scrub the counter tops. We make a handy canning table by putting a slab of plywood astride two sawhorses and cover the plywood with a flannel-backed vinyl tablecloth that is easy to wipe clean with a damp cloth whenever necessary. We then make sure that we have all the tools and accessories required and that they have been scrubbed clean.

Preparing Jars and Lids

Carefully follow the jar manufacturer's directions for preparing jars and lids for canning. If the instructions are not available, you should first wash the jars and lids in hot, soapy water. Rinse them thoroughly, fill them with hot water, and let them stand until you're ready to fill them with fish. It's not necessary to sterilize the jars used in pressure canning because they will be sterilized during the canning process. After rinsing the lids and rings, put them in a shallow pan (a cake pan works well), pour boiling water over them, and leave them in the hot water until you need them. This softens the sealing compound on the lids and facilitates the sealing of the jars.

Basic Raw-Pack Method

Since fish cooks completely during the canning process, it is usually canned raw. Most fish can be put up according to this basic method with excellent results. If you have doubts or questions about any particular species, consult your canner directions or phone your county Extension agent.

Once your fish have been scaled, skinned, or filleted according to your personal preference, follow these steps:

1. Cut the fish into pieces about a half inch shorter than the depth of the jars. Chunks approximately the same diameter as the jars

can be packed individually. Larger fish should be cut into small enough pieces to fit the jars. Small fish can be packed several to a jar.

2. Empty the hot water out of a jar and fill the jar with fish—skin side out. Fillets should be packed firmly, but not compressed. Small fish should be alternated in the jar—head up on one, head down on the next—to adequately fill the jar without leaving gaps.

3. Pack all remaining jars as in Step 2, working quickly. Put unused fish in the refrigerator immediately.

4. Add a teaspoon of salt to each pint jar or a half teaspoon to each half-pint jar.

5. Add hot water to each jar to within a quarter inch of the rim. Slide the blade of a table knife down the inside wall of each jar in several places to allow water to seep into any air pockets.

Your jars of fish are now ready for sealing and processing according to the canner manufacturer's instructions or the sealing and processing directions that follow.

Cold-Brine Pack

Fish can be soaked in a weak brine prior to canning. After preparing the fish as you would in Step 1 of the basic raw-pack method, follow these steps:

1. Dissolve ¾ cup of salt in a gallon of water, which is enough to brine about 25 pounds of cleaned fish.

2. Put the fish in a glass jar or crock and cover with brine. Put a plate on top of the fish to keep it submerged and leave the fish in the brine for one hour.

3. Remove the fish from the brine and drain it for several minutes.

4. Fill jars with fish, leaving about a half inch of headspace. Do not add salt or water.

Your cold-brined fish is now ready for sealing and processing.

Hot-Brine Pack

Another method recommended by some sources is the hot-brine pack. For this method, follow Steps 1, 2, and 3 of the basic raw-pack method. Then do the following:

1. In a large kettle or uncovered canner, make a brine of a half cup of salt to a gallon of water.

2. Submerge the packed jars in the brine. Do not put lids on the jars.

3. Bring the brine to a boil and continue boiling for 20 minutes.
4. Remove the jars from the brine and invert on a rack to drain thoroughly.
5. Turn jars right side up on a table or counter top.

Your hot-brined fish is now ready for sealing and processing.

Precooked Pack

Although the various species of tuna can be canned raw, according to any of the methods described above, some people find the unusual flavor of tuna a bit too strong when canned raw. Precooking helps to eliminate some of the oil in tuna and makes the fish easier to prepare.

Albacore, tuna, and other bloody species should be killed, eviscerated, and bled as soon as possible after they're caught. They should then be iced at once. They can be precooked and canned as soon as you

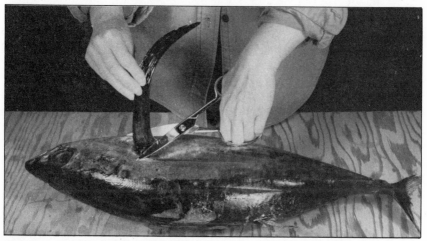

Use shears to remove large pectoral fins from all tuna and similar species.

get them home, or they can be frozen until you're ready to can them.

Fish can be precooked by steaming, pressure-cooking, or baking as follows:

1. Remove heads and tails from fish. Fish too large for easy handling should be cut into roasting-size pieces.
2. To precook by steaming, place fish, belly down, on a rack in a large roasting pan. Add water to the pan. Bring to a boil. Reduce heat to simmer and cover pan. Allow fish to steam two to four hours, depending on size, and add more boiling water as required.
3. To precook in a large-capacity pressure cooker/canner, put fish in pans with perforated bottoms and stack in cooker/canner.

Precooked Pack, Step 4.

Precooked Pack, Step 8.

Precooked Pack, Step 9.

Precooked Pack, Step 14.

107

Add three quarts of water and cook for two hours at 10 pounds pressure.

4. To precook by baking, put fish, belly down, on racks and place in a large, covered roasting pan. Or you can put the fish on racks in one or more large, shallow baking or broiling pans and cover and seal with extra–heavy-duty aluminum foil. Bake at 350° F. for one to two hours, depending on size, or to an internal temperature of 165° F. if you use a meat thermometer.

5. After cooking, allow fish to cool to room temperature. Then put fish in plastic bags and place in a cool room (40° F. or cooler, but not freezing) or refrigerate overnight. If you have a lot of fish and don't have room in your refrigerator, ice them down in coolers, alternating layers of ice and layers of fish in plastic bags.

6. The following day, remove the skin from the fish by scraping it off with a table knife.

7. With a fillet knife, make cuts down each side of the dorsal fin and for the entire length of the fish.

8. Turn the fish on one side and make a lengthwise cut just above the lateral line and another just below the lateral line—on each side of the row of bones that emanate horizontally from the backbone.

9. Start at the cuts made along the lateral line and use the fillet knife to cut top and bottom loins away from the backbone.

10. Turn fish over and repeat Steps 7, 8, and 9.

11. Cut away all dark meat and cut or break loins into canning-size pieces.

12. Pack jars firmly, leaving about a half inch of headspace, but do not compress the fish.

13. Add a half teaspoon of salt to pint jars or a quarter teaspoon to half-pint jars.

14. To pack in water, add boiling water to within a quarter inch of the jar rim. Slide the blade of a table knife down the inside wall of each jar in several places to allow water to seep into any air pockets.

15. To pack in oil, do the same as Step 14, substituting hot (not boiling) bland cooking oil for the boiling water—two to four tablespoonfuls for each pint or one to two tablespoonfuls for each half pint.

Your jars of precooked fish are now ready for sealing and processing.

Preparing and Packing Smoked Fish

Some people successfully can smoked fish without adding any liquid to the jars, but most sources recommend an oil pack for all smoked fish. Also, since canning tends to amplify the effects of smoking, you should slightly alter your smoking process for any fish you plan to can. It might take some experimenting to come up with canned smoked fish that suits your personal tastes, but for starters, try cutting your drying time in the smoker in half. If you normally use two panfuls of wood chips for smoked fish, use only one if you will later can the fish.

Prepare your smoked fish and pack it as follows:

1. Remove skin and bones from the smoked fish.
2. Cut large boneless pieces into jar-length pieces.
3. Pack large pieces into half-pint jars and fill any gaps or holes with smaller pieces and flakes.
4. Heat bland vegetable oil, but do not bring it to a boil.
5. Fill jars with oil to within an inch of the rims.

Your jars of smoked fish are now ready for sealing and processing.

Preparing and Packing Crabs

Although some people put live crabs into boiling water and essentially cook them for canning as they would for freezing or consuming fresh, home economists and food technologists at the University of California and the University of Alaska recommend killing crabs before cooking if they are to be canned.

To prepare and pack crabs for canning, follow these steps:

1. Immerse crabs in ice water for about two minutes. Then break off back legs and claws.
2. Insert fingers in leg holes and remove the back by lifting it off.
3. Grasp the crab's left legs in one hand and right legs in the other and crack the center of the body shell over the edge of the sink or the rim of a pot. Then break the crab in two.
4. Remove gills and all entrails and wash the crab bodies in fast-running cold water. Scrub legs and all shell areas with a stiff brush.
5. In a large kettle, make a brine of ¼ cup of distilled white vinegar and one cup of salt to each gallon of water. Bring brine to a rolling boil.
6. Immerse crabs in boiling brine. Allow brine to return to a boil and boil crabs for 15 more minutes.
7. Remove crabs from brine and cool until they can be handled. Then pick the meat as soon as possible.
8. Use a mallet or pliers to crack leg and claw shells so that the meat can be removed in large pieces. Keep body meat separate from leg and claw meat.

9. Make a fresh, cold brine by adding one cup each of salt and white distilled vinegar to a gallon of water. Stir until salt is dissolved.
10. With leg meat in one bowl and body meat in another, cover picked meat with brine and let stand for about two minutes.
11. Remove meat from brine and press the meat in your hands to remove excess brine and drain meat thoroughly. Do not discard the brine.
12. Pack a total of ¾ cup of meat into half-pint jars by arranging a layer of leg meat on the bottom and around the sides; then fill the center with body meat and top off with more leg meat.
13. Add a tablespoon of the cold brine to each jar.

Your jars of crab are now ready for sealing and processing.

Preparing and Packing Clams

Clams to be used for canning should be kept alive and allowed to self-clean before being shucked, so you'll want to bring home some clean sea water after your clamdigging trip, or you can make your own brine. Refer to Chapter 11 for details.

To prepare clams for the canner, follow these simple steps:

1. After the clams have self-cleaned, shuck them over a pan and save the nectar.
2. Clean the clams as you normally would. Remove entrails from large clams, such as gapers, and skin the necks. Remove all dark meat from necks.
3. Wash clams and neck meat in a brine made of a half cup of salt dissolved in a gallon of water.
4. Dissolve a half teaspoon of citric acid crystals in one gallon of water.
5. Immerse the clams in the citric-acid solution for one minute. Drain thoroughly.
6. Strain the clam nectar (from Step 1) into a pot and bring to a boil.
7. Pack the clams whole or mince or coarse-grind the clams and neck meat, allowing 1½ cups of clam meat for each pint jar.
8. Fill all jars with boiling clam nectar to within a quarter inch of the rims.

Your clams are now ready for sealing and processing.

Sealing and Processing

No matter which pack method you use, seal and process your fish or shellfish as follows:

1. Use a clean, damp cloth to wipe the jar rims free of any pieces of

110

fish, salt, oil, or anything else that might prevent the lids from sealing properly.

2. Remove the lids from their boiling-water bath with tongs and place them atop the jars.

3. Screw the rings onto the jars and tighten by hand only—never with a jar-lid wrench.

4. Arrange the jars on a rack inside the canner. In large-capacity canners, jars can be stacked one atop another. The jars may touch each other, but should not touch the sides or bottom of the canner.

5. Pour boiling water into the canner according to the manufacturer's instructions—usually about two inches of water or about two quarts in a 22-quart canner.

6. Close the canner lid and bring the water to a boil on a relatively high setting.

7. Vent all air from the canner—according to the manufacturer's directions—before closing or putting the weight on top of the vent pipe.

8. Allow the pressure to build to 10 pounds (240° F.) if processing at or slightly above sea level. Add another pound of pressure for every 2000 feet of elevation. Or follow the canner manufacturer's recommendations for pressure and processing time.

9. As soon as proper pressure is reached, mark starting and finishing times on a piece of paper and process according to the manufacturer's instructions or the processing table shown in this chapter.

10. After processing, carefully move the canner off the burner to another burner that's turned off and let stand until the pressure drops to zero.

11. Open the petlock or remove the weight from the vent pipe before opening the canner.

12. Turn the canner lid to the open position and tilt the far end of the lid up to allow vapor to escape before removing the lid.

13. Spread a towel or clean cloth on a table or counter top. Lift jars out of the canner with jar tongs and stand them upright on the cloth. Never place hot jars on a cold counter or table.

14. Let the jars stand away from drafts until they cool to room temperature.

15. Check all lids for proper sealing according to the jar manufacturer's directions. Lids should be slightly depressed and should make a ringing sound when tapped with a spoon. Any jars with bulging lids should be completely reprocessed at once, or if you prefer, you can refrigerate them and use the contents within two

or three days or pack and freeze it for later use.

16. Remove the rings from all properly sealed jars. Then use a dish cloth and warm, soapy water to wash the outsides of the jars. Rinse and dry them, and they are ready for labeling and storing.

Sealing and Processing, Step 13.

Labeling and Storing Canned Fish

You will find jar labels wherever canning supplies are sold, or you can do as we do and use the small, pressure-sensitive address labels available at office supply stores. These normally come 33 labels to a page. They can be quickly and easily typed, peeled off the page, and pressed onto the jars.

Your jars of canned fish and shellfish should then be stored in a cool place, but not where they will be exposed to freezing. If you will be storing them on shelves, use the shelves nearest the floor because the temperature there will be coolest. You should also store the jars in darkness, such as in a closed cabinet or dark pantry. If you don't have a dark storage area, store them in the cardboard cartons in which the jars were originally packed.

Most canned fish and shellfish will keep well for up to a year. Products that are canned in oil should be used within six to nine months. Any jars that lost some liquid during the canning process should be used before others.

Keep a complete inventory list of all your canned fish and shellfish with dates when they were canned. Use the oldest products first and check them off the list as they're used.

Some Variations You Might Try

Some people prefer to pack fish in oil. Personally, we don't like adding calories to our low-calorie canned fish, but if you wish to pack fish in oil, simply substitute oil for water in any steps that call for adding boiling water to the product. Heat bland cooking oil, but do not bring it to a boil. Add one tablespoon of oil to each half-pint jar or two tablespoons to each pint jar.

When canning tuna, you can make an oil pack by adding one to two tablespoons of hot oil to each half-pint jar or two to four tablespoons to each pint jar. Or you can make an oil-and-water pack with equal portions of each.

You can spark up your canned fish by adding various spices and seasonings. You might try canning only a few jars with seasonings added to learn which way you prefer the canned products. When we can salmon, we like to add two tablespoons of tomato catsup to each pint jar. Not only does this enhance the flavor of the fish, but it also helps retain the pink color. You might also try adding a slice of onion and one bay leaf to each pint of canned fish. If you're canning in half-pint jars, use only a half a bay leaf in each jar.

The folks at the Cooperative Extension Service at Michigan State University have come up with several tasty sauces for use when canning fish. One is a tomato sauce made from a half gallon of tomato catsup, a half ounce of ground horseradish, one tablespoon of minced onion, and two tablespoons of salt. All ingredients should be mixed thoroughly, heated, and then poured over the packed fish, leaving about a half inch of headspace. For canning suckers, they recommend adding to each pint jar 1½ teaspoons of vinegar, 1½ teaspoons of prepared mustard, and tomato juice to within about a half inch of the jar rim.

Some Final Safety Reminders

To succeed at canning the catch, you must be careful and you must be sure. Don't guess about anything. If you're unsure about any aspect of canning, phone your county Extension Service and ask questions.

If you suspect that any batch of canned fish or shellfish might not have been properly processed, process it again—for the entire recommended time and pressure. Although slight overprocessing will not normally harm the product being canned, underprocessing is dangerous. If, at any time during processing, the pressure in your canner drops below the recommended pressure, you must build the pressure back up to the right level and start processing all over again—for the entire recommended time and at the recommended pressure.

If, for one reason or another, your canner holds its pressure better at a pound or two above the recommended pressure, it's better if you process at the slightly higher pressure than try to fool around with the burner control. Your adjustments could cause the pressure to drop too much, or in the case of fluctuating pressures, liquids could be drawn from the jars.

If your canner is in good working order and if you follow the manufacturer's directions to properly seal and process fish and shellfish, your product will be tasty, wholesome, and safe. If, however, the product has not been properly canned or if the canner is malfunctioning, botulism is a threat. For these reasons, most canner manufacturers now recommend that pressure-canned, low-acid foods be boiled in an open pan for 10 to 20 minutes before use. This added safety measure denatures botulism-causing toxin so that it will not react with the body.

Canning Processing Table

Fish Or Shellfish	Jar Size	Time At 240° F.
Salmon, all species	pints	100 minutes
Steelhead, lake trout, brown trout (bones in)	pints	125 minutes
Tuna, all species	½ pints	90 minutes
	pints	100 minutes
Filleted fish, most species	½ pints	85 minutes
	pints	95 minutes
Crab	½ pints	65 minutes
Clams	pints	70 minutes

Chapter 8

SMOKING THE CATCH

In his *New Standard Fishing Encyclopedia,* A. J. McClane wrote: "The average sportsman can easily learn the art of smokehouse cookery. Such expensive delicacies as smoked trout, salmon, and eel may be produced with minimum equipment by anybody capable of building a fire."

It's true: smoking the catch is relatively simple, and it does produce some of the tastiest treats to tempt the most discriminating palate. In fact, with the widespread availability of inexpensive little electric smokers, such as those produced by Outers Laboratories and Luhr Jensen, the sportsman need not even be "capable of lighting a fire." If you can push a plug into an electrical outlet, you can fire up an electric smoker.

It is not our intention to tell you everything you ever wanted to know about smoke cookery but were afraid to ask. The subject is rather extensive; indeed, whole books have been written on it. Our purpose is to introduce you to basic fish and brine preparation and basic hot-smoking methods. We want to convince you how simple and inexpensive it is to produce otherwise expensive smoked delicacies. And we want to urge you to build or buy a simple smoker that will enable you to better utilize your catch while adding variety to your snacking and dining. We're sold on smoked fish, and we think you will be too.

Smokers

Smokers are easy to build and can be constructed of a variety of materials. You can make a smoker out of a 55-gallon oil drum, a new metal trash can, an old refrigerator, or even a cardboard box. You can build a smokehouse of wood. We have even built "wilderness smokers" on the banks of Alaskan salmon rivers, using saplings for the framework, polyethylene sheeting for the walls, light canvas tarps for the tops, and chicken wire for racks.

Your heat source can be the coals from a hardwood fire, commercial charcoal briquets, or an electric hotplate. You can even use a small barbeque grill or hibachi to contain your coals during the smoking process.

If you're interested in building a smoker or smokehouse, visit your county Extension Service or the Cooperative Extension Service at a nearby university to obtain plans. McClane's *New Standard Fishing Encyclopedia* also contains plans for several smokers. *The Easy Art Of Smoking Food,* by Chris Dubbs and Dave Heberle (Winchester Press), is an excellent source of smoker plans and has an abundance of smoke-cookery lore and recipes as well. Smoker plans are also included in the following publications:

Freshwater Fish Preparation, Extension Bulletin E-1180, Michigan Sea Grant Publication MICHU-SG-78-101, Cooperative Extension Service, Michigan State University.

Home Smoking And Pickling Of Fish, WIS-SG-71-110, Sea Grant Program, University of Wisconsin.

Smoking Fish At Home—Step-By-Step Guide, VPI-SG-300-2, Cooperative Extension Service, Virginia Polytechnic Institute and State University.

The Fisherman Returns, Publication No. 31, Cooperative Extension Service, University of Alaska.

Fish Smoking, Publication 64, Ohio Department of Natural Resources, Division of Wildlife.

If you haven't the time nor the inclination to build a smoker, we highly recommend purchasing one of the little electric smokers that are now available at most discount department stores, hardware stores, and sporting goods outlets. They can also be purchased through a number of mail-order suppliers of outdoor products. Or you can write directly for information to:

Luhr Jensen & Sons, Inc.
P.O. Box 297
Hood River, OR 97031

Outer Laboratories, Inc.
Onalaska, WI 54650

If you've never done any smoke cooking, we suggest starting with one of these little electric smokers. By following the manufacturer's instructions (included with the smoker) and experimenting with various foods and recipes, you'll not only learn a good bit about the smoking process, but you'll also prepare a lot of palate-pleasing delicacies during your learning.

Despite their low initial cost and low operating cost, these little smokers are durable appliances that do a remarkable job. We owned our first one when we lived in Alaska. After using it for several seasons, we spent one summer working as commercial fish buyers and had our smoker going 24 hours a day so we could greet our fishermen each day with snacks of smoked salmon and cold beer. We left that smoker with a friend when we moved from Alaska, and the last we heard it's still smoking fish every season. We now have another—a Luhr Jensen "Little Chief"—that sees to virtually all our smoking needs.

Basic Smoking Methods

Of the two basic smoking methods—cold smoking and hot smoking—we recommend the latter as the easiest and most convenient for the average home smoker. Cold smoking is a curing and drying process that provides a better-preserved product, but it is considerably more time-consuming than hot smoking. Hot smoking cures and cooks the fish at temperatures of about 165° F., and while it is considered a method of preserving the catch, hot-smoked fish will keep no more than a few days if not refrigerated or further preserved in some other way. Most smoked fish will keep for two to four weeks—sometimes longer—in a refrigerator. Smoked products will last up to three months in a freezer or, if canned, up to a year.

Preparing Fish for the Smoker

As with any other method of fish preservation and preparation, the quality of the finished product depends on how the fish was handled and cared for after it was caught. In short, the best fish for smoking is the fresh fish that has been properly dressed, cleaned, and chilled. You can also use frozen fish, provided that it was properly prepared and packaged for freezer storage and hasn't been stored beyond the recommended limits.

How you dress and cut fish for the smoker depends largely on what size and type of fish you are smoking, what kind of smoker you have, and your personal preferences.

Generally, small fish—pan-size trout, bluegill, smelt, and the like—should be smoked whole. For some home-built smokers, heads should be left on the fish if they are to be hung from hooks or rods. If your smoker is equipped with racks, as are the little electric smokers, remove the heads since they only waste space.

117

Although some strong-tasting species should be skinned, most should have the skin left on. Whole fish and all large-scaled fish (black bass, striped bass, shad, and the like) should be scaled. Large trout, salmon, lingcod, flounder, and other small-scaled species that will be filleted or cut into smoking strips don't have to be scaled, unless you intend to eat the skin.

We recommend removing the skin from larger fish before consuming them because it is often strong in taste. If you're using previously frozen fillets that have been skinned, be sure to oil the smoking racks well before smoking the fish to prevent sticking.

Normally, we're pretty fussy about fish bones, and for that reason, we prefer boneless fillets to all other forms of fish. But with smoked fish, we're not as finicky. During the smoking process, the meat on fillets or strips cut from large fish shrinks slightly, exposing bone ends. It's then an easy matter to find the bones and pull them out or break the meat away from them. With small fish that are smoked whole, the meat can be broken away from the bones with little effort.

To prepare small fish for brining, gut and gill them, scale them if necessary, and remove the heads if they will be smoked on racks. Wash them thoroughly in cold, running water and drain them on paper towels. They are now ready for brining. If you have more than enough to fill the smoker, brine only one batch and refrigerate the rest until you need them.

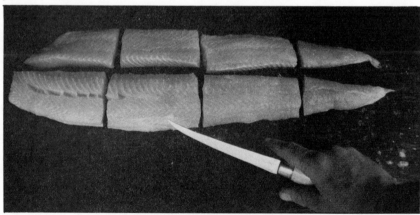

To cut a fillet into smoking chunks or strips, begin by cutting the fillet in half lengthwise, along the natural lateral division. Then make several cuts across the fillet, rendering chunks suitable for brining and smoking. If you prefer smoking strips, divide all chunks except the tail pieces in half lengthwise. Larger fillets require even further division.

Large fish should be scaled if necessary, then filleted. You can leave the fillets whole on fish up to about three pounds, but on larger fish, the fillets should be cut into smaller pieces. We prefer to cut all fillets into smoking strips, regardless of the fish's size. We like strips one to two inches wide and four or five inches long. They are easy to handle in the brine and on the smoker racks, and they glaze nicely on all surfaces. After cutting fillets into smoking strips, we wash them in cold, running water and drain them on paper towels. One smoker load then goes into the brine, and any surplus is refrigerated until it is needed.

If we have a large quantity of fish to smoke, we separate whole fish and smoking strips by size so that all fish or strips in any smoker load will be of approximately equal thickness. This assures that all pieces will be done at the same time. Pieces or whole fish of varying thickness in any smoker load must be checked periodically during the smoking process, and the thinner pieces should be removed first to keep them from becoming too dry and tough.

Preparing a Basic Brine

You'll need a nonmetallic container for brining your catch. A ceramic crock is excellent for such purposes, but crocks are relatively expensive. If you own a crock of sufficient size, by all means use it, but if you must buy a container, you'll find glass or plastic much cheaper. For a full load in one of the little electric smokers, you'll need a brining container with a capacity of one gallon or more. We use a one-gallon glass jar with a wide mouth.

To make a basic brine, dissolve one cup of noniodized salt and one cup of white, granulated sugar in one quart of warm water. When the salt and sugar are completely dissolved, add one quart of cold water and mix. Refrigerate until needed, or if you have a smoker load of fish ready, immerse the fish in the brine and refrigerate.

Small fish and strips or fillets about a half inch thick should remain in the brine for about four hours. Larger strips of an inch or so in thickness should be brined for about eight hours or overnight. Stir the fish several times during the brining process.

You can vary this basic brine by adding herbs, spices, and other seasonings. You'll find numerous recipes in books and pamphlets on smoke cookery, or you can experiment with your own favorite seasonings. We have experimented with several brines and as our basic brine we have settled on the one we described above, but we substitute dark brown sugar for the white sugar. Then we add about a tablespoon—more or less—of freshly ground black pepper, two teaspoons of fines herbes, and two bay leaves. To temper the flavor of strong-tasting fish, we sometimes add a half teaspoon each of garlic powder and onion powder to the brine. For variety, we sometimes sprinkle smoking strips with a little garlic powder or onion powder and freshly ground pepper just before we put them in the smoker. Other brine seasonings we've enjoyed include sweet basil, rosemary, tarragon, and thyme. The flavor of some bland fish can be enhanced by substituting a quart of white wine for one quart of the water in the basic brine. Or for a different flavor, add apple juice to the basic brine.

Glazing and Smoking the Catch

After brining, remove the fish and discard the brine. Since the fish absorbs salt from the brine, make a fresh batch if you have more fish to brine and smoke. Lightly rinse the brined fish under cold water to remove surface salt and spread the fish on paper towels. Use paper towels to pat dry.

Spread the fish or smoking strips on a cookie sheet or on several platters or plates, making sure no pieces touch, and let stand, exposed to air, for about an hour, preferably in a cool room. If you're using a smoker with removable racks, spread the fish on the racks instead of on a cookie sheet or plates. A pellicle or glaze will form that is shiny in appearance and tacky to the touch when the fish is ready for the smoker.

If you're using a smoker equipped with racks, make sure the racks are clean and dry, and before placing the fish on them, spray the racks with Pam vegetable cooking spray to keep the fish from sticking. Place the fish on the racks so that none of the pieces touch one another. Put the racks in the smoker and plug in the electrical cord. Then fill the chip pan with hardwood chips—hickory, alder, or one of the other commercially available products.

Smoking and cooking times depend on the size of the fish or smoking strips, the smoker manufacturer's recommendations, and your personal tastes. So you'll have to experiment with the first few smoker loads to determine the best times for your purposes. If your smoked fish is too dry, reduce the smoking/cooking time; if it isn't dry enough, increase the time.

We find that one-inch-thick strips of salmon, steelhead, and other fatty fish take about eight hours to cure to the consistency we like. Small fatty fish and half-inch-thick strips are done to our liking in four to six hours. Leaner fish, such as bass, bluegill, catfish, lingcod, and flounder, take less time and should be checked often during the smoking process. We find that one-inch-thick strips of lean fish usually take no more than six hours, and thinner pieces are done to perfection in two to four hours.

Two pans of wood chips for each batch of fish are enough to give a good smoky taste to the fish. You might prefer more or less.

After Smoking Your Catch

The brining process extracts moisture from the fish and replaces that moisture with salt. Most of the spoilage bacteria that need the moisture to survive are eliminated in this way. But hot-smoked fish is only partly cured and will spoil if left unrefrigerated for more than a few days. It will keep well for several weeks if it is wrapped in waxed paper or packed in brown paper bags and stored in your refrigerator at a temperature less than 40° F.

If you have a large quantity of smoked fish on hand and cannot possibly consume it all within a few weeks or simply don't have room for it all in your refrigerator, you can freeze it or can it. See the appropriate chapters for directions on freezing (Chapter 6) and canning (Chapter 7).

We should mention, again, that smoked fish that has been stored in a freezer should not be kept in the refrigerator in its air-tight freezer packaging because this could lead to the production of harmful botulism toxin. Rewrap the previously frozen fish in waxed paper or put it in brown paper bags.

Chapter 9

PICKLING THE CATCH

For most of us, our experience with pickled fish is confined to one or two species that are pickled and jarred commercially and sold in supermarkets, delicatessens, and gourmet food shops. And most of us who enjoy pickled fish buy the product for its flavor, with no thought to the original purpose of pickling.

Pickling is among the oldest methods for preserving foods. Our ancestors pickled fish as a way of preserving it, and they certainly didn't confine their efforts to herring, currently the most popular fish among commercial processors. The fact is, they pickled surpluses of all species, and we would do well to follow their examples.

Not only is pickling an excellent way to preserve fish and add variety to our diets, but it is one of the safest of all preservation methods. Vinegar, which contains acetic acid, is a primary ingredient in all pickling recipes, and spoilage bacteria cannot survive in a high-acid environment. A sufficient level of acetic acid, in fact, will even eliminate the threat of botulism.

Vinegar also softens bones, which makes pickling an excellent method for preserving such bony species as shad, pike, and sucker. Some people even leave the bones in other species, such as salmon, trout, lingcod, and flounder, but you need not leave the bones in if you are as anti-fishbone as we are.

You can pickle just about any species with excellent results. So keep this in mind when you have seasonal surpluses of any fish. Fish can be pickled raw or cooked and will keep well in a refrigerator for several months. If you have an abundance of fish, you might wish to can some, which should last up to one year.

Basic Pickling Ingredients and Materials

Although a variety of spices, herbs, and other seasonings can be used when pickling fish, three important ingredients are used in all pickling processes. They are as follows:

1. WATER. It is important that you use good-quality water. For most people, this is no problem since tap water is usually of sufficient quality. But if your water is high in iron, magnesium, or calcium, it can cause pickled fish to discolor and take on an unpleasant taste. So don't use hard water for pickling.
2. VINEGAR. To kill the spores of *Clostridium botulinum*, the vinegar you use must have a minimum acetic acid content of 4.5% before dilution with equal parts of water. To allow a safety margin, use only distilled white vinegar that is at least 5% acetic acid before dilution. Check the label.
3. SALT. Although table salt may be used, it should not contain calcium or magnesium, which will have the same effects as hard water on the finished product. Your best bet is to use pure kosher or dairy salt.

In addition to these basic ingredients, you will need a suitable nonmetallic brining container. A large crock is excellent, or you can use a large, glass jar with a wide mouth or a plastic container of sufficient size.

Finally, you will need containers for storing the pickled fish. We recommend clean, glass jars, such as those used for canning. Most people pack pickled fish in half-pint, pint, and quart jars. Some like to keep a gallon jar full of pickled fish in the refrigerator at all times. The choice is yours. If you're using the canning method, we recommend half-pint or pint jars. For refrigerator storage, pints, quarts, or gallon jars will do. You'll be able to put up about a quarter pound of fish in half-pint jars, a half pound in pint jars, a pound or so in quart jars, and four to five pounds in gallon jars.

Preparing the Catch for Pickling

Fish that are to be pickled should be kept fresh and cold until they're to be used, which means that you must gut, gill, clean, and ice them as soon as they're killed. You can also use frozen fish, provided that they were meticulously cleaned, properly packaged for freezer storage, and have not been in the freezer beyond recommended limits. Freezing is also a good way to keep fish until you have enough for a pickling-size batch.

Scale any fish that will be cooked or canned during the pickling process. Leave the skin on these fish to help hold the meat fibers together. Fish that are to be pickled raw can be skinned or scaled, whichever you prefer.

Small fish can be pickled whole, but after scaling them you should remove their heads, tails, and fins. Rinse them under cold, running water and drain them on paper towels.

Small trout and other slender fish can be cut into one-inch-thick steaks for pickling, if you don't mind the bones. Larger fish that are slightly smaller in diameter than the jars you'll put them in, can be cut into jar-length chunks or one-inch-thick steaks if you will be canning them during the pickling process. Otherwise, these larger fish should be filleted.

Personally, we prefer to fillet even the small fish, thus removing the backbone. We then cut out the ribs, which renders two, small, pickling-size fillets per fish. When we're using larger fish, we fillet them, remove the ribs, and cut the fillets into pickling-size pieces about an inch or so wide and two inches long.

Basic Pickling Methods

There are countless variations and recipes for pickling fish, many of which have been handed down through families, generation after generation. Others are the results of experimentation and modification of existing recipes. You'll find pickling recipes in some seafood cookbooks as well as in pamphlets available from your county Extension agent or the Cooperative Extension Service at your state university.

To get you started, we'll describe four different methods, at least one of which should serve you well, no matter what your personal preferences are or what kind of fish you're using. The first three processes described are for about five pounds of fish each, or enough to fill a gallon jar. If you have more fish, increase the recipes proportionately. The last method described is the canning method and ingredients are sufficient for about 10 to 12 pounds of fish. Before putting up any fish according to this method, please read Chapter 7, "Canning the Catch," and carefully follow all directions in the section on "Sealing and Processing."

Basic Pickling—Raw Fish

Although this method can be used successfully with most species, we recommend it as an excellent choice for shad, salmon, and steelhead.

For five pounds of fish prepared for pickling, make a brine consisting of ¾ cup of salt dissolved in one pint of water and one pint of distilled white vinegar. Place the fish in a nonmetallic container, cover with brine, and store in the refrigerator at 40° F. or colder for five days. Use a plate to hold fish under the brine if necessary.

After fish have been brined, pour off the brine and rinse the fish under cold, running water for about an hour to remove all excess salt. Then drain the fish on paper towels.

While the fish are rinsing, gather together the following ingredients:

4 cups vinegar
2 cups water
3 tablespoons sugar
1 medium onion, thinly sliced
½ cup pickling spices

Dissolve the sugar in the water and add the vinegar.

When the fish is rinsed and drained, wash and dry the brining container. Then put a layer of onion slices in the bottom of the container. Sprinkle some of the pickling spices over the onion and add a layer of fish. Then add another layer of onions, spices, and fish, and continue filling the container in layers until all ingredients have been used. Cover with the sweetened vinegar-and-water solution and let stand in the refrigerator for 24 to 48 hours.

The fish can now be repacked in smaller jars if so desired. Use clean, glass jars with tight-fitting lids and pack in alternating layers of fish and fresh, sliced onion.

To each pint jar, add a bay leaf and a teaspoon of fresh pickling spices. In quart jars, add two bay leaves and two teaspoons of pickling spices. Top off the jar with the vinegar-and-water solution.

If you will pack the whole works in a gallon jar, do that in the first place, instead of using your brining container. But top off the jar with an extra tablespoon or two of pickling spices, a layer of sliced onion, and several bay leaves.

Although fish pickled in this way will be ready to eat within 24 hours, it's best if you let it stand for about a week in the refrigerator.

A moot point, but it should keep well refrigerated for up to six months. For peak flavor and texture, though, use it within six weeks.

Basic Pickling—Cooked Fish (Fatty Species)

If you prefer a cooked product, this method is recommended for all fatty species, such as salmon, trout, shad, and mackerel. Here's what you'll need for about five pounds of fish prepared for pickling:

Salt
1 medium onion, thinly sliced
¼ cup olive oil
1 tablespoon peppercorns
1½ teaspoons mustard seed
2 bay leaves

> 1 tablespoon whole cloves
> 2 cups vinegar
> 2 cups water

After the fish is rinsed and drained, spread a layer of salt in the bottom of a large, shallow, glass baking dish or on a large sheet of foil or waxed paper. Spread the fish on the salt and cover with more salt. Let stand for 30 minutes.

Rinse the fish in cold, running water to remove salt; then place in a large pot or roasting pan and cover with water. Bring to a boil on a medium heat. Reduce the heat and simmer for 10 minutes or until the fish can be pierced easily with a fork.

Remove the fish from the water and place in a large, nonmetallic container. (Use a gallon jar if that's what you'll use to store the fish.)

To a skillet on a medium-high heat, add the olive oil and quickly sauté the sliced onion only until it turns yellow. Then add the water, vinegar, cloves, bay leaves, mustard seed, and peppercorns. When the liquid boils, reduce the heat to low and simmer for 10 minutes. Remove from the heat and let cool to room temperature.

Pour the liquid and seasonings over the fish, making sure the fish is covered. Refrigerate and let stand for 24 to 48 hours.

If you wish, you can repack the fish in smaller jars, adding the fish and fresh, sliced onion in alternating layers. For spicier fish, add a fresh bay leaf and a half teaspoon each of fresh peppercorns and whole allspice to each quart jar—half that for pint jars.

For best results, let stand refrigerated for a week before consuming. Try to use the pickled fish during the peak of its flavor and texture—within four to six weeks.

Basic Pickling—Cooked Fish (Lean Species)

Use this method for all lean species, such as black bass, bluegill, catfish, striped bass, sole, lingcod, and the like.

For five pounds of scaled, whole fillets from small fish or one-inch by two-inch pieces from large fillets (skin on), you'll need the following ingredients:

> Salt
> 4 cups vinegar
> 3 cups water
> 1 cup chopped onion
> 1 clove garlic, minced or pressed
> 3 teaspoons peppercorns
> 2 bay leaves

> 1½ teaspoons ground nutmeg
> 1½ teaspoons whole cloves
> 1½ teaspoons whole allspice
> 2 tablespoons sugar

For later, you'll also need:

> 1 medium onion, thinly sliced
> 4 or 5 bay leaves
> 2½ teaspoons whole allspice
> 1 lemon, sliced

Pour an ample amount of salt onto a platter or large sheet of waxed paper. Rinse fillets or pickling pieces under cold, running water and while they're still moist, roll them in salt until they're completely covered with as much salt as will cling. Pack fish loosely in a nonmetallic container and let stand for two hours.

In a large pot, combine vinegar, water, chopped onion, garlic, peppercorns, bay leaves, nutmeg, cloves, allspice, and sugar. Stir while bringing the mixture to a boil. Reduce the heat and simmer for 10 minutes.

While the mixture is simmering, rinse fish in cold, running water to remove salt. Add fish to the simmering mixture and bring to a boil on a medium-high heat. Reduce the heat to low and simmer for 10 minutes.

Have five glass quart jars or ten pint jars clean and ready for filling. You should have enough fish for four or five quarts or eight to ten pints.

Remove the fish from the liquid. Then strain the liquid into another pot and bring to a rolling boil.

While the liquid is reheating, fill jars with alternating layers of fish and sliced onion. To each quart jar, add a bay leaf, a half teaspoon each of whole allspice and peppercorns, and a slice of lemon—half that for pints. Fill jars with the boiling liquid, cover tightly, and refrigerate.

Your pickled fish will be ready to eat in 24 hours, but for best results, let it stand refrigerated for a week. Although it should keep well for several months, try to use it within four to six weeks.

Basic Pickling—Canning Method

If you have an abundance of fish and a paucity of refrigerator space, you can use this method to produce a product that will keep well for up to a year. But, again, you should carefully read Chapter 7 before attempting to do any canning.

You may use jar-size chunks of fish, steaks, fillets, or pickling strips for this method. All fish should be scaled, with the skin left on.

For each 10 to 12 pounds of fish prepared for pickling, you'll need a pickling mixture made of:

> 8 cups vinegar
> 4 cups water
> ¼ cup sugar
> 2 tablespoons pickling spices

Before sealing and processing the jars, you'll need fresh, sliced onion, bay leaves, whole peppercorns, and whole allspice, so keep them handy.

But before you start the pickling and canning process, wash the fish in cold, running water and immerse it in a brine made of two cups of salt dissolved in a gallon of water. Use a nonmetallic container and let stand for one hour.

In a pot, combine the vinegar, water, and sugar. Put the pickling spices in a tea ball and immerse it in the liquid. Bring to a boil; then reduce the heat and simmer for one hour.

Remove the fish from the brine, rinse in cold water, and drain on paper towels. Pack loosely in half-pint or pint jars.

Mix a quart of the pickling liquid with a quart of hot water. Then add the half-strength liquid to the jars of fish, filling to the rims.

Place the jars in a large kettle and add a couple inches of water to the kettle. Bring to a boil and exhaust the open jars by boiling for 20 minutes.

Remove the jars and invert them on a rack or screen to drain for about five minutes. Turn the jars upright and add two slices of onion, one about five minutes. Turn the jars upright and add two slices of onion, one bay leaf, and a quarter teaspoon each of whole peppercorns and whole allspice to each half pint—double that for pints.

Fill the jars to the rim with full-strength pickling liquid, and your pickled fish is ready for sealing and processing.

Refer to Chapter 7 for sealing and processing directions. Process at 10 pounds for 90 minutes.

Chapter 10

ADDING CRABS TO THE CATCH

Coastal residents and inland anglers vacationing in the coastal states have opportunities to tap another marine resource by harvesting crabs. There is no guarded ritual or mystique involved in crabbing, as some might think, and it is an inexpensive sport with high success rates in most areas. And if the cost of commercially caught crab isn't enough to send you a-crabbing, then the toothsome flavor of the catch should be. Although preferred crabbing techniques will vary from one region to another, most of the techniques described in this chapter will work anywhere, because the various species of crabs are similar in their feeding habits.

Popular American Crabs

While there are a number of different species of crabs locally available along the Atlantic, Gulf, and Pacific coasts, the most popular and abundant species that the sport crabber should consider harvesting are the blue crab and rock crab in the East and the dungeness and red rock crab in the West.

Blue Crab

By far, the most important commercial species and in some areas the species sought more by sportsmen than any other, including fish, is the blue crab. The blue crab ranges as far north as Nova Scotia and south to Florida, and a subspecies occurs in the Gulf of Mexico. The blue crab averages from five to seven inches across the carapace (back) when fully grown. It is distinguished by the brownish green to dark green carapace, white undersides and legs, and varying amounts of blue in the claws. The claws of the adult male are blue. The tips of the adult female's claws are bright red.

Rock Crab

The rock crab has roughly the same range as the blue crab. It is smaller in size than the blue crab, averaging about five inches across the carapace when fully grown. It is easily distinguished from the blue crab by its oval-shaped carapace that is smooth and ivory-colored, with purple or crimson spots.

Dungeness Crab

In popularity and availability, the dungeness is the West Coast's equivalent of the East Coast's blue crab, but here the similarity stops. The dungeness is much larger. In fact, it is among the largest of edible crabs, the males attaining a size of nine inches across the carapace when fully grown. The carapace of the dungeness is brown to reddish or purplish brown, and the legs are long in proportion to the body.

Red Rock Crab

Another West Coast species overlapping in range with the dungeness is the smaller red rock crab. This crab averages only five inches across the carapace, but in quality is just as tasty as the dungeness. The reddish carapace of the rock crab is more brightly hued than that of the dungeness, and the claws and body are heavier in proportion to the legs than in the dungeness.

Crabbing Tides and Seasons

Recommendations for the "best" crabbing tides are as varied as the tides themselves, and you'll find that crabs are fickle creatures that don't always behave according to the experts' advice. Crabs can be taken on high tides, low tides, and slack tides—day or night. They'll come to a bait on an ebb tide or flood tide. They'll gobble your offerings on a spring tide (when sun, moon, and earth are approximately aligned) or on the neap tide (when the sun and moon are in quadrature). Frankly, my dear, crabs don't give a damn—tidewise. The consensus of the experts seems to be in favor of crabbing on a high slack or low slack tide and to avoid an ebbing tide. As nonexperts, we'll recommend that you start on a slack tide, but allow yourself some leeway. If the crabbing is slow, wait for the tide change. You might be surprised to find that you catch many more on the moving tide than you did during the slack period.

Crabbing seasons are more regulated by nature than by bureaucracies. In most areas, crabbing is open to sport or recreational crabbers the year round. Along the Atlantic coast, however, the best crabbing is during the warmer months of the year. During the winter, the crabs move to the deeper channels of bays and burrow into the mud or sand, where they are only available to the commercial crabber's gear.

On the West Coast, crabbing is good throughout the summer months and into the fall until autumn rains begin. As the rains bring great amounts of fresh water into the bays, the salinity of the bay waters decreases, driving the crabs to the saltier waters in the lower reaches of the bays or the open ocean. During midwinter dry spells, when the salinity of the bay waters increases, crabs move into the upper reaches of the bays, and crabbing can be excellent. Then the freshets of spring will again drive them seaward until the rains subside.

In some areas there are regulated seasons for crab pots—traps with fixed entrances that are mostly used by commercial crabbers. It's a good idea to check the regulations for the state where you will be crabbing to find out if there are any other seasonal restrictions on the harvesting of crabs.

Molting

Although the young crab that has spent perhaps two months developing through several stages following hatching is only about a tenth of an inch wide, it grows rapidly during the summer months, molting about every three to five days and adding to its overall size by one third with each molting. It continues to molt throughout its life to its terminal molt. Females will molt from 18 to 20 times, and males will molt 21 to 23 times, which accounts for their larger size.

When a crab starts to molt, its shell will crack between the carapace and abdomen, and the crab simply backs out of its shell. Molting takes about two to three hours, and during the few minutes just before and after the molt, the crab will take on large quantities of water to expand its new shell. During the next 12 hours, the shell will be leathery or papery to the touch, giving rise to the name "paper shell." It takes another 12 to 24 hours for the shell to become hard and brittle.

In some states it is illegal to take some species of crabs in the softshell stage. We recommend taking only the hardshell crabs, regardless of regulations allowing the harvesting of softshell or paper-shell crabs, because the meat of the softshell and paper-shell crabs is watery and not of the best quality and the yield per crab of usable meat will be far lower than with hardshell crabs.

Size Limitations

Some species, notably the blue crab in the East and the dungeness in the West, are regulated by size; that is, the crab must be of a certain size to be considered legal. To determine the size, measure the crab across the carapace. Most sport shops and marinas sell inexpensive gauges for this purpose. Since size regulations will vary from state to state, be sure to consult the specific regulations of the state where you are crabbing.

The simple, inexpensive crab gauge is available at most sport shops in areas where there are size limitations on crabs.

Determining the Sex of a Crab

Some species are not regulated at all. They can be taken at any time with no regard to size, sex, or condition of the shell. Others are closely regulated. In some eastern states, for example, the size limit on male blue crabs differs from that on females. In the Pacific coast states, only hardshell, male dungeness crabs of a specific size may be harvested. So it is important to be able to distinguish the males from the females. It is quite easy to determine the sex of a crab. Turn the crustacean over on its back and examine the flap on the abdomen. The flap on the female is broad, while the flap on the male is quite narrow.

The male crab can be identified by the narrow flap on its abdomen.

132

The female crab is distinguished by the wide flap on its abdomen.

Crabbing Tools and Techniques

In most states, there are few restrictions on the ways crabs can be taken. Most of the common crabbing gear is legal in all parts of the country. Following are some of the more popular methods and descriptions of the equipment required.

Using a Dipnet

Dipnetting is the simplest crabbing technique and requires only one piece of equipment—a long-handled dipnet. Although nets with cotton or nylon mesh will work, experienced crabbers make their own of galvanized chicken wire with one-inch or two-inch mesh. Crabs don't become as easily entangled in the wire mesh as they would in other nets. The dipnet is used only in relatively shallow, clear waters where the crabber can spot his quarry by sight, then simply scoop it up in the dipnet. Dipnetters either wade the shallow water or work from the bow of a boat.

Using Bait and a Handline

Another simple method, and one of the most popular along the East Coast, calls for using a long-handled dipnet as well as a baited line. The advantage it offers over the dipnetting method is that the crabber can ply deeper and murkier waters. Use a stout, braided handline (or rod and reel if you wish), to the end of which you should tie a bait and enough weight to hold bottom. Favorite baits include fresh fish heads, whole fish, and chicken necks and backs. When a crab discovers your bait, you will detect a tugging on the line, not unlike the nibble of a small fish. Steadily and gently bring the line in without jerking it. If the crab is unalarmed and tenacious, it will still be clutching the bait in its claws as you bring it to the surface. Then use the long-handled dipnet to dip beneath the crab and scoop it up.

Using a Crab Trap

Crab traps (also called hand traps) come in several different configurations, but all function similarly. They resemble wire cages with collapsible sides, and they are useful for crabbing in deep water or from bridges and piers where a dipnet is impractical. A bait, usually a whole fish, fish head, or fish carcass, is attached to the floor of the trap. It should be securely tied or wired to prevent a crab from escaping with it. The trap is then lowered into the water by a rope, where it rests on the bottom with the walls of the trap lying flat in the open position. Since the crabber cannot feel his quarry, as in the handline method, he must raise the trap periodically to check it. As the rope is pulled upward, it in turn pulls on the lines attached to the trap walls, thus closing the walls and preventing the crabs from escaping.

Using a Crab Ring

Another kind of trap is the crab ring, which is very effective and popular on the West Coast. It consists of two rings, usually made of ⅝-inch steel and wrapped with strips of rubber inner tube, fiberglass tape, or plastic tape. The bottom ring is usually 26 inches in diameter and has a galvanized wire bottom. The top ring is usually 30 inches in diameter and is connected to the bottom ring with side netting. The side netting is made of net twine that is ⅛-inch in diameter and is 16 inches deep (from the top ring to the bottom ring). The side netting on most crab rings has a stretched-mesh measurement of four inches, to allow the undersize crabs to escape.

There are three ropes of equal length, usually ¼ to ⅜ inch in diameter, attached to the top ring. They are brought together above the top ring and tied to a small ring that is about one inch in diameter. The pulling rope is also attached to this small ring. Just above the small ring a small float is attached to hold the three net ropes up and away from the bait when the crab ring is in use.

The pulling rope should be ⅜ inch in diameter because smaller ropes are hard on the hands when hauling in the heavy crab ring and larger ropes create too much drag in tide currents. The length of the pulling rope and the addition of more floats depends on how the crab ring will be used. If the crabber works from bridges and piers, he will need no other floats, but will require from 50 to 100 feet of pulling rope, depending on the height of the structure and the depth of the water. When crabbing from a boat, the length of the pulling rope depends on the water depth. Here, the crabber also attaches several, usually three, safety floats to the pulling rope. These ropes help to keep the pulling rope vertical and aid the crabber in determining the position of the crab ring. Finally, the crabber attaches a marker buoy to the tag end of the pulling rope. Most crabbers use empty plastic gallon jugs with tightly capped lids for this purpose. Some paint the jugs a bright fluorescent color so that they are easy to spot.

The crab ring, most popular on the west coast, is among the best traps for sport crabbing.

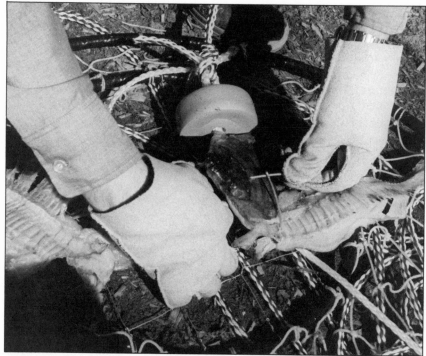

Large, wire safety pin-type bait holders are the simplest means of securing baits in the crab ring.

Baits are attached to the center of the bottom ring in several ways. Large fish heads, fish carcasses, and whole fish can be wired to the mesh of the wire bottom. Wire bait holders, resembling large safety pins, can also be used for this purpose. When baits such as clams and cockles with cracked shells are used, crabbers use net bags with mesh of one inch or smaller, which are wired to the crab ring. Most crabbers use two such bait bags on each crab ring.

The baited ring is lowered to the bottom, the same way that a trap is. If the crabber is working from a bridge or pier, he ties the tag end of his pulling rope to a railing before lowering the crab ring into the water. When the crab ring is on the bottom, he pulls in any slack in the pulling rope and ties it off. From a boat, a crabber simply lowers the ring and tosses the marker buoy overboard.

Crab rings should be checked regularly—about every 10 minutes when there are plenty of crabs in the vicinity and every 20 minutes if the crabbing is slow. To keep crabs from escaping over the sides of the top ring, the crab ring should be brought up fast. Ease any slack out of the pulling rope; then give a sharp pull to raise the top ring, entrapping

136

the crabs. Continue pulling up steadily, hand over hand, so the pressure of the water will keep the crabs in the ring. To keep from getting rope burns and blisters on your hands, wear a pair of heavy-duty, rubber work gloves when crabbing with a crab ring.

In most areas there are limits on the number of such apparatus that any crabber can use. Here in Oregon we are allowed three per crabber. Obviously, the more rings the crabber uses, the better his chances of catching a limit.

If you are using more than one crab ring, don't put them too near one another. If you're working from a bridge or pier, spread your crab rings as far apart as possible. If you're working from a boat, place your rings at least 30 to 40 yards apart and be sure to avoid navigation channels where boats could become entangled in your ropes or could sever your floats from your ropes.

If any crab ring isn't producing within an hour, move it to another location and keep moving it until you find crabs.

One advantage of this type of gear is that the crabber can take along a rod and reel and fish while he's crabbing. And one could do worse than return home with an ice chest full of fresh bay fish and crabs.

Using Crab Pots

Crab pots are traps with fixed entrances. Each pot consists of a metal framework, either cylindrical or box-shaped, with walls, top, and bottom made of galvanized wire. The pot is baited and lowered to the bottom with a pulling rope to which a marker buoy is attached. Since the crabs cannot escape from a crab pot, the crabber need not tend his gear constantly. Instead, he should check the pot once or twice a day, harvesting the legal crabs, releasing unwanted crabs, and replacing baits as required. Crab pots are heavy and hard to handle. Additionally, their use is regulated in some areas. Consequently, they are not as popular with sport or recreational crabbers as are other types of crabbing gear.

The New Crab Snare

As we were working on this book, our good friend, Larry Breniman, stopped by one afternoon to present us with a strange-looking little contraption he had come across that day. As we scratched our heads and wondered what it was, Larry grinned and said, "It's a crab catcher." It looked like nothing we'd ever seen, and our skeptical expressions must have been apparent. Larry, who was raised on a ranch in Oregon's high desert country, said, "I admit, I don't know crabbing. But I do know lassoing. And you use this thing to lasso your crabs." We laughed at our mental images of cowboy crabbers, but as we continued examining the strange gizmo, it became obvious that this was not only an ingenious device, but certainly one of the simplest and least expensive crabbing tools we had ever come across.

The item, being marketed under the name "Surefire Crab Catcher," simply consists of a metal ring, two inches in diameter, to which four heavy-duty monofilament snares are attached. Each snare opening is about six inches, and the whole unit measures about 15 inches across when in the open, crabbing position. The entire unit can be collapsed to fit into a pocket or tackle box, and it weighs a mere two ounces.

Although it can be used on a handline, it was designed for use with a rod and reel. The crabber simply ties a bait to the center ring and adds enough weight to hold bottom. Then he casts out and reels in any slack line. When he feels the telltale tug of a crab, he rears back on the rod, as if setting a hook, and thereby snares the crab by a leg, claw, or the body. And it's possible to catch more than one crab at a time.

The inventor is Harold Bradley of Rockaway, Oregon. We talked to his wife, Luella, who told us that for years Harold has been experimenting with ways to catch crabs off the jetty at nearby Tillamook Bay without using a boat. When he devised his crab catcher he knew he had something that worked, but he didn't know how it would catch on.

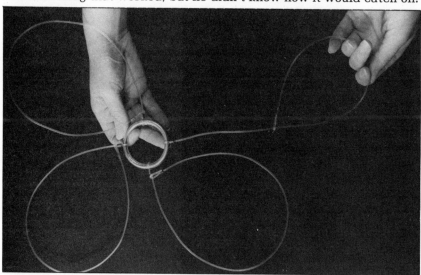

The Surefire Crab Catcher.

Although his sons, Michael and Daniel, are now helping Harold manufacture the crab catchers, they can barely keep up with orders. And it's no wonder, since the unit sells for a mere $3.98. At current crab prices, the Surefire Crab Catcher will pay for itself with its first catch. At this writing, Surefire Sporting Goods is still a small, family business and the Crab Catcher is only available in Oregon and Washington. If you'd like to order one or several, write or phone for current price and order information:

Surefire Sporting Goods
15450 Lakeside Dr.
Rockaway, OR 97136
(503) 322-3390

Crab Baits

Contrary to popular belief, crabs are not scavengers that eat mainly rotten fish, tainted meat, and soured clams. Quite the opposite, they prefer fresh baits. They are efficient predators with a highly developed sense of smell, so the best baits are those that exude oils that create scent trails. Fatty fish are top choices, and the heads and carcasses of mackerel, bonita, albacore, salmon, and mullet are excellent baits. You can also use the carcasses of freshwater species. And whole rough fish are good baits. But if you use whole fish, score the bodies with a fillet knife to release crab-attracting fluids into the water. Clams are a favorite food of crabs, but they are also a favorite food of man. But fresh clams with broken shells or those that die before they can be shucked and cleaned can be frozen and used later as crab bait. Chicken necks and backs are favorite crab baits. They're readily available everywhere, are relatively inexpensive, and are more durable than many other kinds of bait.

Handling Crabs

It's obvious to anyone who has ever seen a crab that these creatures come armed with two claws that can do damage to the unwary crabber. And with all those legs moving in every direction, the crab appears more dangerous and difficult to handle than it actually is.

The crab will first try to escape; if cornered, it will attempt to defend itself. It will pivot to keep its claws in striking position, but its reaction time is slow. So the first recommendation is that you work quickly when handling crabs, moving them as fast as possible from the catching device to the holding container.

Although a crab can reach across or under itself with its claws, you can safely pick it up by the two rearmost legs and your hands will be out of the reach of the claws. You can also grasp the rear center of the body, between the two back legs and safely handle the crab in this way. Some crabbers handle crabs by simultaneously grabbing a claw leg in each hand and spreading those legs away from one another, thus rendering the crab defenseless. If you have a crabbing partner, you can hold the crab by the claw legs and have your partner use a pair of pliers or wire cutters to snip off the small pincer from each claw, which makes the crab totally harmless and safe to handle in any manner.

Keeping Crabs Alive

Crabs should never be kept in buckets, tubs, coolers, or other containers of unoxygenated water, because, like fish, they will soon die from lack of oxygen. If you're crabbing from a boat equipped with an aerated livewell, crabs will stay alive in the livewell.

Most crabbers use bushel baskets, plastic fish baskets, or plastic laundry baskets to keep their crabs alive and well. For best results, cover your crabs with a piece of burlap that has been soaked in salt water. This not only keeps them cool, but also prevents them from crawling out of the container.

If you're wading the shallows and dipnetting crabs, tie a bushel basket or plastic basket inside an inflated inner tube. Then tie one end of a rope to the inner tube and the other end to a belt loop or around your waist and trail your container behind you as you wade.

Cleaning, Cooking, and Cracking Crabs

Many people prepare crabs by dropping them live into boiling water and cleaning them after they're cooked, but we prefer to clean them before cooking them for several reasons.

First, most of the crab, from 77% to as much as 86% is waste. The meat yield on the meatiest of crabs in prime condition is only 23%; on the average blue crab it is only about 14%. Crabs are bulky creatures, and a good bit of the waste material consists of the back and entrails. By cleaning the crab before cooking it, you eliminate about half the waste, thereby enabling you to cook more crab in any single batch.

Another reason for cleaning crabs before cooking them is to increase the salt penetration in the body meat, thus improving the keeping qualities of the meat.

Crab that is cleaned before cooking can also be cooled much quicker, which improves the quality of the meat and makes it much easier to remove from the shell.

Most important to us, though, is that crab that is cooked first and cleaned later often takes on a visceral taste that overwhelms the delicate flavor of the meat. This problem is eliminated by cleaning the crabs before cooking them.

Cleaning Crabs

To the inexperienced person, a crab is an impenetrable fortress. And with its pinching claws, it certainly seems a formidable adversary.

The truth is, crabs are among the easiest of all seafoods to clean, and if you're careful you need not worry about getting a finger caught in a claw. With practice you'll be able to have each crab cleaned and ready for the pot in 30 seconds or less. When we clean crabs we like to wear heavy, rubber work gloves. They make it easier to get a good grip on the crab, and they protect the hands from sharp edges on shells and legs.

Here are the simple steps in cleaning a crab:

1. Approaching the crab from behind, with a hand on each side of the body, quickly and firmly grasp the crab's right legs and claw in your right hand and left legs and claw in your left hand. Grip these appendages as near to the crab's body as possible and squeeze your grip tight enough to immobilize the crab.
2. Place an edge of the crab's carapace on the top edge of a table, counter, or similar object. Now push downward and the carapace will pop off like a jar lid.
3. Still grasping the legs and claws in both hands, break the crab in two by first bending the legs downward, then upward again, until the two halves come apart—as if you were breaking a "green" stick or tree branch.
4. Several shakes of each half into a bucket or sink will remove the viscera. Pull out the grayish gill filaments with your fingers.
5. Now rinse each half under cold, running water to remove any remnants of the viscera, and your crab is ready for the pot.

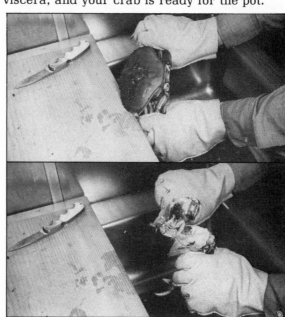

Cleaning Crabs, Step 2.

Cleaning Crabs, Step 3.

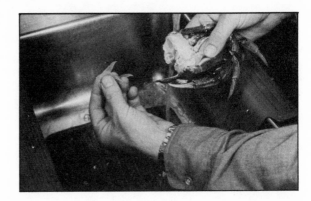

Cleaning Crabs,
Steps 4 and 5.

By the way, you can use the unbroken carapaces for serving crab salads, cocktails, deviled crab, and a number of other dishes. Just scrub them clean, dry them, and put them aside for later.

Cooking and Picking Crabs

You'll need a big soup kettle or similar pot for cooking the crabs, and since it takes a while to bring a large amount of water to a boil, you'll probably want to start the water heating before you begin your cleaing chores. Add a cup of salt to each gallon of water and bring to a rolling boil. Put the crabs into the boiling water, making sure not to put any more in the pot than can be completely covered. Let the water return to a boil, cover the kettle, and continue boiling for 15 minutes, adjusting the heat to maintain a good boil without boiling over. Remove the crabs immediately and drench them in cold water—the colder the better. You can either spray them with cold tap water or plunge them into a kettle of ice water. Now they're ready for picking. If you're having a crab feed, in which the participants will pick their own crabs, they can be left in this form and served chilled with a cocktail sauce and lemon wedges. Or you can serve them hot with lemon butter or any similar melted butter sauce.

For crab Louies, crab salads, crabmeat cocktails, deviled crab, and other recipes calling for picked crab meat, pick the meat now. Break away each leg from the body halves. Break off the claws at the first joint. Then carefully crack the claws and leg segments with a nutcracker. Or you can put them on a cutting board and rap them with a mallet to crack the shells. Carefully remove the meat from the claws and legs, trying to keep it intact in large pieces. These chunks are ideal for cocktails and crab Louies as well as hot dishes such as crab Newburg. Use a nut pick or small cocktail fork to remove the small pieces of meat from the narrow leg segments. Pick away all visible

142

body meat from the shell. Then break the shell with a nutcracker or mallet and remove the remaining filaments of body meat. This meat can be combined with leg meat and claw meat in crab salad, or it can be kept separate for other recipes. It's ideal for deviled crab.

Storing Crab Meat

Crab meat is always best when consumed fresh, preferably the day it's caught. Cooked crab meat will keep well for a couple of days in the refrigerator at a temperature below 40° F. and if it is well-wrapped in a plastic cling wrap or sealed in plastic bags or containers with tight-fitting lids. Crab that is to be kept for more than a couple of days should be canned or frozen, although crab does not freeze as well as most seafoods. For freezing and canning instructions, see Chapters 6 and 7.

11

ADDING CLAMS
TO THE CATCH

Clams are another bonus for the coastal angler or the inland fisherman visiting the coast. Clamdigging is not only fun, but inexpensive, requiring only a minimum of equipment. It also offers the opportunity to explore and discover interesting intertidal life forms, and it is an excellent source of physical exercise that results in the gathering of delicious seafood. In many areas, clams are abundant and in some places are even underharvested. For that reason, limits are usually liberal, allowing diggers to gather these delicacies in good numbers.

Clamdigging Tides

Clams live below the high-tide mark, both in bays and estuaries as well as on the open ocean. Some clams can be found just below the high-tide line and can be dug on just about any low tide, while others live nearer to the low-tide mark and should be dug on minus tides. The clams that require the highest salinities will be found on the open ocean beaches and in the lower reaches of bays and estuaries. Clams that are tolerant of lower salinities can be found further up the estuaries and backwaters of bays and are called upper-bay clams.

The U.S. Coast and Geodetic Survey publishes tide tables each year that provide the times and levels of high and low tides for all coastal areas in the U.S. Many private concerns publish pocket-size booklets based on the U.S.C.G.S. data, and these booklets are available at most coastal sport shops, bait stores, and marinas.

If you plan to dig clams, you will have to pick up a tide table and know how to use it. In the booklet, tables are provided for each month and tides are listed for each day of the month. Tide level is important for determining the best clamdigging tides and which species you might pursue in a given area. Corresponding times will tell you when low tide occurs and when you should plan to be on the digging flats.

Within a tide district, tides will vary in level and time from one place to another. Moreover, in the upper reaches of bays and estuaries, tide levels will differ from those in the lower reaches or on the open ocean and times will be later. Consequently, tide tables contain correction tables that allow you to calculate precisely the tides for any given area within the district.

To illustrate, we live in the city of Coos Bay, Oregon on a large estuary of the same name. The tide table we use is for the Astoria, Oregon tide district, but corrections are provided for the entire Oregon coast. By checking the Astoria tide table and accompanying correction table, we know that high and low tides at the entrance of Coos Bay occur 1 hour and 25 minutes earlier than in Astoria, and the tides in the lower bay are 1½ feet lower than those listed for Astoria. Further up the bay, where we do most of our digging, the tide times precede those in Astoria by only 40 minutes, but are still 1½ feet lower. In the upper bay, near the port of Coos Bay, tide times are the same as those in Astoria and are only ⁸⁄₁₀ of a foot lower.

July
Astoria District Low Tides
Daylight Time

Date	A.M.		P.M.	
	h.m.	ft.	h.m.	ft.
1 Tue	10:45	-1.0	10:54	2.5
2 Wed	11:27	-0.8	11:53	2.3
3 Thu	. . . . .	. . .	12:15	-0.3
4 Fri	0:56	2.0	1:04	0.2
5 Sat	2:01	1.6	1:57	0.8
6 Sun	3:09	1.0	2:59	1.4
7 Mon	4:15	0.4	4:01	1.8
8 Tue	5:19	-0.2	5:03	2.2
9 Wed	6:18	-0.7	6:06	2.3
10 Thu	7:10	-1.2	7:03	2.4
11 Fri	7:59	-1.4	7:55	2.4
12 Sat	8:44	-1.4	8:45	2.4
13 Sun	9:26	-1.3	9:30	2.4
14 Mon	10:05	-1.0	10:13	2.4
15 Tue	10:41	-0.7	10:56	2.4
16 Wed	11:18	-0.3	11:39	2.3
17 Thu	11:55	0.2	. . . . .	. . .
18 Fri	0.28	2.2	12:32	0.7
19 Sat	1:20	2.0	1:12	1.3

20	Sun	2:16	1.8	2:01	1.8
21	Mon	3:15	1.5	2:53	2.2
22	Tue	4:16	1.0	3:49	2.6
23	Wed	5:13	0.5	4:51	2.8
24	Thu	6:06	0.0	5:48	2.8
25	Fri	6:54	-0.5	6:43	2.7
26	Sat	7:39	-0.9	7:31	2.5
27	Sun	8:21	-1.3	8:16	2.3
28	Mon	9:02	-1.4	9:05	2.0
29	Tue	9:44	-1.4	9:53	1.6
30	Wed	10:22	-1.2	10:44	1.3
31	Thu	11:05	-0.8	11:38	1.0

A reproduction of one page from our tide tables for coastal Oregon. At first glance, you will notice an abundance of minus tides, which is characteristic of our summer months. For a variety of reasons, some of these tides are better than others. For example, although July 1 and 2 have minus tides occurring in the late morning and clamming would be reasonably good at those times, these tides were preceded by five days of lower tides in June. We prefer the first of a series of such tides and for that reason would concentrate on the following week. Since sunrise is at about 5:30 A.M. from July 8 through July 11, we would pick any of those days. We would also try to avoid the weekend when the flats would be crowded. For similar reasons, we would try to be on the flats on the mornings of July 28, 29, 30, and 31 about 45 minutes before low tide. For those who can only dig clams on the weekend, we would recommend being on the flats by 8:00 A.M. on July 12, by 8:45 A.M. on July 13, by 6:45 A.M. on July 26, and by 7:30 A.M. on July 27.

In some coastal areas tide changes are minimal—sometimes only a foot or so difference between high and low tides. In other areas and during certain times of the year, tide changes can exhibit great differences; sometimes there can be tide changes amounting to 10 to 15 feet or more. These changes are most noticeable along gently sloping banks in shallow bays and on mud flats, where vast expanses of bottom are exposed during the low tide.

In the tide tables, both high and low tides are established in relation to the low mean tide for a given year. The level for the low mean tide is set at 0.0 feet, and tide levels are listed in feet and tenths of feet above and below that level, either as "plus" tides or "minus" tides. All high tides are plus tides or are above 0.0 feet, but so are some low tides. The minus tides are those that expose the greatest expanses of mud flats and, consequently, are the best clamdigging tides. Generally, the lowest tides of the year are the most productive for the clamdigger.

This is not to say that minus tides are the only clamdigging tides. Indeed, we consider any low tide near the 0.0 mark a good tide for most species. It's just that when we have the great low tides each year—those ranging from -1.0 to -1.9 feet—clam beds that have been covered with water since last year are now exposed. Clam populations there are dense, the clams are larger than average, and we can easily gather our limit within an hour or less.

These lowest tides of the year, known in our part of the country as clamming tides, occur in series of several days at a stretch. We look for those occurring at or shortly after dawn, and we try to get out on the first such tide of a series. In that way we are usually among the first to reach these tidal treasures. For some species, such as razor clams and gapers, these tides are always the most productive. Those tides in the series that occur later in the day always find bigger crowds of diggers on the flats and correspondingly fewer clams to go around.

Some species, most notably, the softshell clam, can be gathered on just about any low tide because they reside nearer to the high-tide mark than other clams. Depending on where we plan to dig, we can find softshells on low tides of up to +3.0 feet.

By using the tide tables and knowing where to find the various species of clams, the clamdigger can plan any outing for a maximum harvest. For example, we sometimes leave home a couple of hours before low slack tide so that we can stop by one of our favorite softshell beds to dig limits before heading on to another area to gather cockles and dig gapers. Or when the low tide is near dawn, we hit the lower-bay beds first and dig softshells afterward, before the incoming tide covers their beds.

Our regulations permit each digger to take a total of 20 bay clams (gaper, butter, littleneck, and cockle), of which no more than 12 may be gapers. In addition, each digger may take a total of 36 softshell and other clams. So, by planning, the two of us can dig a total of 24 gapers and 16 more cockles, littlenecks, or butter clams. To that we can add another 72 softshell clams and return home with 112 clams in all. If we want to dig on the other side of the bay, it's only a short drive from there to the vast mussel beds, where we can each gather 72 of these, bringing the total one-day harvest to 256. It doesn't take many such outings to stock our freezer with plenty of clams for frying, steaming, and mincing for chowders and fritters.

Clamdigging Tools

You'll need something for toting your clams, and most state regulations stipulate that each digger must have his own container. Most of us use buckets or pails, but you can also use a burlap bag, an onion sack, a nylon fish bag, or any other suitable container.

The most universal clamdigging tool is the common long-handled shovel. Short-handled garden spades can be used, but the long-handled shovel is most useful for the widest variety of species. It allows for more leverage and is easier on the digger's back in most situations.

Some diggers like to use the narrow-bladed "clam shovel," but we've found the wider blade of the common shovel to be much better at moving material fast and getting limits in a minimum amount of time. Some species that reside in the upper few inches of mud or sand can be gathered by raking. Although in some parts of the country, diggers use special, long-tined clamdigging rakes, most rakers use common garden rakes, or the smaller, short-tined clamdigging rakes. We would like to point out, here, that raking is an excellent way to gather some species of clams on the open flats, but we urge you not to use a rake on eelgrass beds, where the rake can uproot this important vegetation and cause much environmental damage. Besides, there are easier ways to gather clams in eelgrass (which we'll discuss later) that cause no harm to the grass beds.

Another item we have found handy to have along on most clamdigging outings is a large-capacity plastic bucket with a lid. Since we let some clams, particularly softshells, clean themselves out in salt water, we like to take a big bucketful of clean sea water home with us for this purpose. The lid keeps the water from sloshing out of the bucket as we're driving home.

Dressing for Clamdigging

It should be obvious that clamdigging is not the tidiest of recreational activities. You will be traversing partly submerged grass beds and walking over oozing mud flats. For some species, such as gapers, you'll have to get down on your hands and knees next to the holes you've dug to depths of one to two feet. And you'll have to stick your arm into these muddy holes, that are usually at least partially filled with muddy water, to probe for your quarry with your fingers. So wear old clothes and plan on getting them muddy and full of sand.

Some people like to wear sneakers that they can just toss into the washing machine when they get home. Others prefer rubber boots. While some folks disdain hip boots as cumbersome and uncomfortable for walking any distance, we prefer the hippers when we're digging gapers because they not only help keep pants reasonably clean, but on cold mornings they keep us dry and warm. They also let us cross submerged depressions that would be over the tops of ordinary rubber boots, thus saving time and energy.

On chilly mornings we prefer flannel or wool shirts to jackets or coats, since shirt sleeves can be rolled up easily and tucked out of the way when it comes time to stick an arm into a deep hole full of icy water. For the same reason, we find that insulated vests do a good job of keeping us warm without getting in the way of our work.

Try not to overdress since it's difficult to find some place to stow ex-

148

tra clothing on the mud flats. But do keep in mind that it's almost always a little chillier on the water than it is elsewhere, and the damp air is penetrating. Dress in layers, with the outer layer preferably a long-sleeved wool shirt that will keep you warm in the damp environment. If you get too warm, you can take off a shirt and tie the sleeves around your waist, with the shirt hanging behind you, out of the way.

Finding Clamdigging Areas

Coastal residents usually have no trouble finding clamdigging areas, but newcomers can waste time exploring nonproductive spots. If you have recently moved to a coastal community or are vacationing in an unfamiliar area, several sources of clamdigging information are worth investigating.

If you have the time, you should write to the state fish-and-game agency to inquire about clamdigging in that state. In any specific locale, you should contact the local fish-and-game agent.

Chambers of Commerce and tourist-information centers are other good sources. Often such places have brochures available on clamdigging and some can even provide clamdigging maps.

Sport shop and marina operators should not be overlooked as good sources of clamdigging information. And they will usually have tide tables available, either free or for a nominal fee.

In some coastal communities you will find community colleges and adult education programs offering short courses or workshops in clamdigging. By all means, take advantage of these. Fees are usually low, and the courses often include field trips to the clamdigging flats for firsthand experience.

Another way to find out where the clamdigging areas are is to simply observe. When you see people sloshing across mud flats at low tide, carrying shovels or rakes and buckets, you can be assured that these folks are going after clams.

Parking areas near clam flats are excellent sources of information. There you can see how successful diggers have been, and you will find that most clamdiggers will willingly volunteer information and will point you toward the productive beds.

Popular Clams

There are numerous species of clams, many of which are either too small to be of value to the clamdigger or are impossible to reach with simple tools. Others, too, are only popular in some areas or are only available in rather small geographical regions. So be sure to check locally to find out what kinds of clams are available. Among the most popular clams in coastal America are the softshell clam, gaper clam, butter clam, razor clam, cockle, littleneck clam, and mussel, most of which have several other localized aliases. It is important to learn how to distinguish one clam from another so that you can keep within the harvest limits and so you'll know how to clean and prepare your catch.

Softshell Clam

The softshell clam, also known as the eastern clam, eastern softshell, or mud clam, is available on both the East and West Coasts of the U.S. In some eastern seaboard areas, pollution has reduced the numbers of softshell clams, and in other areas, softshell populations are subtidal and consequently out of reach of the recreational or sport clamdigger. Where it is abundant and available to clamdiggers, notably on the West Coast and from Maine to Massachusetts on the East Coast, it is one of the most popular clams. It is also among the easiest to gather and clean.

The softshell clam can be identified by its thin, brittle, and elongate shell, which is normally a maximum of two to four inches in length. Sometimes softshells do grow larger and are often confused with gapers, which they resemble. Although the neck of the softshell is similar to that of the gaper, it lacks the two leathery flaps on the tip that are present in the gaper.

The softshell is tolerant of lower salinities than are most other clams and, for this reason, will be found further up bays. It is also present in numerous small bays where no other clams occur. On open flats it is found in mud or sandy mud, where you should look for oblong holes up to an inch in diameter. Stick your finger into the hole and if you feel the rubbery siphon or neck recede, you have found a clam. The clam can then be dug with a shovel.

When searching for softshell clams in gravelly or rocky areas, stomp on the ground as you walk, watching for clam spouts.

Softshell clams also occur in gravelly and rocky areas just below the high-tide mark. Here, their holes are difficult if not impossible to find because they are so well camouflaged. You can readily locate the clams

Once you've located softshell clams by their spouts, penetrate the rocky mud with your shovel by rotating the shovel handle in fairly large circles while applying increasing foot pressure to the top edge of the shovel blade.

Once you have sunk the shovel blade into the gravelly mud, gradually ease the handle back in a rocking motion, being careful not to apply so much pressure that the handle breaks.

by stomping on the gravelly ground as you walk and by watching for water spouts. When the clam spouts, mark the location and dig out the clam with a shovel. More often than not, several softshells, sometimes a half dozen or more, will spout at one time. Use two or three rocks to mark each spout; then dig up the clams one at a time.

On the flats, you will often find two clams sharing the same feeding hole, and more often than not you'll find other clams nearby. In gravelly beds, you will almost always find more than one clam in any small area, and it's not uncommon there to dig up several in one shovelful.

Softshell clams can only retract their necks and are normally only 6 to 14 inches beneath the surface, although larger ones might be as deep as 18 inches. Consequently, they are easy to dig.

You can dig softshells on the flats on any 0.0 or minus tide. On upperbay areas, where you find them in gravelly beds, any low tide of +3.0 or lower will normally expose the beds.

Gaper Clam

The gaper, which is also called horse, horseneck, or blue clam, and in our part of the country is known as the Empire clam, is one of the largest of clams, with an average shell length of four to five inches, up to a maximum of about seven inches. Additionally, it has a broad, leathery-skinned neck that is several times as long as its shell when it is fully extended. There is a large gape in the shell where the neck protrudes, hence the name. The shell has a dark covering that is usually quite eroded, exposing chalkier underlayers.

Gapers are found on sand or sandy mud flats in bays. Look for a circular hole up to nearly two inches in diameter. Stick your finger in the

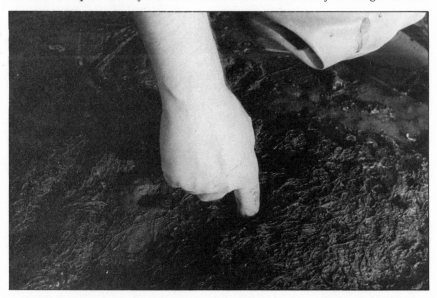

To locate gaper clams, look for large, circular holes on the clam flats. Stick your finger in a hole, and if a clam is present, you'll feel its neck recede.

152

When you've found a gaper clam to dig, use your finger to scribe a line pointing toward the water's edge, with the clam's hole in the center of the line. Then intersect that line with another line perpendicular to the first, keeping the clam's hole at the intersection.

Thinking of the ends of the lines as compass points, with the one nearest the water's edge being "south," begin digging in the "southeast" or "southwest" quadrant several inches "south" of the clam hole.

153

When you have dug to a depth of about one foot, move to the opposite southern quadrant and dig to the same depth. When you have cleared away a substantial amount of mud, run your hand down the clam's hole, pushing mud away from it as you go. Shovel out any excess mud as it collapses into the hole you dug. When you can feel the clam's shell, carefully dig it out with your hand.

The gaper digger is rewarded for his efforts with one of the largest and tastiest of clams. Open holes are dangerous to other clamdiggers, so be sure to fill any you dig.

hole and you will feel the neck retract if a clam is present. With practice, you will soon learn to distinguish the large gapers from the small ones by the feel of the neck.

Since these are large clams with long necks, they are usually found from 10 to 24 inches beneath the surface, sometimes a bit deeper. They can only retract their necks and will not otherwise move to avoid you. But because of the depth at which they are found, they aren't the easiest clams to dig. And on the flats where sand is loosely packed, holes often cave in before the clam is reached, calling for more digging and searching. The reward, however, is well worth the effort, as the gaper is among the tastiest of clams and can be prepared in a variety of ways.

You can dig gapers on any 0.0 or minus tide, but the lowest tides of the season will uncover the best clamming flats, where gapers will be larger and more abundant than elsewhere.

Butter Clam

The butter clam goes by quite a few aliases throughout its range. It is known as the hardshell, quahog, beefsteak, money, Martha Washington, and great Oregon clam.

The butter clam has a very thick, oval shell, averaging two to three inches in length, and the larger ones are often confused with small gapers. Its shell is considerably heavier than the gaper's, and the butter clam does not have the large neck opening in the shell, but this is not easy to determine when examining the clams in their shells. The easiest way to distinguish the butter from the gaper is to check the shell hinge: the former has a shiny black external hinge; the latter has an internal hinge.

The butter clam is sometimes found in the same sandy or muddy flats where gapers, cockles, and littlenecks occur. There, look for small, rectangular holes, up to a half inch or more in length and a quarter inch or more in width. If you feel the neck retract when you poke a finger into the hole, you'll only have to dig to a depth of 12 to 16 inches to reach the clam.

Like the softshell, the butter clam is sometimes found in gravelly areas where it can be located by stomping and watching for water spouts. When we lived in Alaska, we found beds of butter clams so dense that we could fill a five-gallon bucket with clams in a half hour of easy digging.

Butter clams can be dug on any 0.0 or minus tide in most areas but are sometimes found in the gravelly beds slightly above the low mean tide mark. They are easy to clean and are delicious prepared in just about any manner.

Like the softshell, the butter clam is sometimes found in gravelly mud, where digging shallow trenches can unearth whole colonies.

Razor Clam

The razor is a popular West Coast clam that is spotty in population in the southern extremes of its range and locally abundant north of Tillamook Head, Oregon. Because it is a favorite of clamdiggers, digging pressure is heavy throughout much of its range.

The razor clam is so named because of its shell's resemblance to the handle of a straight razor. It is easily distinguished by this oval shape and its smooth, plastic-like appearance. The shell is thin and quite sharp, perhaps another reason for its name. The color is light brown. The razor clam averages from three to five inches in length.

The razor clam is found on open ocean beaches and near the mouths of some bays, where a single tide change can move from two to four feet of sand over the clam beds. For this reason, the razor clam is equipped with a large digger foot that enables it to move and maintain a depth of from 6 to 18 inches. Razor clam beds are identified by dimples or pits in the hard-packed sand above the wave line at low tide. Some diggers also find the beds by walking along the beach in shallow water, tapping the sand with a shovel handle as they go. They watch for the small pit left by the retracting neck of the clam.

Since razor clams always position themselves with their hinges toward the ocean, always dig on the ocean side of the pit or dimple. As soon as you spot a clam pit, shove the blade of the shovel into the sand for its entire length, a couple of inches toward the water from the clam. Then ease your hand down the back of the shovel blade to the tip. Ease the shovel blade out and feel through the sand until you locate the clam.

But remember, if you are to catch this critter, you must move quickly. A razor clam is capable of digging vertically at a rate of up to two feet per minute in soft sand.

Cockle

The cockle, sometimes called cockerel or basket cockle, is the easiest of all clams to identify. Its handsome shell, which averages from 2½ to 3½ inches across, has prominent ridges that radiate outward from the hinge to the slightly scalloped edge of the shell. Color will vary from mottlings of reddish brown against ivory to dark blue-gray.

Since the cockle's hole is not easy to find or recognize, most diggers resort to other methods for finding this clam. Most people rake for them, and others simply rely on finding them incidental to the harvesting of other species.

For several reasons, we don't rake them. First, raking tears up the grass beds where they are most plentiful. On the flats, they are just too difficult to find for our liking. We prefer to slowly walk through the eelgrass beds, usually on our way to and from the gaper clam and butter clam beds, feeling for hard objects beneath our feet. Once the object is detected, the toe of a boot can push enough grass aside to make sure the object isn't a crab. Then by probing down with fingers no more than three or four inches into the sand it doesn't take long to determine if the object is an empty shell or a cockle. In the more productive beds, about nine times out of ten, the object will be a cockle. This is by far the easiest way to "dig" clams, and we recommend the method over any other for gathering cockles. Keep a sharp eye as you walk the eelgrass beds, because sometimes you'll find cockles just resting atop the sand, amidst the blades of grass. To harvest them you need only stoop over and gather them up.

If you prefer to rake cockles on the flats, pick any 0.0 or minus tide. If you want to try finding them with your feet, any low tide that exposes the eelgrass beds will do.

The easiest way to "dig" cockles is to walk slowly over eelgrass beds, feeling for the clams with your feet. When you feel a hard object, push the grass aside with the toe of your boot to make sure it isn't a crab. Then dig out the shallow-bedded cockle with your fingers.

Watch closely as you walk the eelgrass beds because you sometimes find cockles resting atop the sand in the strands of grass.

Littleneck Clam

This tasty little clam, also known as the steamer or cherrystone clam and erroneously called butter clam in some areas, is a favorite among clamdiggers on both the East and West Coasts.

The shell of the littleneck, which grows to an average of only one or two inches, is similar in shape to that of the cockle. It has ridges radiating from the hinge, but the ridges are narrower and not nearly as prominent. Additionally, it has concentric ridges that intersect the radiating ridges at right angles, creating a crosshatching not present in the cockle.

The shell of the littleneck clam (right) can be distinguished from that of the cockle (left) by its narrower radiating ridges and concentric ridges that intersect the radiating ridges, creating a crosshatching not present in the cockle.

159

Like the cockle, the littleneck is found only a few inches below the surface to a maximum depth of six inches. It prefers gravelly beds in bays and resides near rocky outcrops on the open ocean but is never found in soft sand that will shift beneath wave and tidal action.

The littleneck can be harvested on 0.0 or minus tides with shovels or rakes. The small ones are favored as steamers; the larger ones can be fried or minced for chowder and fritters.

Mussel

Mussels are among the most plentiful, easily harvested, and under-utilized shellfish in the U.S. They are abundant on East and West Coasts alike, and they can be prepared in a great variety of ways. Yet, they seem to be fully appreciated only by Europeans who relish their delicate flavor.

The elongate shell of the mussel resembles that of the softshell clam in shape. The bluish-black color of the shell, however, makes the mussel quite easy to distinguish from other clams, as does its habitat. Instead of residing in the sand or mud flats and beaches, the mussel is found, often in great colonies, attached to rocks and ledges on the open ocean and on pilings and abutments in bays.

The pink meat of the mussel is high in protein, minerals, and vitamins. This highly digestible food can be steamed, fried, or minced for chowders and fritters.

The mussel is highly susceptible to pollution, and for that reason should only be harvested from open ocean areas, rather than from bays and backwaters where industrial and residential wastes might be present.

To gather mussels, simply detach them from their rocky lairs at low tide. Pick only those mussels that are nearest the water on steep ledges and rocks, avoiding higher colonies that are exposed to air and sun for long periods between high tides.

Transporting Clams

Although most clams are rather hardy creatures in their natural environment, once removed they are somewhat fragile and vulnerable. And their meat will spoil rapidly if not properly cared for.

If you don't have far to travel between clamming beds and home, you should have no problem getting your catch home alive and well. Wash the shells off in clean sea or bay water as soon as possible after harvesting, removing all visible sand and vegetation. Then you can put the clams in buckets and cover them with an inch or two of clean sea water. Clams will also keep well for a short time in burlap bags that have been soaked in sea or bay water.

If you must transport them for any distance, clams should be shucked and frozen or packed in plastic bags and iced. Unfrozen clams should be kept as near 32° F. as possible. They will keep for several days in a refrigerator or ice chest where the temperature is below 40° F.

Cleaning Clams

Some clams are exceptionally easy to clean, and others require a bit more work. Among the easiest to clean are softshell clams, butter clams, littleneck clams, cockles, and mussels, particularly the smallest ones used for steaming or served on the half shell.

A favorite way to clean small butter clams and all but the largest softshell clams is to let them clean themselves. One way to do this is to put the clams in a bucket with enough clean sea water to cover them. If you have any fear that the water where you gathered your clams might be polluted or if it has been roiled by winds or currents, make a clean brine by adding a cup of salt to each gallon of fresh water.

Add a couple handfuls of cornmeal to each bucket of clams and salt water. Since the clams are unable to digest the cornmeal, they will regurgitate it, along with sand, grit, and other undesirable materials. Depending on the size of the clams, they should pump themselves out in 6 to 12 hours. They can be left overnight in this way if they are kept cool. Self-cleaning clams should be kept out of direct sunlight and should not be left for more than 36 hours. While the clams are self-cleaning, change the water two or three times or until they no longer pump out sand and grit. Cockles and littlenecks can be cleaned the same way, but should not be left in the salt water and cornmeal for more than six hours.

When you change the water and after all clams have been cleaned, look for any clam that will not close its shell when you touch it. Discard such clams immediately or save them for bait or chum.

Another way to let clams clean themselves is to put them in a wire fish basket or nylon mesh fish bag, tie one end of a rope to the container and the other to a dock, and suspend the clams in bay water for 12 to 24 hours. Clams will then be able to pump the sand and grit out of their systems, but you must be sure you have them deep enough in the water so that they will not be exposed on the low tide.

Once the clams have cleaned themselves, they can be steamed and eaten, steamed and frozen for later use, or simply packed in plastic bags and frozen. Or you can shuck the clams before freezing or canning them. If you plan to shuck them, steam them for about a minute to kill them and cause their shells to open. Then trim away the dark meat on the necks and can or freeze the meat either whole or minced.

Larger butter clams that will be used for frying or minced should be shucked. Then cut open the stomach—the small dark area in the clam body—and scrape away all dark material with the point of a knife. Rinse the clam under cold, running water, and it will be ready for freezing, canning, or refrigerating for use within several days.

Another way to clean butter clams is to simply slice them in half with a fillet knife, separating the shell into halves, with half a clam in each side of the shell. The slicing divides the stomach, which can then be scraped clean with the point of a knife. Prepared this way, the clam halves can be dipped in batter and fried in the shell.

Mussels are among the easiest to clean. They will self-clean in clean sea water or salted fresh water in about an hour or two. If you plan to steam them, thoroughly scrub the shells under cold, running water. The only nonedible part of the mussel's body is the byssus thread or beard, which is the clump of black, threadlike material with which the mussel attaches itself to rocks and ledges. The byssus thread can be pulled out or cut away from the mussel before cooking or easily removed after cooking.

To shuck and clean razor clams, gaper clams, and large softshell clams, you'll need a small fillet knife. Holding the clam with the shell hinge in the palm of your hand and the shell opening toward you, quickly insert the knife blade into the shell near the rear of the clam. Press the point of the knife against the inside of the shell, between the clam meat and one side of the shell, and sever the adductor muscle near the clam's digger foot. Run the knife along the shell to the front and cut the adductor muscle near the neck. Trim the meat from the shell half and repeat the process on the other side to remove the clam from its shell.

On razor clams, cut away the black tip of the neck and split the neck lengthwise. Do the same on large softshell clams. Then peel the skin from the neck. On gapers, cut the neck off near the body and split it lengthwise. Cut the black tips off the gaper necks, then blanche the necks in boiling water for about 20 to 30 seconds. Now peel away the leathery skin and wash the neck under cold, running water.

In the clam body, cut away the grayish-colored gills. Then use a fillet knife to split the digger foot lengthwise. Spread the slit digger foot apart with your fingers and remove the crystalline style from the gaper clam. Now, with the slit in the digger foot still spread, press on the dark abdomen from the opposite side and scrape away all dark material with the knife point. Widen the slit beyond the digger foot if necessary.

Trim away dark skin along the mantle edge (rubbery meat near the shell opening) and rinse away all dark material and visible sand and grit under cold, running water.

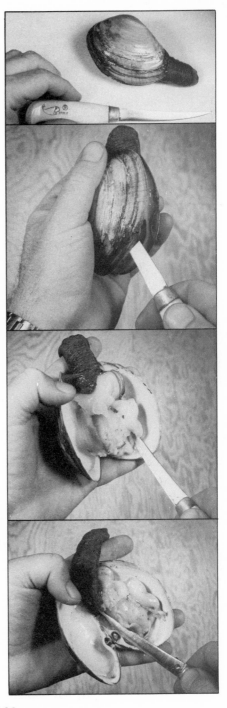

To shuck and clean razor, gaper (pictured), and large softshell clams, you'll need a small fillet knife.

Start by quickly inserting the knife blade into the shell near the rear of the clam to severe the rear abductor muscle.

After severing rear and front abductor muscles on one side of the shell, cut the muscles on the other side.

Cut the skin near the neck that holds the clam to the shell.

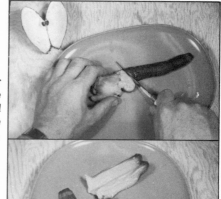

On the gaper clam, cut the neck off near the body. You can now clean either the clam body or neck. Refrigerate clams and necks and continue shucking until all the clams are shucked and ready for cleaning.

Split the gaper necks lengthwise with the fillet knife.

Blanche gaper necks in boiling water for 20 to 30 seconds.

Peel the leathery skin away from the neck meat.

164

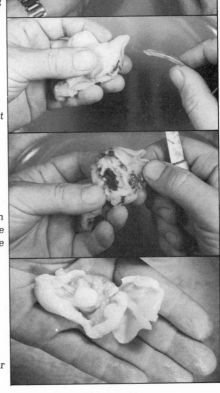

Trim the dark meat away from the tip of the neck and the neck is ready for frying or mincing.

To clean the clam body, start by splitting the digger foot lengthwise.

Remove the crystalline style from the slit digger foot.

With the digger foot slit still open, press on the dark abdomen from the opposite side and scrape away all dark material with the knife point.

Cleaned gaper clam ready for frying or mincing.

The clam is now ready for frying or mincing. Clams to be used for chowder or fritters can be frozen or canned whole or minced. Gaper necks can be left whole for frying or can be minced for chowders or fritters.

The easiest way to mince clams is to run them through a food grinder set for coarse grinding. If you don't have access to a grinder, use a sharp knife to cut the clams into small pieces, being careful to catch all the juices or clam nectar.

When shucking clams that will be minced or will be frozen in liquid, be sure to shuck them over a clean pan or bowl that will catch the nectar that drains from the clam. The nectar can then be strained through clean linen or several layers of clean cheesecloth. Use the nectar in chowders or pour it over clams before freezing them.

The Clamdigger's Bonus

Just as clams are a bonus seafood for the coastal angler, there are other bonuses to be derived from clamdigging, besides the obvious culinary ones.

The mud flats that are home to the various species of clams also harbor many other forms of marine life, many of which are ideal baits for numerous kinds of fish. In the course of digging clams, you are likely to find several kinds of large sea worms, including clam worms (known variously as sandworms, mussel worms, and pile worms), bloodworms, ribbon worms, and lugworms.

On the West Coast, two species of ghost shrimp reside on the mud flats and are often encountered by clamdiggers. They are excellent bait for numerous species of fish.

Small crabs of several varieties are found both on the flats and in the upper-bay areas where they are most plentiful and easily gathered.

Clams are good bait in their own right, but since they are also such good food, we normally keep for bait only those that die before we can

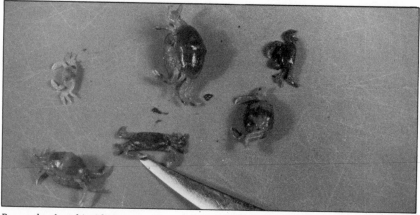

Pea crabs, found inside gaper and some other clams, are considered a gourmet treat and are excellent bait as well.

shuck them or small clams with broken shells. These can also be ground up and used as chum.

One other little critter that bears mentioning is the tiny female pea crab that takes up residence inside gaper clams and is sometimes found in other clams as well. There will almost always be at least one pea crab inside every gaper you dig, and more often than not there will be several. We have found as many as five inside large gapers, both in the body and in the neck of the clam. This harmless little creature grows no larger than an inch in diameter and is in a permanent soft-shell stage. It requires no cleaning and is considered a gourmet treat when sautéed in butter or when lightly breaded and fried quickly. The pea crab is also a dandy bait for surf perch, flounder, sole, and a number of other marine species.

When you're heading out for the clamdigging flats, you might want to carry a bait container along to make use of the various bait species you'll find.

Chapter 12

FRYING THE CATCH

Frying is probably the most popular way to prepare fish, and in our opinion is among the best methods for producing tasty, succulent fish of all sorts. For several reasons, frying is also one of the most misunderstood and abused methods of fish cookery. Most fish is breaded prior to frying, and few people take the time to bread fish properly. Moreover, directions for breading in most cookbooks are terribly misleading, as regards the preparation and frying of fish. Too few people exercise care in the selection and storage of cooking oil, and too many people, including some restaurant chefs, overcook fish, which makes it dry, often tough, and always unsavory. Like most peple, we, too, have had our share of fish-fry disasters, but after a good bit of experimentation we have learned how to fry fish the right way, and we have found some foolproof methods for turning out the finest fried fish every time.

Breading Fish

There are two areas where most people go wrong in breading fish. First, they use breading that is too coarse. Second, they fail to make sure that the breading completely seals the fish.

Recipes for breaded fish often call for bread "crumbs" or cracker "crumbs," and, take it from us, crumbs are too coarse. No matter what material you are using, your breading should be the consistency of meal. Those same recipes will also advise you to "roll" the fish in the breading. While this is okay for lightly breading pan-dressed fish, it is totally inadequate for breading and sealing fillets.

We don't often use bread for making our breadings, because we prefer the texture and flavors of other materials. But when we do use bread, we make sure it is thoroughly dried out. If you live in a dry climate, you can set out several slices of bread on a plate to air dry in an hour or two. In wetter parts of the country or during damp or humid weather, you can dry bread slices by laying them on the racks in an oven, setting the oven at 200° F., and propping the oven door open slightly.

If you use crackers for breading, they, too, must be crisp. Salted crackers will draw moisture and will soften if not kept properly sealed. Many people will use these so-called stale crackers for breading to keep them from going to waste. This is a mistake that can ruin your fish. Dry the crackers before using them the same way you would dry soft bread.

If you have a smoker, you can put soft bread or crackers on the racks and dry them with the heat from the smoker. For a change of pace, try adding some hardwood chips to the smoker and smoke the bread or crackers for about 15 minutes. The breading you will make later will have a slightly smoky flavor.

The breading we use most often is cracker meal, but we rarely use the commercially available meal, which is similar in taste to meal made with saltine crackers. If you like a saltine meal, make your own from saltine crackers or use the store-bought meal to save time. But don't be afraid to experiment with other materials.

We happen to like meal made with Ritz crackers. It produces a naturally golden breading that is mighty tasty. But this isn't the only breading we use. We also make breadings with cheese crackers, Wheat Thins, cornflakes, or cornmeal. When we want a highly seasoned and unusual breading, we make a meal with Dip In A Chip crackers. Every supermarket has an aisle full of variously flavored crackers, any of which are suitable for making cracker meal with a distinctive taste. Try some of them to spark up your fish dinners. You can also make tasty, seasoned breadings from meals made of potato chips, tortilla chips, and corn chips. Try the flavored chips, too, such as barbeque, sour cream and chives, taco, and nacho cheese.

The traditional way to turn crackers or dried bread into meal is to crush them with a rolling pin. If this is the way you'll do it, you can minimize the mess by putting a handful of crackers or a couple slices of bread at a time in a plastic food storage bag and then crushing them. Make sure you pulverize the breading, and as you empty the bag into a bowl, before filling it again with more crackers or bread, put any large chunks or crumbs back into the bag and crush them with the new batch. Remember, for best results, your meal must be of a fine, powdery consistency.

Some people like to use an electric food blender to make cracker meal. For best results, break the crackers in your hands before putting them into the blender and only use a small quantity at a time. Whir them until they appear pulverized. Then turn the blender off and stir the meal to make sure there are no large chunks.

If you own an electric food grinder, you're in luck, because this appliance is the fastest, simplest, and most efficient tool for making cracker meal of perfect consistency. Set the grinder for fine grinding, break the crackers, bread, or chips into small pieces by hand, and feed them into the grinder to create a fine meal that is ideal for breading.

We have found that adding a small quantity of flour to any breading material makes a finer breading and the best possible seal. After experimenting with various ratios, we have settled on one part flour to three parts breading meal.

Prior to breading, fish should be dipped in a breading liquid. Most cooks use egg, milk, or a combination of both for this purpose. But, here again, don't be afraid to experiment. We don't recommend using egg alone because it makes a breading that is too heavy and overwhelming. Beat the eggs well; then thin them with milk, cream, or—our favorite—buttermilk.

For 10 or 12 serving-size fillets, beat two eggs until frothy. Then add three tablespoons of whole milk or four tablespoons of cream or evaporated milk. You can then add your favorite seasonings to the liquid or to the breading. For the same amount of fish, we beat two eggs with a half cup of buttermilk. To that we add a half teaspoon of onion salt, several good dashes of garlic powder, two or three pinches of fines herbes, and freshly ground black pepper. We immerse the fillets in this liquid and refrigerate for a half hour.

If you have some strong-tasting fish on hand, use this buttermilk mixture to eliminate offensive tastes. Add a fresh lemon cut into thin slices and allow the fish to soak, refrigerated, for one to two hours.

To use our breading technique, you'll need more breading meal than you are probably accustomed to using. For 10 or 12 fillets, about a quart of breading will suffice. So mix one cup of all-purpose flour with three cups of meal. Of course, only a small portion of this will end up on the fish, which means you'll have most of it left over, but it won't go to waste. Simply put the leftovers in a plastic freezer container, label it, and store it in your freezer until the next time you need it. When you remove it from the freezer, pour it into a bowl and stir it with a fork to break up any frozen chunks. Drops of breading liquid from prior use will have frozen solid and can be picked out with a fork. The breading can be replenished at the same 3:1 ratio, as required, and can be refrozen time after time with no deterioration of quality. This method of storage not only eliminates waste, but it saves time. By making your breading meal in a fairly large batch, you'll have plenty on hand when you're rushed. And if you experiment with a variety of breadings, you'll accumulate quite a selection to choose from at any time you wish.

To properly bread your fish, put a half-inch-deep layer of breading meal on a sheet of waxed paper on a table or counter top. Remove a fillet from the breading liquid and let the excess drain for a second or two. Lay the fillet atop the breading and pour more breading over the top of the fillet until it is completely covered. Do this with three or four small fillets at once or one or two larger fillets.

Now use the palm of your hand to press the breading onto the fillets, one at a time. If the fillets are thick, press the breading into the sides as well. Then carefully move your fingertips beneath a fillet and lift it from the breading. Jostle it in your fingers, ever so gently, to knock off the caked excess, leaving only a thin but complete coating. Examine all sides of the fillet to make sure there is not even the tiniest spot left unbreaded. If you find any such spots, sprinkle more breading on them and press it into place with your hand.

Arrange the breaded fillets on a plate, platter, or cookie sheet. If you're breading a large quantity of fillets, you can layer them, but it's best to separate the layers with sheets of waxed paper. When all fillets are breaded, refrigerate them for 30 minutes before frying them. This will firm them and "set" the breading so that it will remain intact during frying.

If you're breading steaks, use the same technique. Pan-dressed fish that have been skinned require the same attention, but those with the skin left on should only be lightly breaded. This is one type of fish that can be "rolled" in breading before frying, because the skin will seal in the natural juices. You can also put the breading in a plastic bag, drop your pan-dressed fish into the bag, and shake the bag vigorously until the fish is lightly coated.

Most often, we use the breading made of three parts Ritz cracker meal to one part flour. This is an excellent breading for most fish, particularly salmon fillets, steelhead, large clams, and a variety of saltwater species. Try this one and compare it with a breading made of saltine cracker meal and flour to find out which you like best.

For bland fish, try breading made with three parts cheese cracker meal to one part flour. And be sure to experiment with some of the flavored crackers, mixed in the same 3:1 ratio.

Cornmeal is a popular breading and is excellent for pan-dressed fish and fillets alike. When we're breading pan-dressed trout, bluegills, or other small fish, we mix one part flour with three parts cornmeal. When we have a yen for cornmeal breading on fillets, however, we modify the recipe a bit. We mix two parts cornflake meal (or the com-

171

mercially available cornflake crumbs) with one part yellow cornmeal and one part flour. Then we soak and bread the fillets in our usual manner.

If you've had trouble with breading falling off your fillets when you fried them, you'll be quite pleased when you try our method. And when you experiment with some of the many breading materials available, your palate will be mighty pleased as well.

Cooking Oil

Your choice of cooking oil or fat is important. Since you will be frying fish at a relatively high temperature, you should avoid using animal fats because they smoke and begin to break down at high temperatures. A far better choice is some sort of vegetable oil. Use your favorite or experiment until you find one you like. We have good results with corn oil and safflower oil, but our two favorites are Planter's peanut oil and Sunlite sunflower oil.

Some people like to fry fish, especially pan-dressed fish, in butter, but butter is an animal fat, and it will smoke and burn if you use the right temperature for frying fish. Although margarine does not burn as readily as butter, it will not do as well as vegetable oils. If you want the buttery flavor, try using butter with an equal amount of shortening or your favorite cooking oil.

Cooking oil is reusable, but it should be strained to remove all residue, and it will keep best when refrigerated. We have found that the easiest way to strain cooking oil is to pour it through a layer of linen, and it's a snap if you clamp the material in an embroidery hoop and hold it over the container in which you will store the oil.

Pan Frying

Frying fish in a skillet or frying pan with a small amount of fat or oil is probably the most widely used method. Its popularity notwithstanding, pan frying requires care if it is to be done right.

Your first concern should be with the frying pan itself. A top-quality electric skillet, preferably with a nonstick surface, is a good choice. If you don't have an electric skillet, or if you prefer cooking at the range, use a skillet of heavy-gauge metal that will evenly distribute and maintain heat. Cheap, thin frying pans often warp with use and seldom heat evenly. A heavy aluminum or stainless steel skillet will do, but one of the best frying pans, by far, is a well-seasoned, cast-iron skillet.

Proper temperature of the cooking oil is critical to success. In all but a few instances, the ideal temperature is 350° F. Higher temperatures will cause the breading to fry completely or even burn while the fish only partially cooks. Lower temperatures cause the breading to become oil soaked, and the fish will dry out before the breading browns.

If you're using an electric skillet, simply set it for 350° F. and wait till that temperature is reached before frying any fish. If you're cooking on a stove, you'll probably find that something between a medium and medium-high setting is about right. If you're using a heavy-gauge skillet, though, let it gradually heat up by starting out on a low setting for several minutes before turning it up to frying temperature. This will prevent hot spots on the cooking surface and will help the skillet retain its frying temperature when chilled fillets are added.

When you think the oil has reached the right temperature, test it by dropping in a small piece of bread. The oil should sizzle a bit when the bread touches it, and the bread should turn golden brown on one side in 60 seconds. If it browns too fast, reduce the heat. If it does not brown fast enough, the oil is not yet ready.

You'll only need about an eighth of an inch of oil in the skillet for frying fish. Arrange the fillets in a single layer without crowding them. Leave enough space to allow turning them.

Fry your fillets until the breading is golden brown. Half-inch-thick fillets will be ready for turning in about three or four minutes. Slightly thicker fillets might need five minutes; thinner ones might be done in just under three minutes.

When the fillets are done on one side, turn them carefully to avoid damaging the breading. Use a spatula to gently lift one side of a fillet, while holding the fillet against the spatula with a fork or another spatula. Turn it slowly and fry the second side for an equal amount of time. The fillets will be done when they are fried to a golden brown and when the fish flakes easily when tested with a fork. With practice, you'll learn to fry them to perfection without performing the fork test.

When the fillets are fried, remove them as carefully as you turned them, holding them above the skillet with the spatula and fork to drain excess oil. Then arrange them on paper towels to let them drain for one or two minutes. If you're preparing several batches, spread the fried fillets on a cookie sheet or in a large, shallow baking dish, and put them in an oven set for warm or 200° F. and serve when all fillets are fried.

Most pan-dressed fish should be fried the same way and will be done in eight to twelve minutes, or four to six minutes per side. To be sure, check them with a fork to see that the meat is opaque (all the way to the backbone) and flaky.

Deep Frying

As the term implies, deep frying, or deep-fat frying, is a method of frying fish in deep oil. For deep frying fish, you will need an electric deep fryer or French fryer or any similar straight-sided pan that can be used on a stove. Here, again, cast iron is a good choice, and a Dutch oven is ideal for deep frying. You'll also need a frying basket, and for batter-dipped fish a perforated scoop is handy.

You'll need several inches of oil in your deep fryer—enough to float the fish. But be sure to use a fryer that is deep enough so that you need only fill it half full of oil to allow for the bubbling and spattering without overflowing. As with pan frying, your oil should be at 350° F. for deep frying. Use the same test for proper temperature by frying a small piece of bread to golden brown in 60 seconds.

Breaded fillets should be prepared for deep frying as they are for pan frying. After the breaded fillets have been refrigerated for 30 minutes, arrange them in a single layer in the bottom of the frying basket, being careful not to overload the fryer, which will cause the temperature of the oil to plummet and will oil soak the breading. Ease the basket into the hot oil gradually, until the bubbling and sizzling lessens.

As with other cooking methods, you must make sure not to overcook the fish. But deep frying is one of the fastest ways to prepare fish because the hot oil cooks it on all sides at once, so be especially careful. Depending on the thickness of the pieces, fish should be deep fried to a golden brown and should easily flake when tested with a fork after about three to five minutes in the deep fryer.

Deep frying is a method we recommend for all batter-dipped fish because such coatings call for enough oil to float the fillets above the bottom of the pan or fryer. Do not use a frying basket for batter-dipped fish, though. Instead, carefully and gently drop them into the hot oil by hand and remove them with a perforated scoop or perforated serving spoon. If you prefer, gently lift them from the oil with a pair of tongs.

To prepare fillets for batter dipping, rinse them in cold water and drain them on paper towels. Arrange them on a platter or cookie sheet and refrigerate them for 30 minutes. Dip the chilled fillets, one at a time, into the batter, let the excess drain for a second or two, and drop the fillet into the hot oil.

Simple Beer Batters

Among the most popular batters for fish is beer batter. It produces a crisp, light coating that seals in all the natural juices, and the slightly yeasty taste enhances the flavor of most fish.

Tempura batter made with beer is excellent. You can either follow the recipe below for making your own tempura batter and simply substitute beer for the water, or you can use packaged tempura batter mix that you will find in the Oriental or gourmet food section of your local supermarket. If the latter is your choice, follow the package directions, but substitute beer for the water or other liquid called for.

Another simple and tasty beer batter is made from commercial pancake mix. We prefer Krusteaz brand mix, and to two cups of mix, we add one 12-ounce bottle of beer. We blend the batter thoroughly and beat it gently with an electric mixer until it is smooth.

If you prefer to make your beer batter from scratch or need a batter you can make as much as a day ahead for large fish fries, you'll need the following ingredients for this French-style beer batter:

1½ cups all-purpose flour	2 eggs, separated
1 teaspoon salt	1 cup beer
1 tablespoon melted butter	

Combine the salt and flour; then gradually add the beer, melted butter, and egg yolks. Beat until the batter is smooth, cover, and refrigerate for at least one hour or up to 12 hours. When you're ready to fry the fish, beat the two egg whites until stiff and fold them gently into the batter and you're ready to dip the fillets.

Other Simple Batters

If you don't care for the flavor of a beer batter, try making any of the above batters, but use Seven-Up or any similar soft drink instead of beer. The Seven-Up produces a slightly sweet coating that is quite tasty. If you want a batter that produces the same crispy coating as a beer or Seven-Up batter, but without the yeasty taste of the former or sweet taste of the latter, use club soda as the liquid.

You can also add your favorite seasonings to any of the batters we have described. We always add freshly ground black pepper and usually a dash or two of onion powder and a dash of garlic powder. You can add a pinch of your favorite herbs, and our choice is fines herbes.

Oven Frying

Oven frying is a method of cooking fish developed by Home Economist, Evelene Spencer. It is not actually a frying technique, but rather a way of baking fish in a very hot oven that simulates the flavor and texture of fried fish. The primary advantage of oven frying is that you can prepare a large quantity of fillets at the same time with a minimum amount of attention, which makes this an ideal method when you're feeding a large group or simply don't feel like fooling with the frying pan or deep fryer.

Spencer's original method calls for cutting fillets into serving-size pieces, dipping them in salted milk, and coating them with toasted, fine, dry, bread crumbs. You can also use any of the breadings described earlier. If you wish, you can use any of the commercially available coating products such as Shake 'n Bake for fish.

Once the fillets are breaded, arrange them on a shallow, well-greased baking pan or cookie sheet. Melt butter or margarine or use cooking oil and drizzle a small amount (a few drops will do) over the top of each breaded fillet. Then oven fry (bake) in a preheated oven for 10 to 15 minutes at 550° F.

Since the baking pan gets very hot and essentially fries the bottoms of the fillets while the tops are baking, there's no need to turn them. The fish will be done when they have turned golden brown and flake easily with a fork.

Other Favorite Fried-Fish Recipes

When you have done all the experimenting you care to do or have run out of ideas and recipes, here are a few of our favorites that you might try. For the best results, be sure to follow the methods we described earlier for preparing breaded and batter-dipped fish, no matter what recipe you're using.

Country-Fried Fillets

This recipe from the R. T. French Company makes some mighty tasty, tangy fillets we're sure you'll like.

1$^1/_2$ pounds fillets
$^1/_4$ cup French's prepared mustard
$^1/_2$ teaspoon French's Seafood Seasoning
2 eggs
  French's Country Style Mashed Potato Flakes

Beat eggs with mustard and seafood seasoning. Dip the fillets in the mixture and bread with potato flakes. Deep fry or pan fry until golden brown and flaky.

Makes four servings.

Fish Tempura

Tempura is a crispy, deep-fried, Japanese dish, prepared with a batter that seals in all the natural juices of fish, shellfish, and vegetables. Fish fried in tempura batter is among the tastiest of treats. You can use the tempura batter to prepare fish only, or you can make an entire meal by adding tempura-fried vegetables. Try chunks of green onion, onion rings, sliced or whole mushrooms, carrot strips, turnip strips, and strips of potatoes and yams.

176

To make the tempura batter, you'll need the following ingredients:

1 cup all-purpose flour
1 cup cornstarch
$1/4$ teaspoon baking soda
$1/4$ teaspoon salt

$1/8$ teaspoon pepper
1 well-beaten egg
$1^1/2$ cups water

Combine all dry ingredients in a bowl. Then beat egg and water together. Gradually add the liquid to the dry ingredients and mix thoroughly until smooth.

For best results, use fillets that are about a quarter-inch thick, and cut them into 1-inch by 3-inch strips. Heat oil in the deep fryer to 375° F. and gently drop the batter-dipped fillets into the hot oil, allowing them to fry until golden brown—about two to four minutes.

Drain fillets on absorbent paper towels and keep them warm in an oven until all fillets (and vegetables) are fried. Then serve promptly with tartar sauce or sweet-and-hot mustard.

Deep-Fried Fish Fritters

Use canned or frozen flaked fish, or you can flake the leftovers of any baked, poached, or steamed fish that has not been highly seasoned. If you're using leftovers, be sure to remove all skin and bones and flake the fish by hand or with a fork.

2 cups flaked fish
$1/2$ cup all-purpose flour
2 well-beaten eggs

$1/4$ cup finely chopped green
onions
$1/2$ teaspoon salt
freshly ground pepper to
taste

Mix all ingredients thoroughly. The mixture should be stiff, but should easily drop from a spoon. If consistency is not right, thicken with flour or thin with water.

Heat oil in the deep fryer to 350° F. Drop batter into hot oil, one tablespoonful at a time. Fry for five to eight minutes, or until fritters are golden brown. Remove from oil and drain on absorbent paper towels.

Serve with tartar sauce or hot tomato-cheese sauce.

Makes four servings.

Batter-Dipped Clams on the Half Shell

Here's one of the simplest and tastiest ways to prepare such easy-to-clean clams as butter clams and large softshell clams.

Let clams self-clean according to the directions in Chapter 11. Then use a sharp knife to slice the clams in half, leaving half of each clam in each shell half. Use the point of a knife to scrape away any visible abdominal matter. Keep cleaned clams refrigerated until you're ready to fry them.

Prepare a simple batter by mixing one 12-ounce bottle of beer with two cups of pancake mix and adding one well-beaten egg. Beat the batter until it is smooth.

Preheat a skillet or griddle to 350° F. and grease lightly with cooking oil. Dip the clams, one at a time, in the batter by holding a clam shell, clam side down, and touching the surface of the batter only enough to coat the entire clam and the edge of the shell, forming a complete seal.

Place the clams on the griddle or in the skillet, shell side up, and fry until the batter coating is golden brown—about three to five minutes.

The batter not only makes a tasty coating, but it seals the clams so that they cook quickly in their own nectar and turn out about as savory as a clam can be.

Serve with tartar sauce or Thousand Island dressing.

Clam Fritters

This is one of our favorite ways to serve clams, and all the ingredients you'll need are these:

2 cups minced clams	1^1/$_2$ teaspoons baking powder
1 cup all-purpose flour	^{2}/$_3$ cup clam nectar and cream
1 teaspoon salt	2 tablespoons minced onion
2 well-beaten eggs	

If you're using fresh clams, mince them and save the nectar. Canned or frozen clams should be drained and the liquid reserved. Add light cream or evaporated milk to the nectar to make ^{2}/$_3$ cup.

Mix all dry ingredients in one bowl. Then beat eggs in another bowl with nectar and cream. Combine the liquid and dry ingredients and mix thoroughly. Turn clams into this batter until completely mixed.

Heat ^{1}/$_8$ inch of oil in a skillet to 350° F. or heat a griddle to the same temperature and grease with cooking oil. Spoon the clam-and-batter mixture into the frying pan or onto the griddle, making pancake-shaped fritters about two to three inches in diameter.

Fry until golden brown on each side; then drain on paper towels. Keep fritters warm in the oven until all have been fried.

Serve plain or with lemon wedges, tartar sauce, or Thousand Island dressing.

Makes four servings.

Fish Patties

Here's another recipe for canned or frozen flaked fish. As usual you can also use the flaked leftovers from baked, poached, or steamed fish.

2 cups flaked fish	1 well-beaten egg
1/4 teaspoon garlic salt	1/4 teaspoon pepper
1/2 cup minced fresh onion	1/2 cup cracker meal

Make sure fish is well drained. Combine all ingredients except the cracker meal. Mold into patties; then roll patties in cracker meal.

Fry the patties on a lightly greased griddle or in 1/8 inch of cooking oil in a skillet at 350° F. Patties should brown on one side in about five minutes. Turn them carefully and brown the other side for about five more minutes.

Serve on hamburger buns with lettuce and tartar sauce, with cold dill pickle wedges on the side.

Deep-Fried Fish Balls

Use any flaked fish for this recipe—canned, frozen, or leftover. Here's what you'll need for this unusual and delicious dish:

2 cups flaked fish	1/2 teaspoon salt
2 cups mashed potatoes	1/4 teaspoon pepper
2 tablespoons minced fresh onion	2 well-beaten eggs
	flour
2 tablespoons chopped parsley	

Drain the fish and mix it with the potatoes, eggs, and seasonings. Form into small balls and roll them in flour. Deep fry at 375° F. until golden brown—about three to five minutes.

Makes six servings.

Oven-Fried Fish Sticks

Use any lean, white fish fillets for this recipe. If you want to please a crowd, this is a simple way to prepare a large quantity of fish. Just increase the recipe proportionately. Here's what you'll need:

2 pounds fillets	1 clove garlic, minced
1/2 cup vegetable oil	1 cup finely grated cheddar
1 teaspoon salt	cheese
1/2 teaspoon pepper	1 cup cracker meal

Cut fillets into 1/2-inch by 1-inch by 2-inch sticks. Mix oil with salt, pepper, and garlic; marinate fish in this mixture for two minutes. Lift fish sticks, one at a time, from the oil and let excess drain for a second or two. Then roll fish sticks in grated cheese, then in cracker meal.

Arrange sticks on well-greased baking pan or cookie sheet and oven fry in a preheated oven at 500° F. for about 10 minutes or until golden brown.

Garnish with lemon or lime wedges and parsley sprigs. Serve with tartar sauce.

Makes six servings.

Hush Puppies

No chapter on frying fish would be complete without a recipe for hush puppies. Although hush puppies are mostly served in the South with fried catfish, they're great with just about any kind of fish. Try them with your favorite fried fillets. Here's what you'll need to make a batch:

2 cups white cornmeal	2 tablespoons minced fresh
1 1/2 teaspoons salt	onion
1 teaspoon sugar	2 well-beaten eggs
2 teaspoons baking powder	1/2 cup milk

Combine all ingredients except the eggs and milk. Beat the eggs with the milk and gradually add to the other ingredients. Mix well and form into half-dollar-size balls. Deep fry at 375° F. until golden brown on all sides. Drain on paper towels and serve hot with fried fish.

Makes four servings.

Chapter 13

BAKING THE CATCH

Although baking is the easiest of all fish-cookery methods, you must exercise some care to assure a top-quality product. As with all other methods, you must be careful not to overcook the fish, and if you are preparing any recipe that does not call for a sauce, be sure to baste the fish several times as it bakes to keep it from drying out.

Frozen fish that will not be breaded prior to baking can be baked without being thawed beforehand. If you bake any frozen fish, be sure to allow extra baking time to properly thaw the fish in the oven. A good general rule is to double the normal baking time.

Baking is also a good way to cook fish that will later be flaked and frozen or used in salads, chowders, fish patties, and other flaked-fish recipes.

Basic Baking

Always preheat the oven prior to baking any fish. For most recipes you'll find that 350° F. is the right temperature. Baking times vary according to the size and cut of fish you are baking. Small, pan-dressed fish will normally be done in 25 to 30 minutes. Fillets and steaks should bake from 20 to 25 minutes. But larger, drawn fish that will be baked whole take more time. A three-pound whole fish will take from 45 to 60 minutes to bake until it will flake easily with a fork. Larger fish and roasts cut from large fish take even more time. For these, allow 10 to 15 minutes baking time per pound of fish. A five-pound fish or roast should take between 50 and 75 minutes, and a 10-pound fish will take about twice as long.

When baking whole fish and roasts, check them for doneness when the minimum time is reached. Use a fork to pry the meat fibers apart, all the way down to the backbone. The usual flake test will tell you if the fish is done, but a better way to tell is when the flesh has changed from translucent to opaque. The meat nearest the backbone will be the last to cook, so make sure it is opaque all the way through.

If you're baking fish to be flaked and used in other recipes or frozen for later use, you needn't season the fish, but you should make sure that it is kept moist. If you're working with small, pan-dressed fish, either rub each fish with cooking oil or put a small pat of butter or margarine in the stomach cavity and another pat on top of each fish. Arrange them in a single layer in a shallow baking pan and cover the pan with aluminum foil. Bake for 25 to 30 minutes, but check them after about 20 minutes. After they're baked, let them cool. Then pick the meat away from the bones and freeze it or refrigerate it for use within two days.

Larger fish can be baked the same way. Fish that are too large for your baking pan can be wrapped and sealed in extra-heavy-duty aluminum foil, then placed on a cookie sheet for support and baked 10 to 15 minutes per pound.

Pan-dressed or large drawn fish can be baked in a similar fashion to be served as baked fish, but you will want to season them. One simple and tasty way is to fill the stomach cavities with wedges of onion and chunks of celery. Put a pat of butter in small fish or several pats in large fish. Sprinkle the fish with Lawry's seasoned salt and freshly ground black pepper. Add a dash of garlic powder if you wish. Then lay the fish on a baking rack inside a shallow baking pan. Pour about a quarter inch of white wine in the bottom of the baking pan and cover the pan with aluminum foil. Bake small fish for 25 to 30 minutes and larger fish for 10 to 15 minutes per pound. Check the fish about every 10 minutes and baste them liberally with the wine and juices in the baking pan.

When baking large, fatty fish, such as salmon and large trout, place them upright on an adjustable baking rack to allow oils to drain from the stomach cavity. Score the sides of the fish with a knife along the lateral line, making gashes an inch or so apart and deep enough to penetrate the skin. This will allow oils to drain from the fatty tissues. Do not use butter or margarine; instead, baste the fish with white wine or wine and water in equal amounts.

Stuffed Fish

There are a number of methods for stuffing fish and a variety of suitable stuffings, but baking is the only way to prepare stuffed fish.

If you are using pan-dressed or large, drawn fish, simply prepare your favorite stuffing and fill the stomach cavities of the fish.

You can serve stuffed fillets by arranging the fillets in a baking pan, covering each fillet with a layer of stuffing, and then putting another fillet on top of each, thus sandwiching the stuffing between two fillets for each serving. Liberally dot the fillets with butter before baking.

Thin fillets, such as those from small flounder, sole, perch, and some other fishes, can be made into roll-ups. Spread several spoonfuls of stuffing onto one end of each fillet; then roll the fillet around the stuffing onto one end of each fillet; then roll the fillet around the stuffing and hold it together with a wooden toothpick. Put a pat of butter or margarine on each roll-up prior to baking.

Bake stuffed fish as you would any other fish—in a preheated oven at 350° F. for 25 to 30 minutes for pan-dressed fish, 10 to 15 minutes per pound for large fish, and 20 to 25 minutes for stuffed fillets and roll-ups.

Stuffings for Fish

You can stuff fish with just about any of the stuffings you would use for fowl, so be sure to try your favorites. Other stuffings, such as those calling for crab meat or shrimp, are specifically for fish. Here are some simple stuffings you might try with your favorite fish.

Bread Stuffing

4 cups dry bread cubes
½ cup chopped celery
¼ cup minced fresh onion
¼ cup butter or margarine
¼ teaspoon thyme

1 well-beaten egg
½ teaspoon sage
½ teaspoon salt
¼ teaspoon pepper

Sauté the celery and onion in butter or margarine until tender. Combine all ingredients and mix thoroughly. Makes three cups of stuffing, sufficient for six small, pan-dressed fish; one three-pound, drawn fish; or about two pounds of fillets.

Cornbread Stuffing

6 cups cornbread crumbs
8 strips bacon, diced
½ cup melted butter
  or margarine

½ teaspoon dried chervil
½ teaspoon dried tarragon
  leaves
hot water

Fry bacon until crisp. Remove bacon from skillet with perforated scoop or serving spoon and place on paper towels to drain. Add ¼ cup of the bacon drippings to the melted butter or margarine and combine with cornbread crumbs, herbs, seasonings, and bacon bits. Add enough hot water to make a moist stuffing.

Use this as you would the bread stuffing above or to make roll-ups. Makes enough to stuff a five-pound, drawn fish or a dozen roll-ups.

Crab Meat Stuffing

1 pound crab meat
½ cup minced fresh onion
¼ cup chopped celery
¼ cup chopped green pepper
2 cloves garlic, minced
⅓ cup butter or margarine

2 cups soft bread cubes
3 well-beaten eggs
1 tablespoon chopped parsley
2 teaspoons salt
1 teaspoon pepper

Sauté onion, celery, green pepper, and garlic in butter or margarine until tender. Then combine vegetables and melted butter with all other ingredients and mix thoroughly.

Makes enough stuffing for six, small, pan-dressed fish, 12 fillets, or 12 roll-ups.

Shrimp And Rice Stuffing

3 cups cooked rice
2 cups cooked shrimp
1 cup seedless raisins
¼ pound butter
1½ cups white wine

1 cup quartered, seedless
  grapes
2 teaspoons salt
1 teaspoon pepper
1 teaspoon fines herbes
½ teaspoon sweet basil

Combine all ingredients, except for one cup of the wine. Mix thoroughly and use to stuff large, drawn trout, salmon, striped bass, or other suitable fish of 8 to 10 pounds. Pour remaining cup of wine over the fish and bake in a covered roasting pan, basting from time to time with the liquid that accumulates in the bottom of the pan. Use more wine for basting if necessary.

For larger fish, increase the recipe proportionately.

Other Favorite Baked-Fish Recipes

Although we normally prefer fried fish, we do enjoy baked fish from time to time and over the years have tried a number of different recipes. Here are a few of our favorites.

Foil-Baked Fillets

This is a quick and easy way to bake fish fillets that is especially good for dinner parties. The fillets don't need close supervision while baking, and there is a minimum of after-dinner clean-up required.

You'll need about a half pound of fillets and one 12-inch-by-12-inch piece of aluminum foil for each serving. Arrange each fillet or individual portion of small fillets in the center of a sheet of foil and squeeze an ample amount of fresh lemon or lime juice over it. Then top it with several thin slices of onion. If you wish, you can also add sliced fresh mushrooms and one or two strips of celery. If you're using lean fish, add a pat or two of butter or margarine to each portion. Then season with salt, pepper, and a dash of garlic powder. Seal the foil completely, making sure there are no holes or gaps where moisture can escape. Arrange the foil packets on a cookie sheet and bake in a preheated oven for 20 to 25 minutes at 350° F.

Mayonnaise-Baked Fish

Use large fillets or inch-thick steaks for this tasty dish and sprinkle each piece with Lawry's seasoned salt and lemon pepper. Arrange fish on a lightly greased, shallow baking pan. Then spread a liberal amount of mayonnaise over each piece and sprinkle with paprika. Bake in a preheated oven at 350° F. for 30 to 35 minutes until fish flakes easily with a fork.

Fish Croquettes

Here's a good way to put your canned or frozen flaked fish to use. You can also use the leftovers from baked, poached, or steamed fish.

2 cups flaked fish	2 tablespoons melted butter
1 cup grated cheddar cheese	or margarine
1 teaspoon salt	2 well-beaten eggs
¼ teaspoon pepper	½ cup cracker meal
	juice from half a lemon

Combine all ingredients but the cracker meal and mix thoroughly. Mold into six croquettes and roll them in the cracker meal. Arrange the croquettes in a lightly greased, shallow baking pan or on a cookie sheet and bake in a preheated oven at 350° F. for 25 or 30 minutes or until golden brown.

Serve the croquettes plain or topped with cream sauce. You can also serve them on hamburger buns with lettuce and tartar sauce.

Makes six servings.

Baked Fillets in Mushroom-Cheese Sauce

This is another simple and savory dish that's easy to prepare. It's

185

ideal for those days when you just don't feel like cooking, but would like something that's good to eat.

2 pounds fillets	½ teaspoon pepper
3 tablespoons minced fresh onion	1 can (10¾ ounces) condensed cream of mushroom soup
1 teaspoon salt	1 cup grated cheddar cheese

Cut fillets into serving-size pieces and arrange in a single layer in a well-greased, shallow baking pan. Mix the cream of mushroom soup, onion, salt, and pepper and spread over the fish. Top with grated cheese and bake, uncovered, in a preheated oven at 350° F. for 25 or 30 minutes.

Makes six servings.

Dilled Fish Steaks Baked in Cream

Use three-quarter-inch steaks cut from large trout, salmon, striped bass, or other large fish for this delicious recipe. For every two pounds of steaks, you'll need the following ingredients:

2 tablespoons minced fresh onion	¼ teaspoon pepper
1½ teaspoons dill weed	1 cup light cream or evaporated milk
1 teaspoon salt	butter or margarine

Arrange steaks in a single layer in a well-greased baking pan. Scatter minced onion over the steaks; then sprinkle with salt, pepper, and dill weed. Put a small pat of butter or margarine on top of each steak. Then pour cream over the steaks. Bake in a preheated oven at 350° F. for 25 to 30 minutes or until the fish flakes easily with a fork.

Makes six servings.

Tangy Canned-Fish Casserole

When you're rushed, here's a great casserole that is not only delicious, but easy to prepare.

1 pint canned fish	½ cup mayonnaise
3 tablespoons butter or margarine	½ cup grated cheddar cheese
3 tablespoons flour	2 teaspoons Worcestershire sauce
2 cups fish liquid and milk	2 teaspoons prepared mustard
4 cups sliced, cooked potatoes	¼ cup cracker meal

Drain the canned fish and keep the liquid. Flake the fish with a fork and put aside until later.

Melt the butter or margarine in a small saucepan. Blend the flour and stir until smooth and bubbly. Remove pan from heat and gradually add fish liquid and milk. Return pan to heat and bring to a boil on a medium setting, stirring constantly. Allow sauce to boil for one minute, until smooth and thickened; then remove from heat.

In a well-greased casserole, arrange potatoes, fish, and sauce in alternating layers. Combine mayonnaise, cheese, mustard, and Worcestershire sauce and spread over the top layer in the casserole. Sprinkle with cracker meal and bake in a preheated oven at 375° F. for 30 minutes.

Makes six servings.

Escalloped Seafood

For this great casserole you can use clams, canned fish, or a combination of the two. Clams should be shucked and chopped. Fish should be flaked.

2 cups fish or clams	½ teaspoon Worcestershire
½ cup melted butter	sauce
or margarine	1 cup seafood liquid and milk
½ teaspoon salt	2 cups cracker meal
¼ teaspoon pepper	

If you're using clams, save the nectar. If you're using canned fish, drain and flake the fish and save the liquid.

In a small bowl, combine the cracker meal, seasonings, and melted butter or margarine. Mix thoroughly and spread a third of the mixture in a well-greased casserole. Cover that layer with half the clams or flaked fish. Then add another layer of the cracker meal mixture and the rest of the clams or fish.

Add milk to the clam nectar or fish liquid to make one cup. Add the Worcestershire sauce to this and pour over the casserole. Sprinkle the rest of the cracker meal mixture over the top and bake in a preheated oven at 375° F. for 30 minutes or until brown on top.

Makes six servings.

Clam and Corn Casserole

Here's about the simplest and tastiest clam casserole you'll ever find. It's great after a long day of fishing, when you just don't feel like cooking.

2 cups minced clams
  with nectar
2 lightly beaten eggs
½ cup light cream
1 cup cream-style corn

2 tablespoons melted butter
  or margarine
1 teaspoon salt
½ teaspoon pepper
1 cup cracker meal

Combine all ingredients except for half the cracker meal. Pour into a well-greased casserole, sprinkle on the remaining cracker meal, and bake in a preheated oven at 350° F. for 45 to 60 minutes or until top is brown.

Makes four servings.

Baked Fish Kabobs

For this dish you'll need two pounds of thick fillets. Large trout, salmon, striped bass, pike, catfish, lingcod, or bluefish are all excellent choices.

1 cup catsup
¼ cup brown sugar
2 teaspoons salt

6 tablespoons vegetable oil
¼ cup cider vinegar
Tabasco sauce

Cut fillets into one-inch cubes. Combine catsup, brown sugar, salt, oil, vinegar, and add six to eight drops of Tabasco sauce. Pour mixture over fish and marinate in the refrigerator for two hours.

Remove fish from marinade and put on skewers. Arrange skewers across a shallow baking pan and bake in a preheated oven at 375° F. for about 10 minutes. Baste with marinade; then bake for another 10 minutes.

Makes about six servings.

Deviled Crab

This is one of our favorite ways to enjoy crab meat, and it's an ideal way to utilize home-canned crab. Of course, you can use fresh crab that has been picked and flaked or frozen crab, although we don't recommend freezing crab unless you have no other way of preserving it. At any rate, here's what you'll need:

2 cups crab meat
⅓ cup cracker meal
1 cup light cream
2 well-beaten eggs
4 tablespoons butter
  or margarine
½ teaspoon salt

¼ teaspoon pepper
1 teaspoon powdered mustard
1 teaspoon prepared
  horseradish
4 or 5 drops Tabasco sauce
  dash of cayenne pepper

In a small saucepan, melt two tablespoons of butter or margarine. Gradually add cracker meal and cream and bring to a boil. Remove from heat.

In a bowl, combine all other ingredients except the crab meat and beat. Then flake the crab meat and add it to the bowl and mix thoroughly. Gradually stir the cream–cracker meal mixture into the crab mixture and blend thoroughly.

Pack the mixture equally into four crab-back shells and brush the tops with melted butter. Bake them in a preheated oven at 375° F. for about 20 minutes or until tops brown.

Makes four servings.

Chapter 14

BROILING THE CATCH

Broiling is a method of fish cookery in which the heat is direct and intense. Fish can be broiled indoors beneath the broiling element of an electric range or in the broiler section of a gas range according to the range manufacturer's directions, or they can be charcoal broiled or cooked over the coals outdoors—at home or in camp.

Since broiling is a dry-heat method that tends to dry out thin fillets, use only pan-dressed fish, inch-thick steaks, and thick fillets for broiling. Even then, to retain moisture and to attain the best flavor and texture, you should either use some sort of sauce on the fish or baste it before and during the broiling process.

If you're using frozen fish, always thaw it before broiling.

Range Broiling

Broiling times will vary according to the thickness of the fish and its distance from the heat source. Inch-thick steaks and fillets should be placed about three or four inches from the heat source. Thicker pieces and pan-dressed fish should be placed farther from the heat.

Normally, a broiling pan is used in conjunction with the broiling process. Since the pan heats up while the fish is being broiled, it cooks the underside of the fish. So it generally isn't necessary to turn the fish to broil the down side. Pan-dressed fish and steaks and fillets thicker than one inch, however, should be turned at the halfway point, basted, and broiled for as long as the first side.

Inch-thick steaks and fillets will broil to perfection in about 10 to 15 minutes. Pan-dressed fish and thicker steaks and fillets usually take from 15 to 20 minutes total time. As with other methods, check the fish for doneness by testing with a fork to make sure it is flaky and opaque in appearance.

Fish has a tendency to stick to the broiler pan, so it's a good idea to rub any fish that is to be broiled with cooking oil. This also helps to keep it moist.

If you're following no specific recipe, the simplest basting sauce to use is melted butter or margarine. You can also use one of the seasoned butter sauces, such as lemon butter or herb butter, or you can mix equal parts of melted butter and white wine.

Baste the fish liberally before broiling and about every three to five minutes thereafter. Make sure the rest of the meal is prepared and ready to serve so that the broiled fish can be served sizzling hot.

Broiling Over Coals

Whether you're using a charcoal grill or cooking over the coals of a campfire, you'll want to make sure that your coals are only moderately hot and that you have control over your heat source to prevent charring your meal. And since fish, when cooked, tends to fall apart, you'll have to take measures to keep it intact.

If you're charbroiling at home, make sure you prepare the coals properly and well enough in advance to let them burn down to a moderate heat. We have found that we need to start getting the charcoal ready about 45 minutes prior to cooking time. We start by making a mound of coals in the center of the fire bowl in our grill, and we use enough charcoal so that it can be spread liberally over the fire bowl in a single layer that is slightly wider than the amount of fish we'll be broiling.

We sprinkle the charcoal with charcoal lighting fluid and let the fluid soak into the coals for five minutes. We then sprinkle it lightly again with just enough fluid to get the fire started quickly and set a match to it. We then allow the coals to burn until the surfaces of each briquet are covered with gray ash. Depending on wind conditions, this takes from 20 to 35 minutes. If there is a breeze the coals will burn much faster. We then spread the coals in an even layer in the fire bowl, and we're ready to start cooking fish.

In camp, we rake the coals from our campfire into a cooking pit. Whenever possible, we carry along a bag of charcoal briquets because we have found that by adding a few briquets to our wood-coal fire we have more control over the heat and can make a more even bed of cooking coals.

Inch-thick steaks and fillets should be broiled at a distance of four to five inches from the coals. Pan-dressed fish and thicker pieces should be placed about six inches from the heat.

Steaks and pan-dressed fish can be broiled on the rungs of a grill, but fillets should be arranged between the rungs of hinged wire grills because they are likely to fall apart if turned on a conventional grill.

You can do much to eliminate the problem of fish sticking to the grill if you first rub the fish with cooking oil. Then spray the grill with Pam vegetable cooking spray.

Try to avoid turning any fish unnecessarily when broiling. As a general rule, inch-thick steaks and fillets will be done on one side in about five to eight minutes. They should then be turned and broiled on the other side for the same amount of time. Small, pan-dressed fish will usually take from 5 to 10 minutes on each side.

As with range broiling, use a basting sauce before and during the broiling process to keep the fish moist and to retain its flavor and texture. Melted butter or one of the butter sauces will do nicely.

If you like a smoky flavor, you can add material to your coals that will create more smoke. In camp, try cutting small pieces of "green" willow or alder twigs and putting them atop the coals. Don't use dry twigs, as they will catch fire; whereas, the green twigs merely smolder.

At home, use commercially available hickory or other hardwood chips and soak them in water for about an hour before you're ready to broil your fish. Then, just before putting the fish on the grill, sprinkle a handful of wet chips over the coals. As they burn away, add more wet chips. If any dry out and catch fire, cover them with more wet chips.

If your grill is equipped with a lid or cover, put a handful of wet hardwood chips on the coals and cover the grill for the last minute of cooking time.

Favorite Broiling Recipes

When we're in camp or at home and in the mood for a change of pace, we usually prepare fish according to one of the following recipes. Try them and we're sure that a few will become your favorites, too.

Campfire Fish

Although this is something of a traditional way to prepare a shore lunch or dinner in camp, it's also a simple way to broil fish over charcoal at home, and it's suitable for any meal. Try it for breakfast or brunch, served with scrambled eggs, toast, and lots of hot coffee.

For starters, you'll need a few pan-dressed fish, or a mess of fish for a crowd. Trout of 12 inches or bass of about three quarters of a pound are ideal, and you should plan on one fish per person. If you're using smaller trout, perch, bluegills, or other panfish, you had better plan on two or three fish for each person.

Rub each fish lightly with cooking oil and sprinkle with Lawry's seasoned salt and lemon pepper. Put a pat of butter and a wedge of onion inside the stomach cavity of each fish; then wrap the fish with one or two slices of bacon, depending on the size of the fish. Hold the bacon in place with halves of wooden toothpicks and use the toothpicks to partly close the stomach cavity.

Arrange the fish between the rungs of hinged wire grills and broil over the coals for five to 10 minutes on each side. Since the bacon drippings will keep the fish moist, there is no need to baste.

Barbecued Fish Steaks

This is our favorite way to prepare salmon and steelhead steaks, but it is also an excellent way to charbroil inch-thick steaks from other fish, such as large trout, catfish, striped bass, and sturgeon. Try your favorite fish and see if it isn't better this way. Here's all you'll need:

6 large fish steaks	cooking oil
¼ pound butter or margarine	Lawry's seasoned salt
1 lemon	pepper
¼ teaspoon garlic powder	hickory-flavored barbecue sauce

In a small pan, melt the butter and add the juice of the lemon and the garlic powder. Keep warm until needed.

Rinse steaks under cold water and drain on paper towels. Apply a liberal coating of cooking oil to each steak.

When coals are ready and your grill has been sprayed with Pam, place the steaks on the grill and sprinkle them lightly with the seasoned salt and pepper. Allow them to broil for about four to seven minutes or until almost done. Baste them liberally with butter sauce every minute or two.

Carefully turn the steaks, sprinkle with seasoned salt and pepper, baste, and broil for another five minutes or so.

Brush on an ample coating of barbecue sauce and carefully turn the steaks. Allow them to broil for one minute, while you apply barbecue sauce to the other side. Turn the steaks and broil that side for one more minute. Serve immediately, sizzling hot.

Makes six servings.

Charbroiled Fishburgers

Here's another use for your canned fish and a great way to get out of the hamburger rut. Use canned salmon, steelhead, albacore, striped bass, or any other home-canned fish. You can also flake fish you have frozen or the leftovers from baked, steamed, or poached fish.

2 cups flaked fish
¼ cup fish liquid
½ cup minced fresh onion
½ cup butter or margarine
2 well-beaten eggs
1 teaspoon powdered mustard

1 teaspoon salt
½ teaspoon pepper
1 tablespoon Worcestershire
  sauce
2 tablespoons dried parsley
1 cup cracker meal

Drain and flake the fish and save the liquid. Melt one fourth cup of the butter or margarine in a small skillet and saute the onion until tender.

In a bowl, combine the onion with the fish, fish liquid, eggs, mustard, salt, pepper, Worcestershire sauce, parsley, and one third of the cracker meal. Mix thoroughly and mold into six burgers.

Spread the remaining cracker meal on a sheet of waxed paper and roll burgers in the meal. Remold the burgers, pressing the meal into them so it will adhere. Arrange the burgers on a platter or cookie sheet and brush the tops and sides with melted butter.

Spray the grill with Pam; then arrange the burgers on the grill, buttered side down, about four inches from the coal and charbroil for three to four minutes. Brush the tops with melted butter and gently turn the burgers. Charbroil them for another three to four minutes or until well browned. Serve on hamburger buns with lettuce and tartar sauce.

Makes six servings.

Broiled-in-Foil Fillets

Here's an easy way to charbroil fillets without worrying about them sticking or falling apart. You'll need a covered charcoal grill, or you can make a cover out of heavy-duty aluminum foil.

2 pounds fillets
2 medium onions, sliced
2 green peppers, sliced
½ cup melted butter
  or margarine
2 teaspoons salt

½ teaspoon pepper
¼ teaspoon garlic powder
  juice from one lemon
  paprika

Cut fish into serving-size portions. Cut six 12-inch-square pieces of heavy-duty aluminum foil. Lightly grease the foil and place an individual portion of fish in the center of each. Put an equal amount of sliced onion and sliced green pepper on top of each fish portion and bring the edges of the foil up around the fish, leaving the top open.

Combine the melted butter or margarine, salt, pepper, garlic powder, and lemon juice and stir. Pour an equal amount of this sauce over each portion of fish. Sprinkle with paprika. Fold the foil tops together to form a tight, double-wrapped seal.

Place the six packages on the grill, about five or six inches above the coals. Broil for about 30 to 45 minutes or until the fish flakes easily with a fork. About five minutes before the fish is done, use a fork to put several small punctures in the top of the foil on each package. Cover the grill and broil for the remaining five minutes.

For a smokier flavor, add a handful or two of wet hardwood chips to the coals for this last five minutes.

Makes six servings.

Tangy Charbroiled Fillets

Here's another recipe that calls for fillets, but make sure the skin has been left on them to help hold them together. Simply dress the fish as you normally would, but scale it. Then fillet it and remove the bones and your fillets are ready for charbroiling. If you prefer, you can use steaks instead.

2 pounds fillets	6 drops Tabasco sauce
1/2 cup melted butter or margarine	juice from two lemons
	paprika
1 teaspoon Worcestershire sauce	cooking oil
2 teaspoons salt	
1/2 teaspoon pepper	

Rub fillets with cooking oil and place in hinged wire grills that have been sprayed with Pam.

Make a sauce with the melted butter, Worcestershire sauce, salt, pepper, lemon juice, and Tabasco sauce. Broil fish about four inches from the coals for five to eight minutes, basting frequently with the sauce. Turn the fish and broil for another five to eight minutes, or until it flakes easily with a fork, basting liberally and frequently.

Arrange fillets on a platter, skin side down, sprinkle with paprika, and garnish with wedges of lemon and lime.

Makes six servings.

Charcoal-Smoked Fillets

Here's a dandy way to serve tasty smoked fish that doesn't require a smoker. You can use any kind of fish, but for best results, try salmon, steelhead, whitefish, or sucker. Scale the fish before dressing it; then fillet it and bone it as usual, but leave the skin on. Use fillets that are serving size or cut larger fillets into serving-size portions.

6 serving-size fillets	2 quarts water
1 cup noniodized salt	$^1/_2$ cup cooking oil
1 cup brown sugar	1 pound hardwood chips
2 teaspoons fines herbes	

Soak hickory or other hardwood chips in water for two hours or overnight.

Make a brine by dissolving the salt and sugar in one quart of hot water. Then add one quart of cold water and stir in the fines herbes and other seasonings if you wish. Add the fish to the brine and refrigerate for one or two hours. If fish floats to the top of the brine, put a plate on top to hold the fish under.

Remove fish from brine and rinse lightly in cold, running water. Pat dry with paper towels and let stand on a cookie sheet or cake rack in a cool place for about 45 minutes or until a glaze forms.

When your coals are ready, spray the grill liberally with Pam. Adjust the grill so that it is at the highest setting—at least five or six inches from the coals.

Sprinkle several handfuls of wet hardwood chips on the coals. Then quickly arrange the fillets on the grill and close the lid or cover with heavy-duty aluminum foil. Be sure to leave the draft partly open to keep the temperature up. Check the fish about every 10 or 15 minutes. Brush the tops of the fillets with cooking oil each time you check them and add more wood chips as required to keep the coals smoking. Fillets will be done when they are lightly browned and flaky or in about 60 to 90 minutes.

This is a mildly cured fish, which is usually better than a harder cure if the fish is to be served hot. Heat tends to amplify the effects of the curing process. If, after trying the recipe, you would prefer a harder cure, leave the fish in the brine for three or four hours before rinsing and glazing it. Serve hot with wedges of lemon and thinly sliced fresh onion.

Makes six servings.

Deviled Fish Steaks

Although this is a good recipe for a variety of species, our favorites are halibut and lingcod. Try your favorite white-meat fish. For four large steaks (about a half pound each), you'll need the following ingredients:

2 tablespoons prepared
    mustard
2 tablespoons prepared
    horseradish
2 tablespoons chili sauce

1 tablespoon vegetable oil
1 teaspoon salt
$1/2$ teaspoon pepper

Make a sauce by mixing all the ingredients together. Arrange the steaks on a well-greased broiling pan and spread half the sauce on the steaks.

Broil in your range broiler for five to seven minutes. Carefully turn the steaks and spread the rest of the sauce on them. Broil for another five to seven minutes or until the fish flakes easily with a fork.

Makes four servings.

Broiled Steaks with Garlic French Dressing

As with the above recipe, you can use large steaks from your favorite white-meat fish for this simple recipe. Here's all you'll need:

4 inch-thick steaks
$1/2$ cup French dressing
$1/2$ teaspoon garlic powder
1 tablespoon chopped parsley

salt
pepper
paprika

Place steaks on a well-greased broiler pan and sprinkle with salt and pepper. Mix garlic powder with French dressing and spread half the mixture onto the steaks.

Broil for five to seven minutes. Carefully turn the steaks, brush on the remaining dressing, and broil for another five to seven minutes.

Transfer the steaks to a serving platter and sprinkle with paprika and parsley. Garnish with wedges of lemon and lime and serve sizzling hot.

Makes four servings.

Broiled Fillets in Tomato-Cheese Sauce

Since you will be preparing this recipe in a baking pan instead of on a broiling pan and won't need to turn the fish, use any white-meat fillets of your choice.

2 pounds fillets
2 tablespoons melted butter
1 large onion, minced
1 eight-ounce can tomato
    sauce

1 cup grated cheddar cheese
Lawry's seasoned salt
pepper

197

Cut fillets into serving-size portions and place in a well-greased, shallow baking pan. Brush with melted butter or margarine and sprinkle with seasoned salt and pepper to taste.

Broil in range broiler for about seven or eight minutes. Pour tomato sauce over the fish and top with onions and grated cheese. Broil until the cheese melts and becomes bubbly.

Makes six servings.

Broiled Fish Kabobs

Use small fillets of any fish or cut larger fillets into ¹/₂-inch by 1-inch by 4-inch strips. This is ideal for fillets cut from bluegill, perch, and other small fish.

1 pound small fillets	onion wedges
¹/₂ pound bacon	green pepper wedges
¹/₄ cup melted butter or	salt
margarine	pepper
salad tomatoes	

Cut strips of bacon in half or to lengths equal to the length of the fillets. Salt and pepper the fillets and lay each on top of a strip of bacon. Roll fillets and bacon so that fillets are wrapped in the bacon. Arrange rolled fillets, onion wedges, green pepper wedges, and salad tomatoes alternately on skewers.

Brush kabobs with melted butter or margarine and place on a well-greased broiler pan. Sprinkle with salt and pepper to taste and broil in the range for about five minutes. Carefully turn the kabobs, brush with butter, sprinkle with salt and pepper, and broil for another four or five minutes.

Makes six servings.

15

STEAMING
AND POACHING
THE CATCH

Steaming and poaching are similar methods of fish cookery. Each uses a liquid as the cooking medium, and each produces a moist and flavorful product, ideal for serving hot, for chilling and serving cold, or for flaking and using in salads, chowders, croquettes, creamed fish, and other recipes calling for flaked fish. Steamed and poached fish can also be flaked and frozen for later use.

Basic Steaming

To steam fish you'll need a steaming rack and a covered pan large enough to accommodate it. If you don't have a steaming rack, you can get by with a small colander. Whole fish and large steaks and fillets with the skin on can be steamed on a roasting rack or on one or two cake racks placed in a large roasting pan. Skinned fillets should not be steamed on such racks, though, because as they cook the meat might fall apart and drop through the rungs of the rack.

Steaming is one of the simplest and most foolproof methods of fish cookery because the fish requires very little prior preparation. No breadings or stuffings are used. No oil is required for cooking. Steamed fish not only retains its natural flavors but comes out of the steamer as a moist and flaky product that is very low in calories.

To steam fish, use only enough water to reach the bottom of the steaming rack, without actually touching the fish. Before putting the rack into the pan, add the water and bring it to a rolling boil. Meanwhile, spray the rack with a coating of Pam vegetable cooking spray or lightly coat it with cooking oil to prevent the fish from sticking. Arrange the fish in a single layer on the rack and, when the water is boiling, lower the filled rack into the pan. Cover the pan with a tight-fitting lid and steam the fish until it flakes easily with a fork.

Fillets and steaks that are no more than a half-inch thick and small, pan-dressed fish will steam completely in 5 to 10 minutes. For larger fish, plan on 10 minutes per pound. Steamed fish will cook through without being turned on the rack.

You can enhance the flavor of bland fish by adding various seasonings to the steaming water. Experiment with your favorite herbs and spices or try making a steaming liquid with equal portions of water and dry, white wine. Add several slices of onion separated into rings, a stalk of celery cut into chunks, a bay leaf, and a pinch of fines herbes.

Steamed fish is usually served hot with melted butter, lemon butter, or one of any other suitable hot sauces, such as cream sauce, cheese sauce, tomato-cheese sauce, egg sauce, or mustard sauce.

Steamed fish is also excellent when chilled and served cold with mayonnaise, Thousand Island dressing, or cocktail sauce.

If you're watching your weight, steamed fish is one of the best sources of low-calorie protein. But avoid using any of the usual sauces that will only add calories to the dish. Instead, serve steamed fish lightly seasoned with salt and pepper and perhaps sprinkled with your favorite herbs and a dash of garlic powder or onion powder. Substitute fresh lemon juice or malt vinegar for the sauce and you'll have fish that's mighty tasty and high in nutrition, but low in calories.

Basic Poaching

Poaching is similar to steaming, except that the fish is immersed in the cooking liquid instead of suspended above it. As with steaming, you can poach fish in plain water, or you can use seasoned water, water and wine, or even milk.

Although you can poach fish in any form, large, inch-thick fillets and steaks are the forms most often used. Skin can be left on or removed, but seasonings will penetrate better if the skin is removed.

To poach fish, use a large skillet with a tight-fitting lid and use enough liquid to almost cover the fish, usually about two cups. Plain water should be lightly salted. If you're poaching a bland fish, add your favorite seasonings and either the juice from half a lemon or a tablespoon of cider or malt vinegar. Or you can use the seasoned water-and-wine mixture we recommended for steaming bland fish, substituting onion powder and celery salt for the vegetables. If you're poaching strong-tasting fish, you can greatly improve the flavor by poaching it in milk that has been lightly salted and peppered. You can also add onion powder, celery salt, a bay leaf, and herbs to the milk, but don't use lemon juice or vinegar because these acids will curdle the milk.

Bring the liquid to a boil and arrange the fish in the skillet in a single layer, allowing a half inch or so around each piece. Reduce heat to simmer, cover the skillet, and poach the fish until it flakes, usually 5 to 10 minutes for most fillets and steaks.

As with steamed fish, poached fish is best when served hot with a sauce or chilled and served cold with mayonnaise, Thousand Island dressing, or cocktail sauce. It can also be flaked and used in a variety of hot or cold dishes or frozen for later use.

Some folks like to reduce and thicken the poaching liquid to use as a sauce for the poached fish. To do this, remove the poached fish to another container and add a bit of the liquid. Cover the container and keep it hot in the oven. Bring the liquid in the skillet to a rapid boil and allow it to cook down for about five minutes. Strain the liquid through a kitchen strainer or through several layers of cheesecloth and return it to the skillet to bring it back to a boil on a medium heat. In a small bowl, combine two or three tablespoons of cornstarch with enough water to make a liquid the consistency of heavy cream and mix thoroughly. Gradually add the cornstarch to the poaching liquid a little at a time, stirring rapidly and constantly, until the liquid has thickened to the consistency of a cream sauce or gravy. Serve over the poached fish.

Steaming and Poaching for the Freezer

Steaming and poaching are two excellent ways to prepare fish that is to be flaked and frozen for later use. You can steam fillets, steaks, pan-dressed fish, or large chunks from whole fish. If you're poaching, use fillets or steaks.

Since you might use the fish in any of a number of recipes calling for flaked fish, it is best to avoid using strong seasonings when steaming or poaching for the freezer. Instead, use plain water that has been lightly salted. If you're steaming or poaching lean fish, you can add two or three tablespoons of cooking oil to the liquid if you wish.

Steam or poach the fish as described above; then set it aside to cool. Strain the liquid and refrigerate it until needed. If you're cooking several batches, make up fresh liquid for each.

When the fish is cool enough to handle, flake it and remove all bones, skin, and dark meat. Pack the flaked fish loosely in one-pint freezer containers, leaving 1½ inches of headspace. Pour the reserved liquid over the fish until it's covered. Use a spoon to press the fish into the container as you add the liquid to make sure you remove all air pockets. Refrigerate any leftover liquid.

Put the containers in the freezer and allow the fish to freeze solid overnight. Check them the next day to make sure that all of the fish is covered with the frozen liquid. To any containers in which the fish has risen to the surface during freezing, add another quarter inch of the leftover liquid. Cover the containers and store in the freezer until needed. Use within three months.

Incidentally, this is an excellent way to get additional freezer life out of your frozen fish. As fish reaches the maximum recommended freezer-storage time, thaw it and steam or poach it. Then return the cooked fish to the freezer as we just described.

Steaming Clams and Mussels

Steaming is a favorite way to prepare and serve some clams. Use small softshell or littleneck clams for steaming and allow them to self-clean as described in Chapter 11. You can also steam mussels and serve them the same way as steamed clams.

As with steamed fish, you'll need a steaming rack and a pot with a tight-fitting lid. A popular way is to steam the shellfish in wine. Use a dry, white wine—just enough to reach the bottom of the steaming rack. In most steaming pots, a cup of wine and a quarter pound of butter will make a sufficient liquid.

Bring the liquid to a rolling boil. Place the cleaned clams or mussels that have been scrubbed and had the beards removed in a single layer on the steaming rack. Put the rack in the pot, cover, and steam until the shells open, usually about five minutes. Discard any clams or mussels that haven't opened.

Remove the rack and strain the liquid through linen or several layers of cheesecloth. Then serve the clams or mussels in soup bowls with the liquid poured over them. A half dozen or so clams or mussels per person make an excellent appetizer for any meal. If you plan to use them as the main course, count on one to two dozen per person, depending on the size of the shellfish.

Steaming is also a good way to open reluctant clams, such as cockles and littlenecks, that will be shucked and canned or frozen for later use. In this case, however, use water instead of wine and skip the butter.

Sauces for Steamed and Poached Fish

You'll find that cream sauces and cheese sauces are ideal for steamed and poached fish. Try any of your favorite sauces or those in Chapter 18. We recommend the basic cream sauce for the more flavorful fish, such as salmon. For most poached or steamed white-meat fish, we like egg sauce or mustard sauce. The tomato-cheese sauce is excellent with any white fish and will do wonders to improve the flavor of strong-tasting fish.

Chapter 16

APPETIZERS, SNACKS, AND SALADS

Many varieties of fish and shellfish are ideal for hors d'oeuvres and are equally suitable for serving as snacks. Some make fine salads that can be served with any meal. Here, then, are a few of our favorite recipes for such uses.

Flaked Fish and Cheese Canapés

1 cup flaked fish
1 cup grated cheddar cheese
¼ cup butter or margarine
2 tablespoons minced fresh
   onion

1 teaspoon Worcestershire
   sauce
4 drops Tabasco sauce
½ teaspoon paprika
   juice from half a lemon

Allow cheese and butter to reach room temperature; then cream them. Add drained, flaked fish and seasonings and mix thoroughly.

Spread about two teaspoonfuls of the mixture on Melba toast rounds or your favorite cocktail crackers. Arrange on a cookie sheet and broil about four inches from the heat source until lightly browned—about five minutes.

Makes about 30 canapés.

Broiled Crab Canapés

1 cup shredded crab meat
¼ cup soft butter or
   margarine
½ cup chili sauce

1 cup grated cheedar cheese
6 slices sandwich bread

203

Toast bread on one side under the broiler. Trim away crusts and cut each slice into four squares.

Spread butter on the untoasted side of the bread and put an equal portion of crab meat on each piece.

Top each canapé with a teaspoon of chili sauce and two teaspoons of grated cheese.

Arrange canapés on a cookie sheet and broil until cheese melts. Makes 24 canapés.

Crab-Stuffed Eggs

2 cups chopped crab meat
1 cup mayonnaise
2 tablespoons chili sauce
1 teaspoon chopped green
  pepper

2 teaspoons minced fresh
  onion
1 teaspoon chopped pimiento
16 hard-boiled eggs
  chopped parsley

Use fresh, canned, or frozen crab meat. Drain thoroughly, flake, and chop with a sharp knife. Mix crab meat with all ingredients, except the eggs and parsley.

Slice eggs in half lengthwise and remove yolks. Fill each egg half with the mixture and sprinkle with parsley.

Makes 32 hors d'oeuvres.

Crab Salad

2 cups crab meat
1 cup mayonnaise
$1/2$ cup chopped celery
$1/4$ cup minced onion

$1/2$ cup chopped sweet pickles
$1/2$ teaspoon salt
$1/4$ teaspoon pepper
  juice from half a lemon

Use fresh, canned, or frozen crab meat. Drain and flake the meat, add all other ingredients, and mix thoroughly.

Serve as a salad or snack.

Makes four to six servings.

Flaked Fish Salad

1 cup flaked fish
$1/2$ cup chopped celery
$1/2$ cup chopped sweet pickles
$1/4$ cup minced fresh onion

2 tablespoons pickle juice
$3/4$ cup Miracle Whip or
  similar dressing
$1/2$ teaspoon salt
$1/4$ teaspoon pepper

Use canned or frozen flaked fish or fresh fish that has been poached or steamed, cooled, and flaked. Make sure all bones and skin have been removed and fish has been drained.

Combine all ingredients and mix thoroughly. Serve as a salad on crisp lettuce leaves with sliced tomatoes on the side or as sandwiches on toast with lettuce leaves.

Smoked Fish Salad

1 cup flaked smoked fish	$^1/_2$ cup mayonnaise
2 chopped, hard-boiled eggs	6 medium tomatoes
$^1/_2$ cup chopped celery	6 lettuce leaves
$^1/_4$ cup chopped cucumber	juice from half a lemon
$^1/_4$ cup minced fresh onion	salt and pepper

Flake smoked fish and remove all bones and skin. Combine fish, eggs, celery, cucumber, onion, mayonnaise, and lemon juice and mix thoroughly.

Cut the centers out of the tomatoes. Lightly salt and pepper the tomatoes and fill with the smoked fish mixture. Arrange each stuffed tomato on a lettuce leaf.

Makes six servings.

Tangy Flaked-Fish Spread

1 cup flaked fish	2 tablespoons Worcestershire
$^1/_2$ cup chopped celery	sauce
$^1/_2$ cup chopped sweet pickles	$^1/_2$ cup Miracle Whip or
$^1/_4$ cup chopped green onions	similar dressing
2 tablespoons prepared	$^1/_2$ teaspoon salt
horseradish	$^1/_4$ teaspoon pepper

Use canned or frozen flaked fish or fresh fish that has been steamed or poached, cooled, and flaked. Drain fish and combine with all other ingredients.

Serve with crackers as snacks or hors d'oeuvres or use as a sandwich spread.

Canned-Fish Spread

1 pint canned fish	2 tablespoons Worcestershire
1 eight-ounce package cream	sauce
cheese	$^1/_2$ teaspoon salt

$^1/_2$ cup minced fresh onion
2 tablespoons prepared
  horseradish

$^1/_4$ teaspoon pepper
2 teaspoons parsley
  paprika

Allow cream cheese to soften at room temperature. Drain and flake fish, removing any bones and skin. Combine all ingredients except paprika and mix thoroughly.

Put spread in a serving bowl or mold into a mound on a plate. Sprinkle with paprika and refrigerate for 30 minutes.

Serve with party rye bread, Triscuits, Wheat Thins, or your favorite cocktail crackers.

Clam Dip

1 cup minced clams
1 eight-ounce package cream
  cheese
$^1/_2$ teaspoon salt
1 tablespoon minced fresh
  onion

1 teaspoon Worcestershire
  sauce
4 drops Tabasco sauce
  juice from half a lemon
1 teaspoon chopped parsley

Allow cheese to soften at room temperature. Drain clams and save the nectar. Combine all ingredients except the nectar and blend thoroughly. Add a quarter cup of the nectar to the mixture and beat vigorously or whip in a blender until light and fluffy. Chill, uncovered, in the refrigerator for one hour.

Serve with potato chips, corn chips, or tortilla chips.

Chapter 17

SOUPS AND CHOWDERS

Soups and chowders made from fish and shellfish are sometimes served as appetizers, but most are hearty and delicious enough to be complete meals, served with crackers, buttered toast, or hot, home-made bread and butter. Although they're good any time, we particularly enjoy them during the colder months, especially after a blustery day of fishing when the cold and wind has gone bone-deep. These soups and chowders are among our favorite of all foods.

Old-Style New England Clam Chowder

Although potatoes were not in common use when early American settlers first started making clam chowder, crackers were used as the thickening agent. Since then, chowders have been thickened with flour or overcooked potatoes stirred with a whip. Try this old-style way with our own modifications, and we think it will become your favorite, too.

2 cups minced clams
1 cup water
½ pound salt pork
½ cup minced fresh onion
½ cup chopped celery
1½ cups clam nectar
    and water
6 cups diced potatoes

1 cup milk
10 saltine crackers
3 cups half and half
2 tablespoons butter or
    margarine
1 tablespoon dried parsley
    salt and pepper to taste
    paprika

Dice salt pork and fry until crisp. Remove salt pork and drain on paper towels. Discard all but three tablespoons of the drippings. Combine onion and celery with drippings in a soup pot and cook until tender.

Drain clams and reserve the nectar. Add water to the nectar to make 1½ cups and pour into the pot with celery and onions. Add potatoes and bring to a boil. Reduce heat and simmer until potatoes are tender. Add clams and simmer for another five minutes.

Put crackers in a bowl, pour milk over them, and let stand until the crackers are soft. Beat milk and crackers vigorously until the two are thoroughly blended. Stir milk and crackers, half and half, salt pork, butter, parsley, salt, and pepper into the chowder and heat to the boiling point, stirring constantly. Sprinkle with paprika before serving.

Makes six to eight servings.

Manhattan Clam Chowder

Although we don't particularly care for the Manhattan-style clam chowder, some people prefer it to the New England chowder, so we thought we ought to include this recipe. Try them both and decide for yourself.

2 cups minced clams	¼ cup diced salt pork
1 cup chopped celery	1 cup clam nectar and water
½ cup minced fresh onion	2 cups tomato juice
1 cup diced potatoes	¼ teaspoon thyme
½ cup chopped green peppers	dash of cayenne pepper

Drain clams and reserve the nectar. Fry salt pork until crisp and remove from pan to absorbent paper towels. Add celery, onion, and green pepper to salt pork drippings and cook until tender.

Add water to the clam nectar to make one cup. Then combine cooked vegetables, clams, nectar and water, seasonings, and potatoes in a pot, bring to a boil, and simmer for about 10 minutes or until potatoes are tender.

Add tomato juice, heat to boiling point, and serve.

Makes six servings.

Canned-Fish Soup

For years, we called this salmon soup, because that's the only kind of fish we used. But we've since tried several different species and have enjoyed them all.

Canned albacore is quite different in flavor from the salmon, but equally as good. Other fishes are also quite tasty, so try anything you have on hand.

2 pints canned fish	1 teaspoon salt
1 cup chopped onion	½ teaspoon pepper

1 cup chopped celery
2 tablespoons butter or
    margarine
2 tablespoons flour

4 cups milk
1 cup heavy cream
1 tablespoon dried parsley

Melt butter in a pot, add onions and celery, and cook until tender. Gradually stir in flour until well blended.

Remove from heat and gradually add milk, cream, salt, pepper, and parsley and mix well. Flake fish and add it with the fish liquid to the mixture.

Return pot to the stove, heat to just below the boiling point, and serve with crackers or buttered toast.

Makes six to eight servings.

Angler's Bad-Day Bisque

This dish is named in honor of those days when you return home with a catch that will scarcely feed one person, much less a family. With a single fish or a couple of small ones, you can stretch the catch into a hearty family meal.

Just poach or steam your catch, cool it, and flake it, carefully removing all bones and skin. If it was a really bad day, tap your supply of canned or frozen flaked fish.

2 to 4 cups flaked fish
6 large potatoes, diced
1 cup chopped onion
1 cup chopped celery
¼ pound butter or margarine
4 teaspoons salt

1 teaspoon pepper
2 tablespoons dried parsley
2 cups milk
2 cups half and half
1 dollop sherry
paprika

Put potatoes in a large pot, cover with water, and bring to a boil. Reduce heat and simmer, covered, until potatoes are very tender or slightly overcooked.

Meanwhile, melt butter in a skillet and sauté onion and celery until tender.

When potatoes are well done, pour off water and add milk. Use an egg whip to beat potatoes and milk until the milk is thickened and some chunks of potato yet remain.

Now add all other ingredients except sherry and paprika and mix well. Heat to just below the boiling point, stirring constantly. If the soup is too thick, thin with equal portions of milk and half and half. Just before serving, stir in the sherry and sprinkle with paprika.

Serve with hot rolls, biscuits, or freshly baked bread.

Makes eight to 10 servings.

Bouillabaisse

This hearty dish of French origin is considered one of the great soups of the world. While bouillabaisse prepared in Boston will differ from the Creole version or that served in San Francisco or Seattle, they all share one common characteristic: outstanding flavor. Originally, bouillabaisse contained several varieties of fish and shellfish, including eel and rock lobster. Although different varieties of fish and shellfish are used in various parts of the world, the soup should contain a hefty portion of fish and whatever shellfish are locally and seasonally available.

If you live along the coast, use available fish and shellfish. Whether you live on the coast or inland, you might want to or have to purchase some of the shellfish you'll use in your bouillabaisse. By all means, gather as much of the seafood on your own as you can; then add to it as required with the freshest shellfish you can buy.

Plan to use from four to six pounds of fish and shellfish and to do some improvising and experimenting. In our own bouillabaisse, we use several kinds of fish that we might have fresh or frozen, clams in season, and one, several, or all of a variety of other shellfish we enjoy—oysters, scallops, shrimp, and lobster.

To give you a good foundation, we are giving you three basic recipes: "Boston Bouillabaisse," from *Seafoods 'n Seaports—A Cook's Tour Of Massachusetts*, "Creole Bouillabaisse," from *A Seafood Heritage— From The Rappahannock To The Rio Grande*, and "Kenn & Pat's Bouillabaisse," which is our own version and is subject to change at any moment, depending on what's available.

Although the first two recipes call for saltwater species (as do other bouillabaisse recipes), have no compunctions about using any variety of freshwater and anadromous fishes: black bass, white bass, perch, bluegill, crappie, catfish, walleye, salmon, trout, striped bass, or whatever you have on hand.

Boston Bouillabaisse

1 pound pollock fillets
1 pound cod fillets
1 pound ocean perch fillets
1 pound sea scallops
2 small lobsters (optional)
¾ cup chopped onion
¾ cup sliced celery
1 large clove garlic, minced

⅓ cup butter or margarine
2 cups canned clam broth
1 cup water
2 one-pound cans tomatoes
½ teaspoon thyme
1 large bay leaf, crushed
1 teaspoon saffron (optional)
    salt and pepper to taste

Cut fillets into two-inch chunks. Sauté onion, celery, and garlic in butter until tender, but not brown. Add clam broth, water, tomatoes, herbs, and fish. Bring to a boil and simmer for 10 minutes.

Add scallops and simmer 10 more minutes. Season to taste with salt and pepper.

Meanwhile, boil lobsters. Crack claws and remove meat. Remove meat from tails. Dice lobster meat and add to soup just prior to serving.

Makes eight servings.

Creole Bouillabaisse

1 pound red drum fillets
1 pound sea trout fillets
½ pound peeled & deveined shrimp
1 pint oysters
1 6½-ounce can crab meat
2 tablespoons margarine or butter
2 tablespoons olive oil
¼ cup all-purpose oil
1 cup chopped onion
½ cup chopped celery

1 clove garlic, minced
5 cups water
1 one-pound can tomatoes
½ cup dry white wine
2 tablespoons chopped parsley
1 tablespoon lemon juice
1 bay leaf
½ teaspoon salt
¼ teaspoon saffron
¼ teaspoon cayenne pepper

Thaw fish and shellfish if frozen. Remove skin and bones from fish. Cut each fillet into six or eight portions.

In a four- to five-quart Dutch oven, melt margarine. Add olive oil and blend in flour. Cook, stirring constantly, until mixture turns light brown. Add onion, celery, and garlic and cook, stirring constantly, until vegetables begin to brown.

Gradually stir in water. Cut tomatoes and add them, with the juice. Add wine, parsley, lemon juice, bay leaf, salt, saffron, cayenne pepper, and about a fourth of the fish.

Bring to a boil and simmer for 20 minutes. Add remaining fish and cook for five to eight more minutes.

Add shrimp, oysters, and crab meat. Cook another three to five minutes or until all the seafood is done.

Makes eight servings.

Kenn and Pat's Bouillabaisse

3 pounds fish fillets
1 pint small oysters

2 one-pound cans tomatoes
1 cup water

1 pint clams or mussels
½ pound scallops
½ pound peeled &
    deveined shrimp
1 pint crab meat
2 rock lobster tails
1 cup chopped onion
1 cup chopped celery
2 cloves garlic, minced

1 cup dry white wine
½ teaspoon thyme
1 teaspoon salt
½ teaspoon pepper
¼ teaspoon cayenne pepper
1 tablespoon dried parsley
2 bay leaves
    juice from one fresh lemon
¼ pound butter or margarine

Use whatever fish are seasonally available or what you have on hand, but variety is the key to good bouillabaisse. So for the best results, use fish of different flavors and textures. For example, we might use a pound of lingcod fillets, a pound of salmon, and a pound of largemouth bass. Or we might use catfish, bluegill, striped bass, surf perch, flounder, sole, rockfish, or halibut. We do the same with shellfish by using whatever clams and crab we have available and buying oysters, scallops, shrimp, and lobster.

If oysters are larger than bite size, cut them into one-inch pieces and reserve the nectar. Drain and cut tomatoes into small pieces, reserving the juice. If shrimp are large, cut them into bite-size pieces. Do likewise with large scallops. If crab is canned, drain and discard the liquid, as it is often too strong and overpowering. Shred crab meat.

Use only boneless and skinless fillets and cut all fish into one-inch chunks.

Boil lobster tails in salted water for 10 minutes; cool, crack, and pick meat from tails. Cut lobster meat into half-inch chunks.

Melt butter in a cast-iron Dutch oven or large soup pot. Add onion, celery, and garlic and cook until tender. Add clam and oyster nectar, water, wine, juice from tomatoes, lemon juice, bay leaves, and seasonings and bring to a boil.

Add all fish and shellfish, except crab and lobster, and simmer for 20 minutes. Add tomatoes, crab, and lobster and return to a boil. Serve piping hot with buttered, toasted French bread or garlic bread.

Makes 10 to 12 servings.

18

SAUCES FOR THE CATCH

The right sauce can do wonders to enhance the flavor of fish or shellfish. Most sauces complement the delicate flavors and textures, while some actually improve the flavor of strong-tasting fish. A good sauce will garner as many compliments from your diners as will the fish or shellfish, so be as careful in the preparation of sauces as you are with the main courses.

Tartar Sauce

Somebody must have once said, "A big gob of salad dressing and a little gob of pickle relish does not a sauce tartare make." At any rate, somebody should have said it. We have had some pretty awful tartar sauces at restaurants and elsewhere, so some years ago we began experimenting until we finally came up with a recipe that never fails to get plenty of compliments at our fish fries.

Try our basic recipe and judge for yourself. But please don't substitute salad dressing for the mayonnaise or relish for the chopped pickles. Such substitutions might save a little time and money but will also ruin the sauce. Use either the commercially available sweet cucumber chips or home-canned bread-and-butter pickles in the basic recipe.

Basic Tartar Sauce

2 cups mayonnaise
1 cup chopped sweet pickles
2 tablespoons minced fresh onion
2 tablespoons chopped ripe olives

1 tablespoon dried parsley
1 teaspoon fines herbes
⅛ teaspoon garlic powder
1 tablespoon prepared mustard
juice from half a lemon

Combine all ingredients and mix thoroughly. Store in the refrigerator in a tightly covered container.

Serving Suggestions: Use with any hot fish, particularly fried fish and shellfish.

Dill Tartar Sauce

Prepare the basic recipe, but substitute chopped dill pickles for the sweet pickles, one tablespoon of dill pickle juice for the lemon juice, and dill weed for the fines herbes.

Caper Tartar Sauce

Follow the basic recipe, but use dill pickles instead of the sweet pickles and reduce the amount to ¾ cup; substitute chopped Spanish olives for the ripe olives and add two tablespoons of chopped capers.

Cocktail Sauce

1½ cups chili sauce
3 tablespoons prepared
  horseradish
1 teaspoon fines herbes

4 to 6 drops Tabasco sauce
2 tablespoons Worcestershire
  sauce
juice from half a lemon

Combine all ingredients and mix thoroughly. Store in the refrigerator in a tightly covered container.

Serving Suggestions: Use with chilled seafood cocktails and with fried fish and shellfish. Try with small panfish fillets that have been steamed or poached, then chilled.

Thousand Island Dressing

1 cup mayonnaise
¼ cup chili sauce
¼ chopped sweet pickle
¼ cup minced green onion

1 chopped pimiento
1 chopped, hard-boiled egg
  juice from half a lemon

Mix all ingredients completely. Store in the refrigerator in a tightly capped container.

Serving Suggestions: Serve with chilled poached or steamed fish and with chilled crab meat.

Sour-Cream Cucumber Sauce

1 cup dairy sour cream
1 tablespoon chopped chives
½ cup grated cucumber

1 teaspoon salt
juice of half a lemon
dash of cayenne pepper

Gently add all ingredients to the sour cream and mix, but do not beat or stir vigorously. Keep refrigerated in a covered container.

Serving Suggestions: Use with chilled poached or steamed fish. The sauce is also a good substitute for tartar sauce with fried fish and shellfish.

Lemon-and-Garlic Butter

¼ pound butter or margarine
⅛ teaspoon garlic powder

juice from half a lemon

Melt butter in a small pan and stir in other ingredients.

Serving Suggestions: Use as a basting sauce for range-broiled and charbroiled steaks and fillets. Use as a serving sauce with broiled, steamed, and poached fish, with steamed clams and mussels, and with hot crab meat.

Dill Butter

¼ pound butter or margarine
2 teaspoons dill seed
2 teaspoons chopped chives

1 teaspoon chopped parsley
⅛ teaspoon pepper
juice from half a lemon

Melt butter in a small pan and mix in other ingredients.

Serving Suggestions: Use as a basting sauce for broiled fish steaks and fillets and as a serving sauce for broiled, steamed, and poached fish.

Sea Sauce

1 eight-ounce can tomato
   sauce
¼ cup chili sauce
¼ teaspoon garlic powder
¼ teaspoon oregano

¼ teaspoon Tabasco sauce
¼ teaspoon thyme
⅛ teaspoon sugar
1 pinch sweet basil

Combine all ingredients in a small saucepan and bring to a boil. Reduce heat and simmer for 10 minutes, stirring constantly.

Serving Suggestions: Serve hot over fried, baked, steamed, or poached fish as main courses. Serve with fried or oven-fried finger fillets as an appetizer.

Cream Sauce

3 tablespoons butter or
    margarine
3 tablespoons flour
1½ cups milk

½ teaspoon salt
¼ teaspoon pepper

Melt butter or margarine in a saucepan over low heat. Gradually add flour and seasonings and continue cooking over low heat, stirring mixture until smooth and bubbly.

Remove pan from heat and gradually add milk, stirring until blended. Return pan to stove and bring to a boil over medium heat and boil for one minute, stirring constantly.

Makes about 1½ cups of sauce.

Serving Suggestions: Serve over hot poached, steamed, or baked fish. Combine with one cup of flaked fish and serve over buttered toast or toasted and buttered English muffins.

Cheese Sauce

Follow the basic cream sauce recipe, but prepare in the top of a double boiler. When white sauce is done, place the top of the double boiler over the bottom section, in which water has been brought to a boil.

Stir in one cup of grated cheddar cheese and stir occasionally until the cheese melts and is completely blended with the sauce.

Serving Suggestions: Serve over hot poached, steamed, baked, or broiled fish. Also good over croquettes and some fried fish.

Mustard Sauce

Make the basic cream sauce and add two tablespoons of prepared mustard.

Makes 1½ cups of sauce.

Serving Suggestions: Serve over hot poached, steamed, baked, or broiled fish.

Egg Sauce

Make the basic cream sauce, but combine one tablespoon of powdered mustard with the flour and seasonings during preparation.

When the sauce has boiled for one minute, fold in two chopped, hard-boiled eggs and one tablespoon of dried parsley flakes.

Makes about 2 cups of sauce.

Serving Suggestions: Serve over hot poached or steamed fish.

Mushroom Walnut Sauce

1 cup sliced mushrooms
3 tablespoon butter or
  margarine
1 tablespoon minced fresh
  onion
3 tablespoons flour

2 cups light cream
½ teaspoon dry mustard
½ teaspoon salt
¼ teaspoon thyme
¼ cup toasted walnuts

Melt the butter or margarine in a small saucepan; then add onion and mushrooms and cook over medium-high heat until tender. Stir in flour, mustard, salt, and thyme.

Remove pan from heat and gradually add cream. Mix until thoroughly blended.

Return pan to stove and cook over medium heat, stirring constantly, until sauce thickens. Then mix in the toasted walnuts.

Serving Suggestions: Serve over white-meat fish fillets that have been topped with generous servings of cooked wild rice.

Tomato-Cheese Sauce

1 16-ounce can stewed
  tomatoes
1 can (10¾ ounces) tomato
  soup

½ pound Kraft Velveeta cheese

Drain tomatoes and reserve liquid. Cut tomatoes into small pieces and put in top section of a double boiler. Add tomato soup and a fourth of a cup of the stewed tomato liquid. Stir until completely blended.

Bring water in bottom of double boiler to a rolling boil and reduce heat to low.

Slice cheese and cut into strips. Stir cheese into tomato sauce and heat until cheese is melted and sauce is hot.

If sauce is too thick, gradually add more juice from tomatoes until it is of proper consistency.

Makes about four cups of sauce. Leftovers keep well in the refrigerator and can be reheated in the double boiler.

Serving Suggestions: Excellent served over croquettes and hot poached or steamed fish. Also greatly improves the flavor of some strong-tasting fishes.

SELECTED BIBLIOGRAPHY

Following is a list of helpful publications that are either free or inexpensive, most of which contain helpful hints and useful fish and shellfish recipes.

Country Catfish. B. Finley. 003-020-00089-4. U.S. Government Printing Office. Prepared by National Marine Fisheries Service. 16 pp. (60¢)

Delaware Seafood Recipes Series. Delaware Sea Grant Marine Advisory Service, 1977. 4 pp. (Free)

Fabulous Feasts With Maine Seafoods. Maine Department of Natural Resources. 32 pp. (Free)

A Fine Kettle Of Fish. V. Hacker. No. 17-3600 (77). Wisconsin Department Of Natural Resources, 1977. 64 pp. ($1.00)

Fish And Seafood—Dividend Foods. C. Dunn. WIS-SG-74-118. University of Wisconsin Sea Grant College Program, 1974. 23 pp. (Free)

Fish And Shellfish Over The Coals. B. Finley. 003-020-00052-5. U.S. Government Printing Office. Prepared by National Marine Fisheries Service. 32 pp. (85¢)

Fish Smoking. Ohio Department of Natural Resources. Publication No. 64. (Free)

Great Lakes Fish Cookery. R. Mattingly. No. E-932. Michigan Sea Grant, 1976. 13 pp. (Free)

Great Lakes Fish Preparation. A. E. Reynolds, et al. Michigan State University Cooperative Extension Service and Michigan Sea Grant Advisory Service, 1978. 16 pp. (45¢)

Let's Cook Fish. B. Finley. 003-020-00053-3. U.S. Government Printing Office. Prepared by National Marine Fisheries Service. 60 pp. ($1.25)

A Little Fish Goes A Long Way. B. Finley. 003-020-00074-6. U.S. Government Printing Office. Prepared by National Marine Fisheries Service. 25 pp. (65¢)

The Maine Dish Is Mussels—New Recipes For An Old Favorite. Maine Department of Marine Resources, 1977. 2 pp. (Free)

Making Fish Jerky For Home And Trail. M. Violand. New York Sea Grant Extension Program, 1978. 2 pp. (Free)

The Mussel Is A Marvellous Mollusk. Massachusetts Seafood Council. No. C-106. (Free)

Mussels In Many Ways. J. Peters and S. Marple. UNH Marine Advisory Program, 1974. 4 pp. (Free)

Mussels For Many. R. Alonzo. UNH-SG-AB-103. UNH Marine Advisory Program. 10 pp. (Free)

Ono Hawaiian Shark Recipes. A. Tachibana. UNI HI-Sea Grant-AB-77-03. University of Hawaii, Sea Grant Marine Advisory Program, 1977. 20 pp. (Free)

Outdoor Cooking—Seafood. Cooperative Extension Service, Mississippi State University, 1975. 5 pp. (Free)

A Seafood Heritage From America's First Industry. B. Finley. 003-020-000101-7. U.S. Government Printing Office. Prepared by National Marine Fisheries Service. 22 pp. (80¢)

A Seafood Heritage From The Plains To The Pacific. B. Finley. 003-020-00124-6. U.S. Government Printing Office. Prepared by National Marine Fisheries Service. 32 pp. ($1.10)

A Seafood Heritage From Plymouth To The Prairies. B. Finley. 003-020-00122-0. U.S. Government Printing Office. Prepared by National Marine Fisheries Service. 32 pp. ($1.10)

A Seafood Heritage From The Rappahannock To The Rio Grande. B. Finley. 003-020-0018-1. U.S. Government Printing Office. Prepared by National Marine Fisheries Service. 32 pp. ($1.10)

Seafoods 'n Seaports—A Cook's Tour Of Massachusetts. Massachusetts Seafood Council. No. C-101. 32 pp. ($1.00)

Smelt—Dip Net To Dish. J. Murray and T. Arneson. #4. Minnesota Sea Grant Extension Program, Lake Superior Basin Studies Center, 1977. (Free)

Smoked Shark And Shark Jerky For Home And Trail. J. Richards and R. Price. Marine Brief #14. Sea Grant Marine Advisory Program, University of California, 1977. 2 pp. (Free)

Smoking Fish At Home. M. Tate, et al. No. 2669. Sea Grant Marine Advisory Program, University of California, 1975. 6 pp. (Free)

Smoking Fish At Home—A Step By Step Guide. Cherrie L. Kassem. VPI-SG-300-2. Cooperative Extension Service, Virginia Polytechnic Institute and State University. 6 pp. (Free)

Spiced And Pickled Seafoods. R. Price. Marine Brief #6. Sea Grant Marine Advisory Program, University of California, 1975. 2 pp. (Free)

Tastes Of Chesapeake Bay. Maryland Seafood Marketing Authority. (Free)

There Are Other Fish In The Sea. Massachusetts Seafood Council. 10 pp. (Free)

Time For Seafood. B. Finley. 003-020-00108-4. U.S. Government Printing Office. Prepared by National Marine Fisheries Service. 16 pp. (Free)

Try Flounder—The Ocean's Platter. R. Smith. MAS-7. Delaware Sea Grant Marine Advisory Service, 1976. 4 pp. (Free)

The Uncommon Cookbook. P. Coggins, editor. MSG-B-8-75. Maine Sea Grant, 1976. 40 pp. ($1.50)

PUBLICATIONS SOURCES

Write to the following sources to order publications included in the Selected Bibliography.

Delaware Sea Grant Marine Advisory Service
College of Marine Studies
University of Delaware
Newark, DE 19711

Maine Department of Marine Resources
State House
Augusta, ME 04333

Maine Sea Grant Publications
Ira C. Darling Center
University of Maine
Walpole, ME 04573

Maryland Seafood Marketing Authority
Department of Economic & Community Development
1748 Forest Dr.
Annapolis, MD 21401

Massachusetts Seafood Council
253 Northern Ave.
Boston, MA 02210

Michigan Sea Grant Program
4117 I.S.T. Building
2200 Bonisteel Blvd.
Ann Arbor, MI 48109

Michigan State University
Cooperative Extension Service
Ag Hall
East Lansing, MI 48824

Minnesota Sea Grant Extension Program
109 Washburn Hall
Duluth, MN 55812

Mississippi State University
Cooperative Extension Service
4646 W. Beach Blvd., Suite 1-E
Biloxi, MS 39531

New York Sea Grant Extension Program
Cornell University
Fernow Hall
Ithaca, NY 14853

Ohio Department of Natural Resources
Fountain Square
Columbus, OH 43224

Superintendent of Documents
U.S. Government Printing Office
Washington, DC 20402

UNH Marine Advisory Program
Marine Program Building
University of New Hampshire
Durham, NH 03824

University of California
Sea Grant Marine Advisory Program
554 Hutchinson Hall
Davis, CA 95616

University of Hawaii
Sea Grant Marine Advisory Program
2540 Maile Way
Spalding 252B
Honolulu, HI 96822

University of Wisconsin
Sea Grant College Program
1800 University Ave.
Madison, WI 53706

Virginia Polytechnic Institute and State University
Cooperative Extension Service
Blacksburg, VA 24061

Wisconsin Department of Natural Resources
Bureau of Fish Management
Box 7921
Madison, WI 53707

INDEX

226